Shakespeare's England

Shakespeare's England

LIFE IN ELIZABETHAN & JACOBEAN TIMES

EDITED & INTRODUCED BY R.E. PRITCHARD

The History Press

First published in 1999
This edition published in 2010

The History Press
The Mill, Brimscombe Port
Stroud, Gloucestershire, GL5 2QG
www.thehistorypress.co.uk

British Library Cataloguing in Publication Data.
A catalogue record for this book is available from the British Library.

ISBN 978 0 7509 3211 0

Typesetting and origination by The History Press
Printed in Great Britain

CONTENTS

ACKNOWLEDGEMENTS

British Library: 1 (MS Eg. 1222.f.73); Bodleian Library: 2, 7, 9, 10, 11, 16, 21 (A.3.15.6–14), 3 (Mal.632), 6 (R.205), 8 (Douce M.399), 12 (4° 17.11.Art), 14 (A.5.287), 20 (Mal.6012), 22 (Mal.632), 25 (G.A. Ireland 4° 82); Pepysian Library, Magdalene College, Cambridge: 4, 5, 24; Staatriche Museen, Kassel: 13; Guildhall Library: 15, 18; Museum of London: 17; Courtauld Institute: 19; British Museum: 23 (117a).

INTRODUCTION

To hold . . . the mirror up to nature; to show . . . the very age and body
of the time his true form and pressure.

Shakespeare, *Hamlet* (1600–3)

This collection of writings by and about Shakespeare's contemporaries, drawn from books, plays, pamphlets and a handful of poems, has been selected both because the passages are interesting and entertaining in themselves, and because of the insight they give us into how some Elizabethans and Jacobeans, the well known and the obscure, perceived the England of their times. A wide range of topics touched on by Shakespeare is included: love and marriage, work and leisure, Court and country, religion and crime, home life and overseas; throughout, a shared world-view becomes apparent.

While some of the famous appear, the emphasis here is on lesser-known writers and passages. In some ways, the greater writers are greater because they penetrate more incisively and eloquently into the essential spirit of their age; but the lesser writers may provide more of the cultural and linguistic context, often give a more generally informative picture of what was going on, and provide their own distinctive pleasures and judgements. Some writers of the time – Holinshed in his *Chronicles*, Spenser in *The Faerie Queene*, Shakespeare in his Histories and *King Lear* – strove, through poetic mythology and history, to engage with and shape 'England', as not just a place or uncertain political structure but an evolving and not readily definable cultural identity. The writings here suggest the day-to-day feel of it, then.

It is notable that the writers are almost all men from the minority upper and middle social orders: women and the lower social orders were generally less literate, with fewer opportunities to write, let alone publish. Their views and experiences achieved little public expression then (though matters improved later in the seventeenth century). Consequently, even if this were a much larger volume, a complete picture of English society at the time would hardly be possible.

Likewise, when encountering these writers' reflections on life, we should remember that (as Hamlet would know) all mirrors distort, and that generally they were less concerned with objective reporting than with making money or a reputation, entertaining, persuading, or reflecting the prejudices of various readerships. Some might consciously engage in long-term political, religious or cultural struggles, and most reveal unexamined assumptions. Inevitably, their culture speaks through them. As such, these writings are part of the history of their times, reflecting and helping to shape their society and its values; they are not objective socio-cultural analyses.

With this in mind, each chapter has a concise, contextual introduction, indebted in varying degrees to the work of recent historians, as represented in the select list of further reading. For greater convenience, spelling, punctuation and typographical conventions have been modernized, and glossing of obscure words and phrases is inserted in the text, in square brackets, rather than tucked away at the back. Such modernization, however, tends to conceal what the original appearance might suggest, that different linguistic practices derive from different cultures and assumptions; even where the words are the same, the meanings may vary. These voices echo out of the past: while much is very recognizable, we may not catch everything they say. (In 'Pierre Menard', Jorge Luis Borges warns us of 'the elementary idea that all epochs are the same, or that they are different'.)

Writing at this time intended for publication had to be approved and entered in the Stationers' Register; after that, it was widely available, from the bookstalls near St Paul's churchyard, from provincial booksellers and, especially in the case of pamphlets, from country pedlars (like Autolycus in *The Winter's Tale*). The expansion of education produced an increasingly wide readership (more could read than could easily write), at all levels of society. The day of the professional writer – seeking profitable subjects (a printer might offer 'forty shillings and an odd pottle of wine'), catering for different markets – had arrived. Most readers were looking for serious material: religious writing (theology, debate, sermons) was predominant, and history, travel, medical and instructional works sold well. *Docere et delectare*, 'profit and delight', were the watchwords. There was also a growing market for entertainment – satirical pamphlets, accounts of crime and scandal, poems and ballads, almanacs, playscripts, jestbooks, and fiction (though the realist novel did not appear until much later). By the turn of the century, perhaps two hundred books were published each year.

Most writers' work was shaped by their education, where the grammar schools and universities concentrated on style as demonstrated in the Latin classics and rhetoric. Writers were trained in the formal disposition of material and the conscious selection of style appropriate to subject and purpose, and encouraged to develop copiousness – accumulation and variation – while variety of metaphor, simile and phrase, and verbal patterning, were particularly appreciated. Classical literary models lay behind much of their writing; increasingly important, however, was the influence of spoken English, of voice ('Language most shows a man: speak, that I may see thee,' wrote Ben Jonson): in the writing of the time, much of the vocabulary, structure and rhythms reflect the pressure and requirements of vigorous speech rather than of grammatical correctness.

At all levels, there is an appreciation of rhetoric, of style, of vigour, of the capacity to combine the colloquial and direct with the extravagant or formal. Whatever the views the writers seek to propagate, whatever the accuracy of their reportage, it is the strength of, and their pleasure in, their writing that is apparent, that in turn serve to increase our pleasure in reading, and to extend our imaginative sympathy and understanding of life both then and now.

1

ENGLAND AND THE ENGLISH

This earth, this realm, this England.
Shakespeare, *Richard II* (1596)

In the sixteenth century, people were interested in 'perspective' paintings, in which the subject changed appearance according to the observer's viewpoint. Likewise, there are different perspectives on the life of these times. One would portray 'merry England', an increasing national confidence, the glamour of Court and high fashion, the splendour of great mansions, the power and beauty of the drama, literature and music, the eloquence of religious prose and concern for religious principle, the charm of traditional customs and a relatively lightly populated, bird-rich countryside, and remarkable, energetic and colourful individuals. Another would present a typical third-world developing country, with gross disparities of wealth, with the powerful few plundering the commonwealth, the numerous poor with low life-expectancy, traditional cultural patterns crumbling under the pressure of new and more efficient agricultural and economic practices, inflation outpacing wages, child labour, infectious diseases, religious intolerance and widespread superstition. As in all good perspective paintings, each has its own validity – and may be glimpsed, sometimes between the lines, in this volume's writings.

The population was starting to grow again, with increasing rapidity, from nearly three million to about four-and-a-half million in Shakespeare's lifetime. A high birth rate mostly surpassed a high death rate from endemic diseases such as pneumonia and tuberculosis and epidemics of plague, typhus and viral diseases, exacerbated by poor hygiene and periods of acute dearth. Pressure on land and food resources produced a busy land market and sharp increases in land rents and food prices (the price of grain doubled in Shakespeare's lifetime), while wages and accommodation increased very little.

Traditional hierarchies remained, but were significantly affected by economic change. The great magnates of the aristocracy and upper gentry, a tiny minority owning some 15 to 20 per cent of the land, did well from the sale of Church estates in the 1530s and Crown estates in the 1560s and 1580s; inflation, and the growing cost of the conspicuous consumption, especially of luxury goods, expected of the upper orders, enforced the selling-off of land, while the acquisition of estates by lawyers, successful businessmen, large farmers and even yeomen, opened the way to social promotion into the gentry and governing classes. Smallholders, small tradesmen and poor cottagers did worse; these were very bad times for the urban poor.

Unaccustomed social mobility accompanied geographical mobility, as people moved around from village to village or to town or even (especially) to London, in pursuit of work, accommodation or food. Most people lived in the country, southeast of a line from the Humber to the Severn, working in agriculture or related trades. There were a few moderate-sized towns (around 1600, Norwich numbered some 30,000, Bristol 20,000, Newcastle 16,000), and many little market towns; poor roads discouraged transport, so marketing and service activities were decentralized.

Agriculture was the main activity; here we may note the importance of the cloth industry, though this struggled in the later sixteenth century, as broadcloth (produced mostly in the southwest) declined, while lighter fabrics and worsteds from Essex and Norfolk did better. Stone quarrying increased, to build the 'prodigy houses' of the rich; woodburning and charcoal diminished the woodlands, but coal was increasingly mined, and the iron industry expanded in the Weald, South Wales and the Midlands, as did lead (for the houses' roofs, waterpipes and window-frames), tin and copper (cooking utensils),

2

glass for more windows, and drinking ('glasses, glasses is the only drinking,' said Falstaff), and lace for ruffs, cuffs and collars (and starch to stiffen them).

More great houses, and more homelessness; more production, more deprivation; more rich, and more poor; and a general, steady improvement for 'the middling sort'. As is the way, a great deal of the new techniques, investment and skilled labour that helped in the industrial transformation of early modern England were imported from the more advanced countries (the Netherlands, Flanders, France); but at last, in a process of profound economic, social and cultural change, one of Europe's more backward countries was catching up.

ENGLAND: THE EARTH, AND THE FULLNESS THEREOF

The air of England is temperate but thick, cloudy and misty, and Caesar witnesseth that the cold is not so piercing as in France. For the sun draweth up the vapours of the sea which compasseth the island, and distils them upon the earth in frequent showers of rain, so that frosts are somewhat rare; and howsoever snow may often fall in the winter time, yet in the southern parts (especially) it seldom lies long on the ground. Also the cool blasts of sea winds mitigate the heat of summer.

By reason of this temper, laurel and rosemary flourish all winter, especially in the southern parts, and in summertime England yields apricots plentifully, musk melons in good quantity, and figs in some places, all which ripen well, and happily imitate the taste and goodness of the same fruits in Italy. And by the same reason all beasts bring forth their young in the open fields, even in the time of winter. And England hath such abundance of apples, pears, cherries and plums, such variety of them and so good in all respects, as no country yields more or better, for which the Italians would gladly exchange their citrons and oranges. But upon the sea coast the winds many times blast the fruits in the very flower.

The English are so naturally inclined to pleasure, as there is no country wherein the gentlemen and lords have so many and large parks only reserved for the pleasure of hunting, or where all sorts of men allot so much ground about their houses for pleasure of gardens and orchards. The very grapes, especially towards the south and west, are of a pleasant taste, and I have said that in some counties, as in Gloucestershire, they made wine of old, which no doubt many parts would yield at this day, but that the inhabitants forbear to plant vines, as well because they are served plentifully and at a good rate with French wines, as for that the hills most fit to bear grapes yield more commodity by feeding of sheep and cattle. . . .

England abounds with sea-coals upon the sea-coast, and with pit-coals within land. But the woods this day are rather frequent and pleasant than vast, being exhausted for fire and with iron-mills, so as the quantity of wood and charcoal for fire is much diminished in respect of the old abundance; and in some places, as in the Fens, they burn turf, and the very dung of cows. Yet in the meantime England exports great quantity of sea-coal to foreign parts. In like sort England hath infinite quantity, as of metals, so of wool and woollen clothes to be exported. The English beer is famous in Netherland and lower Germany, which is made of barley and hops; for England yields plenty of hops, howsoever they also use Flemish hops. . . .

England abounds with corn [wheat], which they may transport, when a quarter (in some places containing six, in others eight, bushels) is sold for twenty shillings, or under; and this corn not only serves England, but also served the English army in the civil wars of Ireland, at which time they also exported great quantity thereof into foreign parts, and by God's mercy England scarce one in ten years needs supply of foreign corn, which want commonly proceeds of the covetousness of private men, finding great commodity in feeding of sheep and cattle than in the plough (requiring the hands of many servants), can by no law be restrained from turning cornfields into enclosed pastures, especially since great men are the first to break these laws.

England abounds with all kinds of fowl as well of the sea as of the land, and hath more tame swans swimming in the rivers than I did see in any other part. It hath multitudes of hurtful birds, as crows, ravens and kites, and they labour not to destroy the crows consuming great quantity of corn, because they feed on worms and other things hurting the corn. And in great cities it is forbidden to kill kites and ravens, because they devour the filth of the streets. England hath very great plenty of sea and river-fish, especially above all other parts abundance of oysters, mackerel and herrings, and the English are very industrious in fishing, though nothing comparable to the Flemings therein.

Fynes Moryson, *An Itinerary* (1617)

Rough Uneven Ways Draw Out Our Miles

Now to speak generally of our common highways through the English part of our isle (for of the rest I can say nothing), you shall understand that in the clay or cledgy soil they are often very deep and troublesome in the winter half. Wherefore by authority of Parliament an order is taken for their yearly amendment, whereby all sorts of the common people do employ their travail for six days in summer upon the same. And albeit that the intent of the statute is very profitable for the reparations of the decayed places, yet the rich do so cancel their portions, and the poor do so loiter in their labours, that of all the six, scarcely two days' work are well performed and accomplished in a parish on these so necessary affairs. Besides this, such as have land lying upon the sides of the ways do utterly neglect to ditch and scour their drains and water-courses for better avoidance of the winter waters . . . whereby the streets do grow to be much more gulled [rutted] than before, and thereby very noisome for such as travel by the same. Sometimes also, and that very often, these days' works are not employed upon those ways that lead from market to market, but each surveyor amendeth such byplots and lanes as seem best for his own commodity and more easy passage unto his fields and pastures. And whereas in some places there is such want of stones as thereby the inhabitants are driven to seek them far off in other soils, the owners of the lands wherein those stones are to be had, and which have hitherto given money to have them borne away, do now reap no small commodity [profit] by raising the same to excessive prices, whereby their neighbours are driven to grievous charges, which is another cause wherefore the meaning of that good law is very much defrauded. Finally, this is another thing likewise to be considered of, that the trees and bushes growing by the streets' sides do not a little keep off the force of the sun in summer for drying up of the lanes. Wherefore if order were taken that their boughs should continually be kept short, and the bushes not suffered to spread so far into the narrow paths, that inconvenience would also be remedied, and many a slough prove hard ground, that yet is deep and hollow.

Of the daily encroachments of the covetous upon the highways I speak not. But this I know by experience, that whereas some streets within these five and twenty years have been in most places fifty foot broad, according to the law, whereby the traveller might escape the thief, or shift the mire, or pass by the laden cart without damage of himself and his horse, now they are brought unto twelve, or twenty, or six and twenty at the most, which is another cause also whereby the ways be worse, and many an honest man encumbered in his journey. But what speak I of these things whereof I do not think to hear a just redress, because the error is so common, and the benefit thereby so sweet and profitable to many by such houses and cottages as are raised upon the same.

William Harrison, *Description of England* (1587)

SHALL I NOT TAKE MINE EASE IN MINE INN?

(I)

The world affords not such inns as England hath, either for good and cheap entertainment after the guests' own pleasure, or for humble attendance on passengers, yea, in very poor villages, where if Curculio of Plautus should see the thatched houses he would fall into a fainting of his spirits, but if he should smell the variety of meats his starveling look would be much cheered. For as soon as a passenger comes to an inn, the servants run to him, and one takes his horse and walks him till he be cold, then rubs him and gives him meat; yet I must say that they are not much to be trusted in this last point, without the eye of the master or his servant to oversee them. Another servant gives the passenger his private chamber, and kindles his fire, the third pulls off his boots and makes them clean. Then the host or hostess visits him, and if he will eat with the host or at a common table with others, his meal will cost him sixpence, or in some places but fourpence (yet this course is less honourable and not used by gentlemen); but if he will eat in his chamber he commands what meat he will, according to his appetite, and as much as he thinks fit for him and his company, yea, the kitchen is open to him, to command the meat to be dressed as he best likes, and when he sits at table, the host or hostess will accompany him, or if they have many guests will at least visit him, taking it for courtesy to be bid sit down. While he eats, if he have company especially, he shall be offered music, which he may freely take or refuse, and if he be solitary, the musicians will give him the good day with music in the morning. It is the custom, and no way disgraceful, to set up part of supper for his breakfast. In the evening, or in the morning after breakfast (for the common sort use not to dine, but ride from breakfast to suppertime, yet coming early to the inn for better resting of their horses), he shall have a reckoning in writing, and if it seem unreasonable, the host will satisfy him, either for the due price or by abating part, especially if the servant deceive him any way, which one of experience will soon find. Having formerly spoken of ordinary expenses by the highway, as well in the particular journal of the first part as in a chapter of this part, purposely treating thereof, I will now only add, that a gentleman and his man shall spend as much as if he were accompanied with another gentleman and his man, and if gentlemen will in such sort join together to eat at one table, the expenses will be much diminished. Lastly, a man cannot more freely command at home than he may do in his inn, and, at parting, if he give some few pence to the chamberlain and ostler, they wish him a happy journey.

Fynes Moryson, *An Itinerary* (1617)

(II)

If the traveller have an horse, his bed doth cost him nothing, but if he go on foot he is sure to pay a penny for the same; but whether he be horseman or footman, if his chamber be once appointed he may carry the key with him, as of his own house, so long as he lodgeth there. If he loseth aught while he abideth in the inn, the host is bound by a general custom to restore the damage, so that there is no greater security anywhere for travellers than in the greatest inns in England.

Their horses in like sort are walked, dressed and looked unto by certain ostlers or hired servants, appointed at the charges of the goodman of the house, who in hope of extraordinary reward will deal very diligently, after outward appearance, in this their function and calling. Herein nevertheless are many of them blameworthy, in that they do not only deceive the beast oftentimes of his allowance by sundry means, except their owners look well to them; but also make such packs with slipper merchants which hunt after prey (for what place is sure from evil and wicked persons?) that many an honest man is spoiled of his goods as he travelleth to and fro, in which feat also the counsel of the tapsters or drawers of drink, and chamberlains is not seldom behind or wanting.

Certes, I believe that not a chapman or traveller in England is robbed by the way without the knowledge of some of them; for when he cometh into the inn and alighteth from his horse, the ostler forthwith is very busy to take down his budget [bag] or capcase [wallet] in the yard from his saddlebow, which he peiseth [weighs] slyly in his hand to feel the weight thereof; or if he miss of this pitch, when the guest hath taken up his chamber, the chamberlain that looketh to the making of the beds will be sure to remove it from the place where the owner hath set it, as if it were to set it more conveniently somewhere else, whereby he getteth an inkling whether it be money or other sort wares, and therefore giveth warning to such odd guests as haunt the house and are of his confederacy, to the utter undoing of many an honest yeoman as he journeyeth by the way. The tapster in like sort for his part doth mark his behaviour, and what plenty of money he draweth when he payeth the shot, to the like end: so that it shall be an hard matter to escape all their subtle practices. Some think it a gay matter to commit their budgets at their coming to the goodman of the house, but thereby they oft bewray [deceive] themselves. For albeit their money be safe for the time that it is in his hands (for you shall not hear that a man is robbed in his inn), yet after their departure the host can make no warranties of the same, sith his protection extendeth no farther than the gate of his own house; and there cannot be a surer token unto such as pry and watch for these booties, than to see any guest deliver his capcase in such a manner.

In all our inns we have plenty of ale, beer and sundry kinds of wine, and such is the capacity of some of them that they are able to lodge two hundred or three hundred persons and their horses at least, and thereto with a very short warning make such provision for their diet, as to him that is unacquainted withal may seem to be incredible. Howbeit of all in England there are no worse inns than in London, and yet many are there far better than the best I have heard of in any foreign country, if all circumstances be duly considered.

William Harrison, *Description of England* (1587)

ENGLAND AND THE ENGLISH

TRAVELLERS IN A VILLAINOUS INN

ROCHESTER, KENT. AN INN YARD.

First Carrier. Heigh-ho! an it be not four by the day, I'll be hanged; Charles's wain [the Plough constellation] is over the new chimney, and yet our horse not packed. What, ostler!

Ostler (within). Anon, anon.

First Carrier. I prithee, Tom, beat Cut's saddle; put a few flocks [tufts of wool] in the point [saddle-strap], poor jade is wrung in the withers [galled on the shoulder-ridge] out of all cess.

ENTER SECOND CARRIER.

Second Carrier. Peas and beans are as dank here as a dog, and that is the next way to give poor jade the bots [worms]; this house is turned upside down since Robin Ostler died.

First Carrier. Poor fellow never joyed since the price of oats rose; it was the death of him.

Second Carrier. I think this be the most villainous house in all London road for fleas; I am stung like a tench.

First Carrier. Like a tench! By the mass, there is ne'er a king christen could be better bit than I have been since the first cock.

Second Carrier. Why, they will allow us ne'er a jordan [chamber-pot], and then we leak in your chimney; and your chamber-lye [urine] breeds fleas like a loach.

First Carrier. What, ostler! Come away, and be hanged; come away!

Second Carrier. I have a gammon of bacon and two razes [roots] of ginger to be delivered as far as Charing Cross.

First Carrier. God's body! the turkeys in my pannier are quite starved. What, ostler! A plague on thee! hast thou never an eye in thy head? Canst not hear? An 'twere not as good deed as drink to break the pate on thee, I am a very villain. Come, and be hanged! Hast no faith in thee?

ENTER GADSHILL [A THIEF].

Gadshill. Good morrow, carriers. What's o'clock?

First Carrier. I think it be two o'clock.

Gadshill.	I prithee lend me thy lantern to see my gelding in the stable.
First Carrier.	Nay, by God! Soft! I know a trick worth two of that, i'faith.
Gadshill.	I pray thee lend me thine.
Second Carrier.	Aye, when, canst tell? Lend me thy lantern, quoth'a? Marry, I'll see thee hanged first.
Gadshill.	Sirrah carrier, what time do you mean to come to London?
Second Carrier.	Time enough to go to bed with a candle, I warrant thee. Come, neighbour Mugs, we'll call up the gentlemen; they will along with company, for they have great charge.

EXEUNT CARRIERS.

Gadshill.	What ho, chamberlain!
Chamberlain (within).	At hand, quoth pickpurse. . . . (Enter chamberlain) Good morrow, Master Gadshill. It holds current that I told you yesternight: there's a franklin in the Weald of Kent hath brought three hundred marks with him in gold; I heard him tell it to one of his company last night at supper . . .
Gadshill.	Give me thy hand: thou shalt have a share in our purchase, as I am a true man.

Shakespeare, *Henry IV, Part I* (1597)

DEGREE AND CHANGE

We in England divide our people commonly into four sorts, as gentlemen, citizens or burgesses, yeomen, and artificers or labourers. Of gentlemen, the first and chief (next the king) be the prince, dukes, marquesses, earls, viscounts, and barons; and these are called gentlemen of the great sort, or (as our common usage of speech is) lords and noblemen; and next unto them be knights, esquires and last of all they that are simply called gentlemen . . .

Citizens and burgesses have next place to gentlemen, who be those that are free within the cities, and are of some substance to bear office in the same. . . . In this place also are our merchants to be installed, as amongst the citizens (although they often change estate with gentlemen, as gentlemen do with them, by a mutual conversion of the one into the other), whose number is so increased in these our days that their only maintenance is the cause of the exceeding prices of foreign wares, which otherwise, when every nation was permitted to bring in their own commodities, were far better cheap and more plentifully to be had. . . . I do not deny but that the navy of the land is in part maintained by their traffic, and so are the high prices of wares kept up, now they have gotten the only sale of things into their hands. . . . The wares that they carry out of the realm are for the most part broadcloths and carfies [prepared cloth] of all colours, likewise cottons, friezes [coarse woollen cloth], rugs, tin, wool, lead, fells [hides], etc; which being shipped at sundry ports of our coasts are borne from thence into all quarters of the world, and there either exchanged for other wares or ready money, to the great gain and commodity of our merchants. And whereas in times past their chief trade was into Spain, Portugal, France, Flanders, Dansk, Norway, Scotland and Iceland only, now in these days, as men not contented with these journeys, they have sought out the East and West Indies, and made voyages not only unto the Canaries and New Spain, but likewise into Cathay [China], Moscovia [Russia], Tartary and the regions thereabout, from whence, as they say, they bring home great commodities.

Yeomen are those which by our law are called *Legales homines*, freemen born English, and may dispend of their own free land in yearly revenue to the sum of forty shillings sterling [£2]. This sort of people have a certain pre-eminence, and more estimation than labourers and artificers, and commonly live wealthily, keep good houses and travel to get riches. They are also for the most part farmers to gentlemen, and with grazing, frequenting of markets and keeping of servants (not idle servants as the gentlemen do, but such as get both their own and part of their masters' living) do come to great wealth, insomuch that many of them are able and do buy the lands of unthrifty gentlemen, and often setting their sons to the schools, to the universities, and to the Inns of Court; or otherwise leaving them sufficient lands whereupon they might live without labour, do make them by those means to become gentlemen; these were they that in times past made all France afraid, and the kings of England in foughten battles were wont to remain among them (who were their footmen) as the French kings did amongst their horsemen, the prince thereby showing where his chief strength did consist.

The fourth and last sort of people in England are day labourers, poor husbandmen, and some retailers (which have no free land), copy holders, and all artificers, as tailors, shoemakers, carpenters, brickmakers, masons, etc. As for slaves and bondmen we have none. This therefore have neither voice nor authority in the commonwealth, but are to be ruled and not to rule other; yet they are not altogether neglected, for in cities and corporate towns, for default of yeomen, they are fain to make up their inquests of such manner of people. And in villages they are commonly made churchwardens, sidesmen, ale-conners, constables, and many times enjoy the name of headboroughs [parish constables].

Unto this sort also may our great swarms of idle serving men be referred, of whom there runneth a proverb: young serving men, old beggars; because service is none heritage. These men are profitable to none, for, if their condition be well perused, they are enemies to their masters, to their friends and to themselves: for by them oftentimes their masters are encouraged unto unlawful exactions of their tenants, their friends brought unto poverty by their rents enhanced, and they themselves brought unto confusion by their own prodigality and errors, as men that, having not wherewith of their own to maintain their excesses, do search in highways, budgets [wallets], coffers, mails [packs] and stables, which way to supply their wants. How divers of them also, coveting to bear an high sail, do insinuate themselves with young gentlemen and noblemen newly come to their lands, the case is too much apparent, whereby the good natures of the parties are not only a little impaired, but also their livelihoods and revenues so wasted and consumed that, if at all, yet in not many years they shall be able to recover themselves.

William Harrison, *Description of England* (1587)

NOBLEMEN

Noblemen or gentlemen ought to be preferred in fees, honours, offices and other dignities of command and government before the common people. They are to be admitted near and about the person of the Prince to be of his Council in war, and to bear his standard.

We ought to give credit to a noble or gentleman before any of the inferior sort. He must not be arrested or pleaded against upon cozenage [fraud]. We must attend him and come to his house, and not he to ours. His punishment ought to be more favourable and honourable upon his trial, and that to be by his peers of the same noble rank. He ought in all sittings, meetings and salutations to have the upper hand and greatest respect. They must be cited by bill or writing to make their appearance. In criminal cases, noblemen may appear by their attorney or procurator. They ought to take their recreations of hunting, hawking, etc., freely, without control in all places. Their imprisonment ought not to be in base manner, or so strict as others.

They may eat the best and daintiest meat that the place affordeth, wear at their pleasure gold, jewels, the best apparel and of what fashion they please, etc. Beside, nobility stirreth up emulation in great spirits, not only of equalling others but excelling them; as in Cimon, the elder Scipio Africanus, Decius the son, Alexander, Edward our Black Prince, and many other. It many times procureth a good marriage, as in Germany; where a fair coat and crest is often preferred before a good revenue.

It is a spur in brave and good spirits to bear in mind those things which their ancestors have nobly achieved. It transferreth itself to posterity; and as for the most part we see the children of noble personages to bear the lineaments and resemblance of their parents, so in like manner they possess their virtues and noble dispositions, which even in their tenderest years will bud forth and discover itself.

Henry Peacham, *The Compleat Gentleman* (1634)

THE DAILY ROUND

ONE OF THE CLOCK

It is now the first hour and time is, as it were, stepping out of darkness and stealing towards the day; the cock calls to his hen and bids her beware of the fox, and the watch, having walked the streets, take a nap upon the stall; the bellman calls to the maids to look to their locks, their fire and their light, and the child in the cradle calls to the nurse for a dug; the cat sits watching behind a cupboard for a mouse, and the flea sucks on sweet flesh, till he is ready to burst with blood; the spirits of the studious start out of their dreams, and, if they cannot fall asleep again, then to the book and the wax candle; the dog at the door frays the thief from the house, and the thief within the house may hap to be about his business. In some places bells are rung to certain [religious] orders; but the quiet sleeper never tells the clock. Not to dwell too long upon it, I hold it the farewell of the night and the forerunner to the day, the spirit's watch and reason's workmaster. Farewell.

TWO OF THE CLOCK

It is now the second hour and the point of the dial hath stepped over the first stroke, and now time begins to draw back the curtain of the night; the cock again calls to his hen, and the watch begin to bustle toward their discharge; the bellman hath made a great part of his walk, and the nurse begins to huggle the child to the dug; the cat sits playing with the mouse which she hath catched, and the dog with his barking wakes the servant of the house; the studious now are near upon waking, and the thief will be gone, for fear of being taken; the foresters now be about their walks, and yet stealers sometimes cozen the keepers; warreners [rabbiters or gamekeepers] now begin to draw homeward, and far dwellers from the town will be on the way to market; the soldier now looks to the *corps de garde* [guardroom], and the corporal takes care for the relief of the watch; the earnest scholar will now be at his book, and the thrifty husbandman will rouse towards his rising; the seaman will now look out for light, and, if the wind be fair, he calls for a can of beer; the fishermen now take the benefit of the tide, and he that bobs for eels will not be without worms. In sum, I hold it much of the nature of the first hour, but somewhat better. And to conclude, I think it the enemy of sleep and the entrance to exercise.

THREE OF THE CLOCK

It is now the third hour, and the windows of heaven begin to open, and the sun begins to colour the clouds in the sky before he show his face to the world. Now are the spirits of life, as it were, risen out of death; the cock calls the servants to their day's work, and the grass horses are fetched from the pastures; the milkmaids begin to look towards their dairy, and the good housewife begins to look about the house; the porridge pot is on for the servants' breakfast, and hungry stomachs will soon be ready for their victual. The sparrow begins to chirp about the house, and the birds in the bushes will bid them welcome to the field; the shepherd sets his pitch on the fire, and fills his tar-pot ready for his flock; the wheel and the reel begin to be set ready, and a merry song makes the work seem easy; the ploughman falls to harness his horses, and the thresher begins to look towards the barn; the scholar that loves learning will be hard at his book, and the labourer by great [piece-worker] will be walking towards his work. In brief, it is a parcel of time to good purpose, the exercise of nature and the entrance into art. Farewell.

FOUR OF THE CLOCK

It is now the fourth hour, and the sun begins to send her beams abroad, whose glimmering brightness no eye can behold. Now crows the cock lustily and claps his wing for the joy of the light, and with his hens leaps lightly from the roost; now are the horses at their chaff and provender, the servants at breakfast, the milkmaid gone to the field, and the spinner at the wheel, and the shepherd with his dog are going toward the fold; now the beggars rouse them out of the hedges, and begin their morning craft – but if the constable come, beware the stocks! The birds now begin to flock, and the sparrowhawk begins to prey for his eyrie. The thresher begins to stretch his long arms, and the thriving labourer will fall hard to his work; the quick-witted brain [lawyer] will be quoting of places, and the cunning workman will be trying of his skill; the hounds begin to be coupled for the chase, and the spaniels follow the falconer to the field. Travellers begin to look toward the stable, where an honest ostler is worthy his reward; the soldier now is upon discharge of his watch, and the captain with his company may take as good rest as they can. In sum, thus I conclude of it: I hold it the messenger of action and the watch of reason. Farewell.

FIVE OF THE CLOCK

It is now five of the clock, and the sun is going apace upon his journey; and fie, sluggards who would be asleep. The bells ring to prayer and the streets are full of people, and the highways are stored with travellers. The scholars are up and going to school, and the rods are ready for the truants' correction; the maids are at milking and the servants at the plough, and the wheel goes merrily – while the mistress is by. The capons and the chickens must be served without door, and the hogs cry till they have their swill; the shepherd is almost gotten to his fold, and the herd[sman] begins to blow his horn through the town. The blind fiddler is up with his dance and his song, and the alehouse door is unlocked for good fellows; the hounds begin to find after the hare, and horse and foot follow after the cry. The traveller now is well on his way, and if the weather be fair he walks with the better cheer; the carter merrily whistles to his horse, and the boy with his sling casts stones at the crows; the lawyer now begins to look on his case, and if he gives good counsel, he is worthy of his fee. In brief, not to stay too long upon it, I hold it the necessity of labour and the note of profit. Farewell.

SIX OF THE CLOCK

It is now the first hour, the sweet time of the morning, and the sun at every window calls the sleepers from their beds; the marigold begins to open her leaves, and the dew on the ground doth sweeten the air. The falconers now meet with many a fair flight, and the hare and the hounds have made the huntsman good sport; the shops in the city begin to show their wares, and the market people have taken their places. The scholars now have their forms, and whosoever cannot say his lesson must presently look for absolution; the forester now is drawing home to his lodge, and if his deer be gone he may draw after cold scent; now begins the curst [shrewish] mistress to put her girls to their tasks, and a lazy hilding will do hurt among good workers. Now the mower falls to whetting of his scythe, and the beaters of hemp give a 'Ho!' to every blow; the ale-knight is at his cup ere he can well see his drink, and the beggar is as nimble-tongued as if he had been at it all day; the fishermen now are at the crayer [small fishing-boat] for their oysters, and they will never tire crying while they have one in their basket. I hold it the sluggard's shame and the labourer's praise. Farewell.

SEVEN OF THE CLOCK

It is now the seventh hour, and time begins to set the world hard to work: the milkmaids in their dairy to their butter and their cheese, the ploughmen to their ploughs and their barrows in the field, the scholars to their lessons, the lawyers to their cases, the merchants to their accounts, the shopmen to 'What lack you?', and every trade to his business. Oh, 'tis a world to see how life leaps about the limbs of the healthful; none but finds something to do: the wise to study, the strong to labour, the fantastic to make love, the poet to make verses, the player to con his part, and the musician to try his note. Everyone in his quality and according to his condition sets himself to some exercise, either of the body or the mind; and therefore, since it is a time of much labour and great use, I will thus briefly conclude of it: I hold it the enemy of idleness and employer of industry. Farewell.

EIGHT OF THE CLOCK

It is now the eighth hour, and good stomachs are ready for a breakfast. The huntsman now calls in his hounds, and at the fall of the deer the horns go apace; now begin the horses to breathe and the labourer to sweat, and, with quick hands, work rids apace. Now the scholars make a charm [chattering noise] in the schools [debating-chambers], and *ergo* [therefore] keeps a stir in many a false argument; now the chapmen fall to furnish the shops, the market people make away with their ware, the tavern-hunters taste of the 'tother wine, and the nappy [strong] ale makes many a drunken noll [head]. Now the thresher begins to fall to his breakfast and eat apace, and work apace rids the corn quickly away; now the piper looks what he hath gotten since day, and the beggar, if he hath hit well, will have a pot of the best; the traveller now begins to water his horse, and, if he were early up, perhaps a bait [something to eat] will do well. The ostler now makes clean his stables, and, if guests come in, he is not without his welcome. In conclusion, for all I find in it, I hold it the mind's travail and the body's toil. Farewell.

NINE OF THE CLOCK

It is now the ninth hour, and the sun is gotten up well toward his height, and the sweating traveller begins to feel the burden of his way. The scholar now falls to conning of his lesson, and the lawyer at the bar falls to pleading of his case; the soldier now makes many a weary step in his march, and the amorous courtier is now almost ready to go out of his chamber; the market now grows to be full of people, and the shopmen now are in the heat of the market. The falconers now find it too hot flying, and the huntsmen begin to grow weary of their sport; the birders now take in their nets and their rods, and the fishermen now send their fish to the market. The tavern and the alehouse are almost full of guests, and Westminster and Guild Hall are not without a word or two on both sides. The carriers now are loading out of town, and not a letter but must be paid for ere it pass; the crier now tries the strength of his throat, and the bearward leads his bear home after his challenge; the players' bills are now almost all set up, and the clerk of the market begins to show his office. In sum, in this hour there is much to do, as well in the city as the country; and therefore to be short, I will thus make my conclusion: I hold it the toil of wit and the trial of reason. Farewell.

TEN OF THE CLOCK

It is now the tenth hour, and now preparation is to be made for dinner: the trenchers must be scraped and the napkins folded, the salt covered and the knives scoured and the cloth laid, the stools set ready and all for the table. There must be haste in the kitchen for the boiled and the roast, provision in the cellar for wine, ale and beer. The pantler and the butler must be ready in their office, and the usher of the hall must marshal the serving-men; the hawk must be set on the perch, and the dogs put into the kennel, and the guests that come to dinner must be invited against the hour. The scholars now fall to construe and parse, and the lawyer makes his client either a man or a mouse. The chapmen now draw home to their inns, and the shopmen fall to folding up their wares; the ploughman now begins to grow towards home, and the dairymaid, after her works, falls to cleansing of her vessels. The cook is cutting sops for broth, and the butler is chipping of loaves for the table; the minstrels begin to go towards the taverns, and the cursed crew visit the vile places. In sum, this I conclude of it; I hold it the messenger to the stomach and the spirit's recreation. Farewell.

ELEVEN OF THE CLOCK

It is now the eleventh hour: children must break up school, lawyers must make home to their houses, merchants to the exchange, and gallants to the ordinary [eating-house]; the dishes set ready for the meat, and the glasses half full of fair water. Now the market people make towards their horses, and the beggars begin to draw near the towns; the porridge, put off the fire, is set a-cooling for the ploughfolk, and the great loaf and the cheese are set ready on the table. Colleges and halls ring to dinner, and a scholar's commons is soon digested; the rich man's guests are at curtsy and 'I thank you'; and the poor man's feast is, 'Welcome, and God be with you'. The page is ready with his knife and trencher, and the meat will be half cold ere the guests can agree on their places; the cook voids the kitchen, and the butler the buttery, and the serving-men stand all ready before the dresser. The children are called to say grace before dinner, and the nice [fussy] people rather look than eat. The gates be locked for fear of the beggars, and the minstrels called in to be ready with their music; the pleasant wit is now breaking a jest, and the hungry man now puts his jaws to their proof. In sum, to conclude my opinion of it, I hold it the epicure's joy and the labourer's ease. Farewell.

TWELVE OF THE CLOCK

It is now the twelfth hour, the sun is at his height, and the middle of the day. The first course is served in, and the second ready to follow; the dishes have been read over, and the reversion [surplus] set by; the wine begins to be called for, and who waits not is chidden; talk passeth away time, and when stomachs are full discourses grow dull and heavy, but after fruit and cheese, say grace and take away. Now the markets are done, the Exchange broke up, and the lawyers at dinner, and Duke Humphrey's servants make their walks in Paul's [Sir John Beauchamp's tomb in St Paul's, believed to be the tomb of Humphrey, Duke of Gloucester, was the rendezvous of the penniless, workless, idlers and foodless]; the shopmen keep their shops, and their servants go to dinner. The traveller begins to call for a reckoning, and goes into the stable to see his horse eat his provender; the ploughman now is at the bottom of his dish, and the labourer draws out his dinner out of his bag. The beasts of the field take rest after their feed, and the birds of the air are at juke [chirping] in the bushes; the lamb lies sucking while the ewe chews the cud, and the rabbit will scarce peep out of her burrow; the hare sits close asleep in her meuse [hole in a hedge], while the dogs sit waiting for a bone from the trencher. In brief, for all I find of it, I thus conclude in it: I hold it the stomach's pleasure and the spirit's weariness. Farewell.

MIDNIGHT

Now is the sun withdrawn into his bedchamber, the windows of heaven are shut up, and silence with darkness have made a walk over the whole earth, and time is tasked to work upon the worst actions. Yet virtue, being herself, is never weary of well doing, while the best spirits are studying for the body's rest. Dreams and visions are haunters of troubled spirits, while nature is most comforted in the hope of the morning. The body now lies as a dead lump, while sleep, the pride of ease, lulls the senses of the slothful; the tired limbs now cease from their labours, and the studious brains give over their business; the bed is now the image of the grave, and the prayer of the faithful makes the pathway to Heaven.

Lovers now enclose a mutual content, while gracious minds have no wicked imaginations; thieves, wolves and foxes now fall to their prey, but a strong lock and a good wit will aware much mischief, and he that trusteth in God will be safe from the Devil. Farewell.

Nicholas Breton, *Fantastickes* (1626)

CLOTHES AND FASHIONS

The fantastical folly of our nation, even from the courtier to the carter, is such that no form of apparel liketh us no longer than the first garment is in wearing, if it continue so long and be not laid aside to receive some other trinket newly devised by the fickle-headed tailors, who covet to have several tricks in cutting, thereby to draw fond customers to more expense of money. For my part, I can tell better how to inveigh against this enormity than describe any certainty of our attire, sithence such is our mutability, that today there is none to the Spanish guise, tomorrow the French toys are most fine and delectable, ere long no such apparel as that which is after the high Almain [German] fashion; by and by the Turkish manner is best liked of, otherwise the Morisco gowns, the barbarian [North African] sleeves, the mandilion [loose overcoat] worn to Colley Weston-ward, and the short French breeches make such a comely vesture that, except it were a dog in a doublet, you shall not see any so disguised as are my countrymen of England.

And as these fashions are diverse, so likewise it is a world to see the costliness and the curiosity, the excess and the vanity, the pomp and the bravery, the change and the variety, and finally the fickleness and the folly, that is in all degrees. Insomuch that nothing is more constant in England than inconstancy of attire. Oh, how much cost is bestowed nowadays upon our bodies, and how little upon our souls! How many suits of apparel hath the one, and how little furniture hath the other! How long time is asked in decking up of the first, and how little space is left wherin to feed up the latter! How curious, how nice also are a number of men and women, and how hardly can the tailor please them in making it fit for their bodies! How many times must it be sent back again to him that made it! What chafing, what fretting, what reproachful language doth the poor workman bear away! And many times when he hath done nothing to it at all, yet when it is brought home again it is very fit and handsome. Then must we put it on, then must the long seams of our hose be set by a plumbline, then we puff, then we blow, and finally sweat till we drop, that our clothes may stand well upon us. . . . I say most nations do not unjustly deride us, as also for that we do seem to imitate all nations round about us, wherein we be like to the polypus [octopus] or chameleon; and thereunto bestow most cost upon our arses, and much more than upon all the rest of our bodies, as women do, likewise upon their heads and shoulders.

In women also it is most to be lamented, that they do now far exceed the lightness of our men (who nevertheless are transformed from the cap even to the very shoe), and such staring attire as in time past was supposed meet for none but light housewives [hussies] only, is now become an habit for chaste and sober matrons. What should I say of their doublets with pendant codpieces [small ornamental bags] on the breast, full of jags and cuts, and sleeves of sundry colours? Their galligaskins [wide, loose breeches], to bear out their bums and make their attire to fit plumb round (as they term it) about them? Their farthingales [hooped petticoats] and diversely coloured nether stocks of silk, jersey and such like, whereby their bodies are rather deformed than commended? I have met with some of these trulls in London so disguised that it hath passed my skill to discern whether they are men or women. . . . Thus it is now come to pass that women are become men, and men transformed into monsters . . .

William Harrison, *Description of England* (1587)

HEAD TO FOOT

[HATS]
Sometimes they wear them sharp on the crown, perking up like a sphere, or shaft of a steeple, standing a quarter of a yard above the crown of their heads, some more, some less, as please the fantasies of their minds. Othersome be flat and broad on the crown, like the battlements of a house. Another sort have round crowns, sometimes with one kind of band, sometime with another, now black, now white, now russet, now red, now green, now yellow, now this, now that, never content with one colour or fashion two days together. And thus in vanity they spend the Lord his treasure, consuming their golden years and silver days in

wickedness and sin. And as the fashions be rare and strange, so are the things whereof their hats be made diverse also: for some are of silk, some of velvet, some of taffeta, some of sarsenet [fine silk], some of wool, and, which is more curious, some of a certain kind of fine hair, far fetched and dear bought you may be sure. And so common a thing it is, that every servingman, countryman and other, even all indifferently, do wear of these hats. For he is of no account or estimation among men, if he have not a velvet or a taffeta hat, and that must be pinked [snipped] and cunningly carved of the best fashion. And good profitable hats be they, for the longer you wear them, the fewer holes they have. Besides this, of late there is a new fashion of wearing their hats sprung up amongst them, which they father upon the Frenchmen, namely, to wear them without bands, but how unseemly (I will not say how assy) a fashion that is, let the wise judge. Notwithstanding however it be, if it please them, it shall not displease me. Another sort, as fantastical as the rest, are content with no kind of hat without a great bunch of feathers of divers and sundry colours, peaking on top of their heads, not unlike (I dare not say) cockscombs, but as sterns [flags] of pride and ensigns of vanity, and these fluttering sails and feathered flags of defiance to virtue (for so they are) are so advanced in Ailgna [England] that every child hath them in his hat or cap.

[RUFFS]

They have great and monstrous ruffs, made of cambric, holland [linen], lawn or else of some other the finest cloth that can be got for money, whereof some be a quarter of a yard, yea, some more, very few less, so that they stand a full quarter of a yard (and more) from their necks, hanging over their shoulder points, instead of a veil. But if Aeolus with his blasts, or Neptune with his storms, chance to hit upon the crazy bark of their bruised ruffs, then they go flip flap in the wind like rags flying abroad, and lie upon their shoulders like the dishcloth of a slut. But wot you what? The Devil, as he in the fullness of his malice first invented these great ruffs, so hath he now found out also two great stays to bear up and maintain this his kingdom of great ruffs (for the Devil is king and prince over all the children of pride). The one arch or pillar whereby his kingdom of great ruffs is underpropped is a certain kind of liquid matter which they call Starch, wherein the Devil has willed them to wash and dive his ruffs well, which when they be dry will then stand stiff and inflexible about their necks. The other pillar is a certain device made of wires crested for the purpose, whipped over either with gold thread, silver or silk, and this he calleth a supportasse or underpropper. This is to be applied round about their necks under the ruff, upon the outside of the band, to bear up the whole frame and body of the ruff from falling and hanging down.

[DOUBLETS]

Their doublets are no less monstrous than the rest: for now the fashion is to have them hang down to the midst of their thighs, or at least to their privy members, being so hard-quilted and stuffed, bombasted [padded] and sewed, as they can very hardly either stop down or decline themselves to the ground, so stiff and sturdy they stand about them.

Now what handsomeness can be in these doublets which stand on their bellies, like or much bigger than a man's codpiece (so as their bellies are thicker than all their bodies beside), let wise men judge. For, for my part, handsomeness in them I see none, and much less profit.

And to be plain, I never saw any wear them but I supposed him to be a man inclined to gormandise, gluttony and suchlike. . . . Certain I am there was never any kind of apparel ever invented that could more disproportion the body of man than these doublets with great bellies hanging down beneath their pudenda (as I have said) and stuffed with four, five or six pound of bombast in the least. I say nothing of what their doublets be made, some of satin, taffeta, silk grogram [coarse silk and wool], chamlet [silky wool], gold, silver and what not, slashed, jagged, cut, carved, pinked and laced with all kind of costly lace of divers and sundry colours . . .

[FOOTWEAR]

To . . . their nether-stocks they have corked shoes, pinsnets [thin slippers] and fine pantofles [high-heeled slippers], which bear them up a finger or two from the ground, whereof some be of white leather, some of black, and some of red; some of black velvet, some of white, some of red, some of green, raced, carved, cut and stitched all over with silk and laid on with gold, silver and suchlike; yet, notwithstanding, to what good uses serve these pantofles, except it be to wear in a private house or in a man's chamber, to keep him warm (for this is the only use whereto they best serve, in my judgement)? But to go abroad in them as they are now used altogether, is rather a let or hindrance to a man than otherwise, for shall he not be fain to knock and spurn at every stone, wall or post, to keep them on his feet?

But if they would consider that their clothes (except those that they wear upon their backs) be none of theirs, but the poor's, they would not heap up their presses and wardrobes as they do. Do they think that it is lawful for them to have millions of sundry sorts of apparel lying rotting by them, when as the poor members of Jesus Christ die at their doors for want of clothing? God commandeth in his law that there be no miserable poor man nor beggar amongst us, but that everyone be provided for and maintained of that abundance which God hath blessed us withal. But we think it a great matter if we give them an old ragged coat, doublet or a pair of hosen, or else a penny or two, whereas notwithstanding we flow in abundance of all things. Then we think we are halfway to heaven, and we need to do no more. If we give them a piece of brown bread, a mess of porridge (nay, the stocks and prison, with whipping cheer now and then, is the best portion of alms which many gentlemen give) at our doors, it is counted meritorious, and a work of supererogation, when we fare full delicately ourselves, feeding on many a dainty dish.

Philip Stubbes, The Anatomy of Abuses (1583)

THE TOP OF FASHION

Gentlewomen virgins wear gowns close to the body, and aprons of fine linen, and go bareheaded, with their hair curiously knotted and raised at the forehead, but many, against the cold (as they say) wear caps of hair that is not their own, decking their heads with buttons of gold, pearls, and flowers of silk, or knots of ribbon. They wear fine linen, and commonly falling bands and often ruffs, both starched, and chains of pearl about the neck, with their breasts naked. The graver sort of married women used to cover their head with a French hood of velvet, set with a border of gold buttons and pearls; but this fashion is now left, and they most commonly wear a coif [light cap] of linen, and a little hat of beaver or felt, with their hair somewhat raised at the forehead. Young married gentlewomen sometimes go bare-headed, as virgins, decking their hair with jewels and silk ribbons, but more commonly they use the foresaid linen coif and hats. All in general wear gowns hanging loose at the back, with a kirtle and close upperbody, of silk or light stuff, but have lately left the French sleeves borne out with hoops of whalebone, and the young married gentlewomen no less than the virgins show their breasts naked.

Fynes Moryson, *An Itinerary* (1617)

WHO'S BEEN DOING YOUR HAIR THEN?

There are no finer fellows under the sun, nor experter in their noble science of barbing than they [barbers] be. And therefore in the fullness of their overflowing knowledge (oh, ingenious heads, and worthy to be dignified with the diadem of folly and vain curiosity!) they have invented such strange fashions and monstrous manners of cuttings, trimmings, shavings and washings that you would wonder to see. They have one manner of cut called the French cut, another the Spanish cut; one the Dutch cut, another the Italian; one the new cut, another the old; one of the bravado fashion, another of the mean fashion; one a gentleman's cut, another the common cut; one cut of the Court, another of the country, with infinite the like varieties which I overpass. They have also other kinds of cuts innumerable; and therefore when you come to be trimmed, they will ask you whether you will be cut to look terrible to your enemy or amiable to your friend, grim and stern in countenance or pleasant and demure (for they have divers kinds of cuts for all these purposes, or else they lie).

Then, when they have done all their feats, it is a world to consider how their mustachios must be preserved and laid out, from one cheek to another, yea, almost from one ear to another, and turned up like two horns toward the forehead. Besides that, when they come to the cutting of the hair, what snipping and snapping of the scissors is there, what tricking and trimming, what rubbing, what scratching, what combing and clawing, what trickling and toying, and all to tawe out [extort] money, you may be sure.

And when they come to washing, oh, how gingerly they behave themselves therein. For then shall your mouth be bossed with the lather or foam that riseth off the balls (for they have their sweet balls wherewithal they use to wash); your eyes closed must be anointed

25

therewithal also. Then snap go the fingers, full bravely, God wot. Thus this tragedy ended, comes me warm cloths to wipe and dry him withal; next, the ears must be picked, and closed together again artificially, forsooth; the hair of the nostrils cut away, and everything done in order comely to behold. The last action in this tragedy is the payment of money.

Philip Stubbes, *The Anatomie of Abuses, Part Two* (1583)

SKIN DEEP

(I)

Maquerelle [the Court bawd, offering two ladies a potion].   This it doth, it purifieth the blood, smootheth the skin, enliveneth the eye, strengtheneth the veins, mundefieth [cleans] the teeth, comforteth the stomach, fortifieth the back, and quickeneth the wit, that's all. . . . Eat me of this posset, quicken your blood, and preserve your beauty. Do you know Doctor Plaster-face? By this curd, he is the most exquisite in forging of veins, sprightening of eyes, dyeing of hair, sleeking of skins, blushing of cheeks, surfling [whitening with sulphur mixture] of breasts, blanching and bleaching of teeth, that ever made an old lady gracious by torchlight, by this curd, la! . . . Men say! Let them say what they will: life o' woman! they are ignorant of your wants. The more in years the more in perfection they grow; if they lose youth and beauty, they gain wisdom and discretion; but when our beauty fades, goodnight with us! There cannot be an uglier thing to see than an old woman, from which, O pruning, pinching and painting, deliver all sweet beauties!

John Marston, *The Malcontent* (1604)

(II)

Divers women use Sublimate [of mercury] diversely prepared for increase of their beauty. Some bray [pound] it with quicksilver in a marble mortar with a wooden pestle; and this they call argentatum. Others boil it in water and therewith wash their face. Some grind it with pomatum, and sundry other ways. But this is sure, that which way soever it be used, it is very offensive to man's flesh. . . . Sublimate is called dead fire, because of his malignant and biting nature, the composition whereof is salt, quicksilver and vitriol, distilled together in a glassen vessel.

This the chirurgeons [surgeons, doctors] call a corrosive, because if it be put upon man's flesh it burneth in a short space, mortifying the place, not without great pain to the patient. Wherefore such women as use it about their face have always black teeth standing far out of their gums like a Spanish mule, an offensive breath, with a face half scorched, and an unclean complexion. All which proceed from the nature of Sublimate. So that simple women, thinking to grow more beautiful, become disfigured, hastening old age before the time, and giving occasion to their husbands to seek strangers instead of their wives, with divers other inconveniences.

Richard Haydocke (trans. from Giovanno Lomazzo), *A Tracte Containing the Artes of curious Paintinge, Caruinge and Building* (1598)

2

WOMEN AND MEN

More belongs to marriage than four bare legs in a bed.
(Sixteenth-century proverb)

Most people got married. One could consent to marriage at the age of seven, though it could not be consummated until twelve (for girls) and fourteen (for boys), but such marriages were extremely rare. The aristocracy and upper gentry, concerned with estates, money and status, and the very poor, with no such concerns, tended to marry earlier than the majority, among whom men generally married at twenty-seven and women at twenty-five. Apart from some wealthy families, marriages were not usually enforced or prevented, and parents and associates mostly acted as negotiators and facilitators. Dowries, marriage portions and parental approval were important, but mattered less than general compatibility: the companionate marriage was hoped for more than the romantic or economic.

Courtship proceeded by familiar patterns, with visits and exchanges of rings and gloves. In an age lacking reliable contraception and with increasing moral pressure from the authorities and community, premarital sexual activity was limited in its scope, though many promised couples anticipated marriage (at least one-fifth of brides were pregnant; when hard times broke off intended marriages, the illegitimacy rate – usually $2\frac{1}{2}$ per cent – increased, to about 4 per cent in 1600). The dual standard, of greater sexual freedom for men, prevailed generally, with unprotected women and servant girls considered fair game. After marriage there was, among the lower orders especially, some degree of sexual freedom and irregularity practised by both sexes (despite the church courts' penances); in London, with its large population of transients and young apprentices forbidden to marry, there was not a little prostitution.

Nuptial contracts took various forms: promises made in the future tense, before witnesses (*verba de futuro*) were not binding unless followed by sexual intercourse; promises made in the present tense before witnesses (*verba de praesenti*) constituted a sufficient contract. From Elizabeth's time, weddings no longer took place in the church porch, but inside; people wore new clothes, though the bride did not necessarily wear white; celebrations could be protracted and very lively Marriage marked a real change in status for both parties, establishing them in the community, with new rights and duties. The nuclear family (one couple and children) was the norm; households included servants, apprentices and children placed by other families.

In such a hierarchic, patriarchal society, the husband's authority was axiomatic, with the wife having few legal rights. There was, however, a sense of the relationship being one of complementarity; for many, marriage was also an economic partnership, especially for poor farmers, tradesmen and the labouring poor. Many women actively engaged in work beyond housework, and widows frequently continued their husbands' businesses.

There was a high birth-rate; although about one-quarter of children died before the age of ten, well over one-third of the population consisted of dependent children. Perhaps 1 per cent of mothers died in childbirth (things were worse in unhealthy London); the average woman might expect six or seven pregnancies, not all successful. Giving birth was a major female ritual, taking place in a darkened room accompanied by gossips and midwives (usually local wives or widows, approved by the church), and celebrated then and at churchings (thanksgiving/purification ceremonies and occasions for women's parties). Gentry women frequently employed wet-nurses, which increased their chances of early re-impregnation (Anne, wife of John Donne, would-be courtier, MP and priest, who married – without parental consent – at seventeen, had eleven pregnancies in fourteen years, dying after the second stillbirth). While there was practically no divorce, and very rare annulments (though the poor might simply run away), the high mortality rate produced many relatively young widowers and widows, who regularly remarried, often several times.

The period also marks the beginning of the controversy regarding the nature, rights and status of women; provoked by the loosening of traditional social restraints, economic change, the spread of literacy and religious debate, this became part of the social near-revolution of later Stuart times.

LOVE, MARRIAGE AND CHILDREN

The stage is more beholding to love than the life of man. For as to the stage, love is ever matter of comedies, and now and then of tragedies; but in life it doth much mischief, sometimes like a siren, sometimes like a fury. . . . There was never proud man thought so absurdly well of himself as the lover doth of the person loved; and therefore it was well said, That it is impossible to love and be wise. Neither doth this weakness appear to others only and not to the party loved, but to the loved most of all, except the love be reciproque [returned]. For it is a true rule, that love is ever rewarded with the reciproque or with an inward and secret contempt. . . .

He that hath wife and children hath given hostages to fortune; for they are impediments to great enterprises, either of virtue or mischief. Certainly, the best works, and of greatest merit for the public, have proceeded from unmarried or childless men, which both in affection and means have married and endowed the public. Yet it were great reason that those that have children should have greatest care of future times, unto which they know they must transmit their dearest pledges. . . . A single life doth well with churchmen, for charity will hardly water the ground where it must first fill a pool. . . . Certainly, wife and children are a kind of discipline of humanity; and single men, though they be many times more charitable, because their means are less exhaust[ed], yet, on the other side, they are more cruel and hard-hearted (good to make severe inquisitors), because their tenderness is not so often called upon. . . . Wives are young men's mistresses; companions for middle age; and old men's nurses. So as a man may have a quarrel to marry when he will.

Women and Men

But yet he was reputed one of the wise men, that made answer to the question, when a man should marry: A young man not yet, an older man not at all.

The joys of parents are secret, and so are their griefs and fears: they cannot utter the one, nor they will not utter the other. Children sweeten labours, but they make misfortunes more bitter: they increase the cares of life, but they mitigate the remembrance of death.

Francis Bacon, *Essayes* (1597–1625)

The Paradise of Married Women

Wives in England are entirely in the power of their husbands, their lives only excepted . . . yet they are not kept so strictly as they are in Spain or elsewhere. Nor are they shut up, but they have the free management of the house or housekeeping, after the fashion of those of the Netherlands, and others their neighbours. They go to market to buy what they like best to eat. They are well dressed, fond of taking it easy, and commonly leave the care of household matters and drudgery to their servants. They sit before their doors, decked out in fine clothes, in order to see and be seen by the passers-by. In all banquets and feasts they are shown the greatest honour; they are placed at the upper end of the table, where they are the first served; at the lower end, they help the men. All the rest of their time they employ in walking or riding, in playing at cards or otherwise, in visiting their friends and keeping company, conversing with their equals (whom they term, gossips) and their neighbours, and making merry with them at childbirths, christenings, churchings and funerals; and all this with the permission and knowledge of their husbands, as such is the custom. Although the husbands often recommend to them the pains, industry and care of the German or Dutch women, who do what the men ought to do both in the house and the shop, for which services in England men are employed, nevertheless the women usually persist in retaining their customs. This is why England is called the paradise of married women.

Van Meteren, *Nederlandische Historie* (1575), in W.B. Rye, *England as seen by Foreigners* (1865)

LAUNCHING GENTLEMEN'S DAUGHTERS

I would have their breeding like to the Dutchwoman's clothing, tending to profit only and comeliness.

Though she never have a dancing-schoolmaster, a French tutor nor a Scotch tailor to make her shoulders of the breadth of Bristol Causeway, it makes no matter; for working in curious Italian purls [lacy loops] or French borders, is not worth the while. Let them learn plain works of all kind, so they take heed of too open seaming. Instead of song and music, let them learn cookery and laundry. And instead of reading Sir Philip Sidney's *Arcadia*, let them read the *Grounds of Good Housewifery*. I like not a female poetess at any hand. Let greater personages glory their skills in music, the posture of their bodies, their knowledge in languages, the greatness and freedom of their spirits, and their arts in arraigning men's affections at their flattering faces. This is not the way to breed a private gentleman's daughter.

If the mother of them be a good housewife and religiously disposed, let her have the bringing up of one of them. Place the other two forth betimes, and before they can judge of a good manly leg: the one in the house of some good merchant, or citizen of civil and religious government; the other in the house of some lawyer, some judge or well-reported Justice or gentleman of the country, where the serving man is not too predominant. In any of these she may learn what belongs to her improvement, for sempstry [sewing], for confectionery [making preserves] and all requisites of housewifery. She shall be sure to be restrained of all rank company and unfitting liberty, which are the overthrow of too many of their sex. . . .

The merchant's factor [agent] and citizen's servant of the better sort cannot disparage [discredit] your daughters with their society; and the judges', lawyers' and Justices' followers are not ordinary serving men, but men of good breed, and their education for the most part clerkly, whose service promiseth their further and future advancement.

Your daughter at home will make a good wife for some good yeoman's eldest son, whose father will be glad to crown his sweating frugality with alliance to such a house of gentry. The young man's fingers will itch to be handling of taffeta; and to be placed at the table; and to be carved unto by Mistress Dorothy, it will make him and the good plain old Joan, his mother, to pass over all respect of portion or patrimony.

For your daughter at the merchant's, and her sister, if they can carry it wittily, the City affords them variety.

The young factor, being fancy-caught in his days of innocency, and before he travels so far into experience as into foreign countries, may lay such a foundation of first love in her bosom as no alteration of climate can alter. So likewise may Thomas, the foreman of the shop, when beard comes to him, as apprenticeship goes from him, be entangled and belimed with the like springes [traps], for the better is as easily surprised as the worst. . . . With a little patience your daughter may light upon some Counsellor at Law who may be willing to take the young wench in hope of favour with the old Judge. An attorney will be glad to give all his profits of a Michaelmas Term, fees and all, but to woo her through a crevice. And the parson of the parish, being her lady's chaplain, will forswear eating of tithe-pig for a whole year for such a parcel of glebe land at all times.

William Powell, *Tom of all Trades, or the Plain Pathway to Preferment* (1631)

AGAINST THE NOBLY DESCENDED MUSEUS

The well-born Museus wedded hath of late
A butcher's daughter fat, for pounds and plate:
Which match is like a pudding, sith in that
He puts the blood, her father all the fat.

John Davies of Hereford, *Wit's Bedlam* (1617)

COURTING, AND CAUGHT

[The mother's] instructions being thus given, and the plot laid for the fetching in of this kind fool into Lob's pound [trap or cage], the next day he cometh in and is on all hands more kindly welcomed and entertained. After dinner, having had great cheer, the mother falls in talk with the other guests, and this frolic novice gets him as near to the daughter as he can, and while the other are hard in chat, he takes her by the hand and thus begins to court her.

'Gentlewoman, I would to God you knew my thoughts.'

'Your thoughts, sir,' quoth she, 'how should I know them except you tell them me? It may be you think something you are loth to tell.'

'Not so,' saith he, 'yet I would you knew it without telling.'

'But that,' saith she, 'is unpossible.'

'Then,' quoth he, 'if I might do it without offence, I would adventure to tell you them.'

'Sir,' saith she, 'you may freely speak your pleasure, for I do so much assure me of your honesty, that I know you will speak nothing that may procure offence.'

'Then thus,' saith he, 'I acknowledge without feigning, that I am far unworthy of so great favour as to be accepted for your servant, friend and lover, which art so fair, so gentle and every way so gracious, that I may truly say that you are replenished with all the good gifts that nature can plant in any mortal creature. But if you would vouchsafe me this undeserved grace, my good will, diligence and continual forwardness to serve and please you should never fail, but I would therein equal the most loyal lover that ever lived, I would esteem you more than anything else, and tender more your good name and credit than mine own.'

'Good sir,' quoth she, 'I heartily thank you for your kind offer, but I pray you speak no more of such matter, for I neither know what love is, nor care for knowing it. This is not the lesson that my mother teacheth me nowadays.'

'Why,' saith he, 'if you please she shall know nothing of it, yet the other day I heard her talk of preferring you in marriage to Master G.R.'

'How say you to that?' quoth she.

'Marry,' thus answers the gentleman, 'if you would vouchsafe to entertain me for your servant, I would never marry, but rely on your favour.'

'But that,' saith she, 'should be no profit to either of us both, and besides it would be to my reproach, which I had not thought you would seek.'

'Nay,' quoth he, 'I had rather die than seek your discredit.'

'Well, sir,' saith she, 'speak no more hereof, for if my mother should perceive it, I were utterly undone.'

And it may be her mother makes her a sign to give over, fearing that she doth not play her part well. At the breaking up of their

Women and Men

amorous parley, he conveys into her hand a gold ring, or some such toy, desiring her to take it and keep it for his sake; which at the first (according to her mother's precepts) she doth refuse, but upon his more earnest urging of it, she is content to take it in the way of honesty, and not on any promise or condition of any further matter.

When it is brought to this pass, the mother makes motion of a journey to be made the next morning, some ten or twelve miles off, to visit or feast with some friend, or to some fair, or whatsoever other occasion presents itself. To this motion they all agree, and afterward sit down to supper, where he is placed next the daughter, who carries herself so toward him with her piercing glances that the young heir is set on fire therewith.

Well, morning comes, they mount on horseback, and by the opinion of them all there is never a horse in the company that can carry double but his, so that he is appointed to have the maiden ride behind him, whereof he is not a little proud, and when he feels her hold him fast by the middle (which she doth to stay herself the better) he is even ravished with joy. After their return home, which will be the same night, the mother, taking her daughter aside, questions with her touching all that had passed between the amorous gallant and her, which when her daughter hath rehearsed, then proceeds the wily grandam thus.

'If he court thee any more, as I know he will, then answer him that thou hast heard thy father and me talking of matching thee with Master G.R., but that thou hast no desire as yet to be married. If he then offer thee to make thee his wife, and use comparisons of his worth and wealth, as if he were every way as good as he, thank him for his good will and kindness, and tell him that thou wilt speak with me about it, and that for thine own part thou couldst find in thy heart to have him to thy husband rather than any man else.'

Upon this lesson the daughter sleeps, revolving it all night in her mind. The next morning she walks into the garden, and this lusty younker follows, when, having given her the time of day, he falls to his former suit. She wills him to give over such talk, or she will leave his company.

'Is this love you bear me,' quoth she, 'to seek my dishonesty? You know well enough that my father and mother is minded to bestow me otherwise.'

'Ah, my sweet mistress,' saith he, 'I would they did so far favour me herein as they do him; I dare boldly say and swear it, and without vainglory utter it, that I am every way his equal.'

35

'Oh sir,' answers she, 'I would he were like you.'

'Ah, sweet mistress,' saith he, 'you deign to think better of me than I deserve, but if you would further vouchsafe me the other favour, I should esteem myself most happy.'

'In troth, sir,' saith she, 'it is a thing I may not do of myself, without the counsel and consent of my parents, to whom I would gladly move it, if I thought they would not be offended. But it should be better if yourself would break the matter unto them, and be sure, if that they refer the matter to me, you shall speed so soon as any.'

He, being ravished with these words, and yielding her infinite thanks, trots presently to the mother to get her good will. To be short, with a little ado the matter is brought about, even in such sort as he would desire, they are straightway contracted and immediately wedded, both because her friends fear that the least delay will prevent all, and because he is so hot in the spur that he thinks every hour a year till it be done. Well, the wedding night comes, wherein she behaves herself so by her mother's counsel that he dares swear on the Bible that he had her maidenhead, and that himself was the first that trod the path. . . .

R[obert]. T[ofte]. (trans. from Antoine de la Sale?), *The Batchelars Banquet* (1603)

POETRY AND PASSION

Who would have learned to write an excellent passion [love poem] might have been a perfect tragic poet had he but attended half the extremity of his [the Earl of Surrey's] lament. Passion upon passion would throng one on another's neck. He would praise her beyond the moon and stars, and that so sweetly and ravishingly as I persuade myself he was more in love with his own curious-forming fancy than her face; and truth it is, many become passionate lovers only to win praise to their wits.

He praised, he prayed, he desired and besought her to pity him that perished for her. From this his entranced mistaking could no man remove him. Who loveth resolutely will include everything under the name of his love. From prose he would leap into verse, and with these or suchlike rhymes assault her.

WOMEN AND MEN

If I must die, Oh, let me choose my death:
Suck out my soul with kisses, cruel maid;
In thy breasts' crystal balls embalm my breath;
Dole it all out in sighs when I am laid.
Thy lips on mine like cupping-glasses clasp,
Let our tongues meet and strive as they would sting;
Crush out my wind with one straight girting grasp;
Stabs on my heart keep time whilst thou dost sing.
Thy eyes like searing irons burn out mine,
In thy fair tresses stifle me outright,
Like Círce change me to a loathsome swine,
So I may live for ever in thy sight.
　　Into heaven's joys none can profoundly see,
　　Except that first they meditate on thee.

Sadly [seriously] and verily, if my master said true, I should, if I were a wench, make many men quickly immortal. What is't, what is't for a maid fair and fresh to spend a little lipsalve on a hungry lover? My master beat the bush and kept a coil and a prattling, but I caught the bird: simplicity and plainness shall carry it away in another world. God wot he was Petro Desperato when I, stepping to her with a Dunstable [plain] tale, made up my market. A holy requiem to their souls that think to woo a woman with riddles.

Thomas Nashe, *The Unfortunate Traveller* (1594)

A SHOWY WEDDING

So the marriage day being appointed, all things prepared meet for the wedding, and royal cheer ordained, most of the lords, knights and gentlemen thereabout were invited thereunto; the bride being attired in a gown of sheep's russet and a kirtle of fine worsted, her head attired with a biliment [ornament] of gold, and her hair as yellow as gold hanging down behind her, which was curiously combed and plaited according to the manner of those days. She was led to church between two sweet boys, with bride-laces and rosemary tied about their silken sleeves; the one of them was son to Sir Thomas Parry, the other to Sir Francis Hungerford. Then was there a fair bride-cup of silver and gilt carried before her, hung about with silken ribbons of all colours; next was there a noise [group] of musicians, that played all the way before her; after her came all the chiefest maidens of the country, some bearing great bridecakes and some garlands of wheat finely gilded, and so she passed unto the church. . . .

The marriage being solemnised, home they came in order as before, and to dinner they went, where was no want of good cheer, no lack of melody: Rhenish wine at this wedding was as plentiful as beer or ale, for the merchants had sent thither ten tuns of the best in the Steelyard [storehouse in London].

This wedding endured ten days, to the great relief of the poor that dwelt all about; and in the end the bride's father and mother came to pay their daughter's portion, which when the bridegroom had received, he gave them great thanks . . .

Thomas Deloney, *Jacke of Newberie* (1597)

BEDDING THE BRIDE

Now bring the Bryde into the brydall boures.
Now night is come, now soone her disaray.

Edmund Spenser, *Epithalamion* (1594)

When bedtime is come, the bridemen pull off the bride's garters, which she had before untied that they might hang down and so prevent a curious hand coming too near her knee. This done, and the garters being fastened to the hats of the gallants, the bridemaids carry the bride into the bedchamber, where they undress her and lay her in bed. The bridegroom, who by the help of his friends is undressed in some other room, comes in his nightgown as soon as possible to his spouse, who is surrounded by mother, aunts, sisters and friends, and without any further ceremony gets into bed. Some of the women run away, others remain, and the moment afterwards they are all got together again. The bridemen take the bride's stockings, and the bridemaids the bridegroom's; both sit down at the bed's feet and fling the stockings over their heads, endeavouring to direct them so as that they may fall upon the married couple. If the man's stocking thrown by the maid fall upon the bridegroom's head, it is a sign she will quickly be married herself; and the same prognostic holds good of the woman's stockings thrown by the man. Oftentimes these young people engage with one another upon the success of the stockings, though they themselves look upon it to be nothing but sport.

While some amuse themselves agreeably with these little follies, others are preparing a good posset, which is a kind of caudle, a potion made up of milk, wine, yolks of eggs, sugar, cinnamon, nutmeg, etc. This they present to the young couple, who swallow it down as fast as they can to get rid of so troublesome company; the bridegroom prays, scolds, entreats them to be gone, and the bride says ne'er a word, but thinks the more. If they obstinately continue to retard the accomplishment of their wishes, the bridegroom jumps up in his shirt, which frightens the women and puts them to flight. The men follow them, and the bridegroom returns to the bride.

Henri Misson, M. Misson's Memoirs and Observations in his Travels over England
(trans. 1719)

A FAIR THING TO BE MARRIED

Crispinella.   O, i'faith, 'tis a fair thing to be married, and a necessary. To hear this word 'must'! If our husbands be proud we must bear his contempt; if noisome [smelly] we must bear with the goat under his armholes, and, which is worse, if a loose liver we must live upon unwholesome reversions. Where, on the contrary, our husbands, because they may and we must, care not for us. Things hoped with fear and got with strugglings are men's high pleasures, when duty pales and flats their appetite.

John Marston, The Dutch Courtesan (1605)

IN DEFENCE OF WOMEN

[In 1615 Joseph Swetnam brought out *The Arraignment of Lewde, idle, froward, and unconstant women*; various answering tracts appeared under women's names.]

(I) THE WORTHINESS OF WOMEN

The material cause [of women's creation], or matter whereof woman was made, was of a refined mould, if I may so speak: for man was created of the dust of the earth, but woman was made of a part of man, after that he was a living soul; yet was she not produced from Adam's foot, to be his too low inferior, nor from his head, to be his superior, but from his side, near his heart, to be his equal; that where he is Lord, she may be Lady. And therefore saith God concerning man and woman jointly, 'Let them rule over the fish of the sea, and over the fowls of the heaven, and over every beast that moveth upon the earth' (Genesis 1.26): by which words he makes their authority equal, and all creatures to be in subjection to them both. This being rightly considered doth teach men to make such account of their wives as Adam did of Eve, 'This is bone of my bone, and flesh of my flesh' (Genesis 2.23). As also, that they neither do or wish any more hurt unto them than unto their own bodies; for men ought to love their wives as themselves, because he that loves his wife, loves himself . . .

Marriage is a merri-age, and this world's Paradise, where there is mutual love. Our blessed Saviour vouchsafed to honour a marriage with the first miracle that he wrought (John 2), unto which miracle, matrimonial estate may not unfitly be resembled. For as Christ turned water into wine, a far more excellent liquor, which, as the Psalmist saith, 'makes glad the heart of man' (Ps. 104.15), so the single man is by marriage changed from a bachelor to a husband, a far more excellent title; from a solitary life unto a joyful union and conjunction, with such a creature as God hath made meet for man, for whom none was meet till she was made. . . . 'A virtuous woman,' saith Solomon, 'is the crown of her husband' (Prov. 12.14), by which metaphor he showeth both the excellency of such a wife, and what account her husband is to make of her.

Rachel Speght, *A Mouzell for Melastomus* (1617)

(II) THE WEAKNESS OF MEN

I will not say that women are better than men, but I will say, men are not so wise as I would wish them to be, to woo us in such fashion as they do, except they should hold and account of us as their betters. . . . Suitors do ever in their suits confess a more worthiness in the persons to whom they sue. These kinds of suits are from Nature, which cannot deceive them: Nature doth tell them what women are, and custom doth approve what Nature doth direct. . . .

WOMEN AND MEN

In no one thing men do acknowledge a more excellent perfection in women than in the estimate of offences which a woman doth commit: the worthiness of the person doth make the sin more markable. What a hateful thing it is to see a woman overcome with drink, when as in a man it is noted for a sign of good fellowship. And whosoever doth observe it, for one woman which doth make a custom of drunkenness you shall find a hundred men. It is abhorred in women, and therefore they avoid it; it is laughed at and made but as a jest among men, and therefore so many practise it. Likewise if a man abuse a maid and get her with child, no matter is made of it but as a trick of youth; but it is made so heinous an offence in the maid, that she is disparaged and utterly undone by it. So in all offences, those which men commit are made light and as nothing, slighted over; but those which women do commit, those are made grievous and shameful. . . .

What is, or are, the causes then why men are so overtaken by women? You set down the causes in your fourth page; there you say, 'They are dangerous for men to deal withal, for their faces are lures, their beauties baits, their looks are nets, and their words are charms,' and all to bring men to ruin. *Incidit in Scyllam qui vult vitare Charybdim*, whilst he seeketh to avoid one mischief he falleth into another. It were more credit for men to yield our sex to be more holy, wise and strong, than to excuse themselves by the reasons alleged: for by this, men are proved to have as little wit as they are charged to exceed in wickedness. Are external and dumb shows such potent baits, nets, lures, charms to bring men to ruin? Why? Wild asses, dotterels [plovers/simpletons] and woodcocks are not so easily entangled and taken. Are men so idle, vain and weak as you seem to make them? . . . When men complain of beauty, and say, 'That woman's dressings and attire are provocations to wantonness, and baits to allure men,' it is a direct means to know of what disposition they are: it is a shame for men in censuring of women to condemn themselves. But a common inn cannot be without a common sign: it is a common sign to know a lecher, by complaining upon the cause and occasion of his surfeit: who had known his disease but by his own complaint?

'Ester Sowernam', *Ester hath hang'd Haman* (1617)

WOMANLY MEN, MANLY WOMEN

I know not how the world's degenerate,
That men or know or like not their estate:
Out from the Gades [Cadiz] up to the eastern morn,
Not one but holds his native state forlorn.
When comely striplings wish it were their chance
For Caenis' distaff to exchange their lance,   [after raping Caenis,
And wear curled periwigs, and chalk their face,   Poseidon granted
And still are poring on their pocket glass,   her wish to be a man]
'Tired with pinned ruffs and fans and partlet strips,
And busks and farthingales about their hips,
And tread on corkèd stilts a prisoner's pace,
And make their napkins for their spitting place,
And gripe their waist with a narrow span;
Fond Caenis that wouldst wish to be a man,
Whose mannish housewives like their refuse state,
And make a drudge of their uxorious mate,
Who like a cot-quean [effeminate] freezes at the rock, [stays fearfully at
Whiles his breeched dame doth man the foreign stock . . .   the distaff]
Joseph Hall, Virgidemiarum (1598)

WAR OF THE SEXES: ATTACK AND COUNTERATTACK

Cucking Stool.   The way of punishing scolding women is pleasant enough. . . . They set up a post upon the bank of a pond, or river, and over this post they lay, almost in equilibrio, . . . two pieces of wood, at one end of which the chair hangs just over the water; they place the woman in this chair, and so plunge her into the water, as often as the sentence directs, in order to cool her immoderate heat. . . .

Horns.   I have sometimes met in the streets of London a woman carrying a figure of straw representing a man crowned with very ample horns, preceded by a drum, and followed by a mob, making a most grating noise with tongs, gridirons, frying-pans and saucepans. I asked what was the meaning of all this; they told me, that a woman had given her husband a sound beating for accusing her of making him a cuckold, and that upon such occasions some kind neighbour of the *poor innocent injured creature* generally performed this ceremony.

Henri Misson, Memoirs and Observations (trans. 1719)

AN OLD JOKE: OF CUCKOLDS

A company of neighbours that dwelt all in a row, in one side of a street: one of them said, 'Let us be merry, for it is reported that we are all cuckolds that dwell on our side of the street, except one.' One of the women sat musing, to whom her husband said, 'Wife, what, all-a-mort! Why art thou so sad?' 'No,' quoth she, 'I am not sad, but I am studying which of our neighbours it is that is not a cuckold.'

John Taylor, Bull, Beare, and Horse (1638)

A LOVE AFFAIR IN A COUNTRY HOUSE

Suppertime came and passed over, and not long after came the handmaid of the Lady Elinor into the great chamber, desiring F.J. to repair unto their mistress, the which he willingly accomplished; and being now entered into her chamber, he might perceive his mistress in her night's attire, preparing herself toward bed; to whom F.J. said, 'Why, how now, Mistress? I had thought this night to have seen you dance, at least or at last, amongst us?' 'By my troth, good servant,' quoth she, 'I adventured so soon unto the great chamber yesternight, that I find myself somewhat sickly disposed, and therefore do strain courtesy, as you see, to go the sooner to my bed this night; but before I sleep,' quoth she, 'I am to charge you with a matter of weight,' and taking him apart from the rest, declared that (as that present night) she would talk with him more at large in the gallery adjoining to her chamber. Hereupon F.J., discreetly dissimulating his joy, took his leave and retired into the great chamber, where he had not long continued before the Lord of the castle commanded a torch to light him to his lodging, whereas he prepared himself and went to bed, commanding his servant also to go to his rest.

And when he thought his servant as the rest of the household be safe, he arose again, and taking his nightgown, did under the same convey his naked sword, and so walked to the gallery, where he found his good mistress walking in her nightgown and attending his coming. The moon was now at the full, the skies clear, and the weather temperate, by reason whereof he might the more plainly, and with the greater contentation, behold his long desired joys, and spreading his arms abroad to embrace his loving mistress, he said, 'Oh my dear lady, when shall I be able with the least desert to countervail the least part of this your bountiful goodness?'

The dame (whether it were of fear indeed, or that the wiliness of womanhood had taught her to cover her conceits with some fine dissimulation) start back from the knight, and shrieking (but softly) said unto him, 'Alas, servant, what have I deserved, that you come against me with naked sword as against an open enemy?'

F.J., perceiving her intent, excused himself, declaring that he brought the same for their defence, and not to offend her in any wise. The lady being therewith somewhat appeased, they began with more comfortable gesture to expel the dread of the said late affright, and sithence to become bolder of behaviour, more familiar in speech, and most kind in accomplishing of common comfort. But why hold I so long discourse in describing the joys which (for lack of like experience) I cannot set out to the full? Were it not that I know to whom I write, I would the more beware what I write. F.J. was a man, and neither of us are senseless, and therefore I should slander him (over and besides a greater obloquy to the whole genealogy of Aeneas) if I should imagine that of tender heart he would forbear to express her more tender limbs against the hard floor. Suffice that of her courteous nature she was content to accept boards for a bed of down, mats for cambric sheets, and the nightgown of F.J. for a counterpoint to cover them; and thus with calm content, instead of quiet sleep, they beguiled the night, until the proudest star began to abandon the firmament, when F.J. and his mistress were constrained also to abandon their delights, and with ten thousand sweet kisses and straight embracings, did frame themselves to play loth to depart. Well, remedy was there none, but Dame Elinor must return to her chamber, and F.J. must also convey himself, as closely as might be, into his chamber, the which was hard to do, the day being so far sprung, and he having a large base court to pass over before he could recover his stairfoot door. And though he were not much perceived, yet the Lady Frances being no less desirous to see an issue to these enterprises than F.J. was to cover them in secrecy, did watch, and even at the entering of his chamber door perceived the point of his naked sword glistering under the skirt of his nightgown; whereat she smiled and said to herself, 'This gear goeth well about.'

Well. F.J. having now recovered his chamber, he went to bed, and there let him sleep, as his mistress did on the other side. Although the Lady Frances, being thoroughly tickled now in all the veins, could not enjoy such quiet rest, but, arising, took another gentlewoman of the house with her, and walked into the park to take the fresh air of the morning.

George Gascoigne, *A Discourse of the Adventures passed by Master F.J.*
(1573)

TENDING THE NEW-BORN

After that the infant is once born, by and by the navel must be cut three fingers' breadth from the belly and so knit up. Then, as Avicenna writeth, let be strewed on the head of that that remaineth the powder of bole armoniac [Armenian clay], sanguis draconis [dragon's blood, red resin], sarcocolla [Ethiopian resin] and myrrh; and common of each like, and much beaten to powder, strew on the cut of that piece that remaineth. Then upon that, bind a piece of wool dipped in oil olive, that the powder fall not off. Some use first to knit the navel and after to cut it so much as is before rehearsed. . . .

Now to return to our purpose. When that the navel is cut off and the rest knit up, anoint all the child's body with oil of acorns, for that is singularly good to confirm, steadfast, and to defend the body from noisome things which may chance from without, as smoke, cold and such other things, which if the infant be grieved withal straight after the birth, being yet very tender, it should hurt it greatly.

After this anointing, wash the infant with warm water; and with your finger (the nail being pared) open the child's nostrils and purge them of the filthiness. *Item.* It shall be good to put a little oil into the eyes. And also that the mother, or the nurse, handle so the child's sitting place that it may be provoked to purge the belly. And chiefly it must be defended from over much cold or over much heat. . . .

Furthermore, when the infant is swaddled and laid in the cradle, the nurse must give all diligence and heed that she bind every part right and in his due place and order, and that with all tenderness and gentle entreating, and not crookedly and confusedly; the which must be done oftentimes in the day, for it is in this as in young and tender imps [sprigs], plants and twigs, the which even as you bow them in their youth, so will they evermore remain unto age. And even so the infant, if it be bound and swaddled, the members lying right and straight, then shall it grow straight and upright; if it be crookedly handled, it will grow likewise. And to the ill negligence of many nurses may be imputed the crookedness and deformity of many a man and woman which otherwise might seem well-favoured as any other.

Eucharius Röesslin (trans. by Richard Jonas) *The Byrth of Mankynde*
(twelve editions, 1545–1634)

GOOD CHEER FOR GOSSIPS

But when the time draws near of her lying down, then must he [the husband] trudge to bid gossips such as she will appoint, or else all the fat is in the fire. Consider then what cost and trouble it will be to him, to have all things fine against the christening day, what store of sugar, biscuits, comfits and carraways, marmalade and marchpane [marzipan], with all kinds of sweet suckets and superfluous banqueting stuff. . . . Besides the charge of the midwife, she must have her nurse to attend and keep her, who must make for her warm broths and costly caudles, enough both for herself and her mistress, being of the mind to fare no worse than she . . .

Then every day after her lying down will sundry dames visit her, which are her neighbours, her kinswomen, or other her special aquaintance, whom the goodman must welcome with all cheerfulness, and be sure there be some dainties in store to set before them, where they about some three or four hours, or possibly half a day, will sit chatting with the child-wife, and by that time the cups of wine have merrily trolled about, and half a dozen times moistened their lips with the sweet juice of the pulped grape, they begin thus one with another to discourse.

'Good Lord, neighbour, I marvel how our gossip Free doth, I have not seen the good soul this many a day.'

'Ah, God help her,' quoth another, 'for she hath her hands full of work, and her heart full of heaviness. While she drudges all the week at home, her husband like an unthrift never leaves running abroad, to the tennis court and dicing houses, spending all that ever he hath in such lewd sort. Yea, and if that were the worst it is well. But hear ye, gossip, there is another matter spoils all, he cares no more for his wife than for a dog, but keeps queans [whores] even under her nose.'

'Jesu,' saith another, 'who would think he were such a man, he behaves himself so orderly and civilly, to all men's sights.'

'Tush, hold your peace, gossip,' saith the other, 'it is commonly seen, the still sow eats up all the draff. He carries a smooth countenance, but a corrupt conscience. That I know F. well enough, I will not say he loves mistress G. Go to, gossip, I drink to you.'

'Yea,' saith another, 'there goes foul lies if G. himself loves not his maid N. I can tell you their mouths will not be stopped with a bushel of wheat that speak it.'

Then the third, fetching a great sigh, saying, 'By my troth, such another bold bettress [betrayer] have I at home. For never give me credit, gossip, if I took her not the other day in close confidence with her master, but I think I beswaddled [beat] my maid in such sort, that she will have small list to do so again.'

'Nay, gossip,' saith another, 'had it been to me, that should not have served her turn, but I would have turned the quean out of doors to pick a salad [to live as best she could]. For, wot ye what, gossip, it is ill setting fire and flax together. But I pray you tell me one thing: when saw you our friend mistress C.? Now, in good sooth, she is a kind creature, and a very gentle peat [a real pet]. I promise you I saw her not since you and I drank a pint of wine with her in the fish market.'

'O gossip,' saith the other, 'there is great change since that time, for they have been fain to pawn everything they have, and yet, God knows, her husband lies still in prison.'

'O the passion of my heart,' saith another, 'is all their great and glorious show come to nothing? Good Lord, what a world is this.'

'Why, gossip,' saith another, 'it was never like to be otherwise, for they loved ever to go fine, and fare daintily, and, by my fay, gossip, this is not a world for those matters, and thereupon I drink to you.'

This is commonly their communication, where they find cheer according to their choice.

R[obert]. T[ofte]., *The Batchelars Banquet* (1603)

SMALL MERCY

On the twentyfifth day of March 1626 it pleased the Lord to afflict my son John so that he was very sick and ate nothing for one whole week, but only took some cold beer. The night before he died, he lay crying all that night, 'Mame [mummy], O John's hand! O John's foot!' for he was struck cold all one side of his body; and about three o'clock in the morning Mistress Trotter that watch[ed] with him wakened my wife and I and told us he was a-departing now. And my wife started up and looked upon him; he then being aware of his mother, he said, 'Mame, John fall down, opaday. Mame, John fall down, opaday.' And the next day he had two or three fits, that we thought he would have died at that time, and at eleven o'clock at night he said unto the maid, 'Jane, some beer,' and she gave him some beer. Then he said, 'Opaday!' These are the last words that my sweet son John spake; and so ended this miserable life on Tuesday the fifth day of April 1626.

Nehemiah Wallington, *A Record of the Mercies of God*
(London Guildhall Library, MS 204)

3

HOUSE AND HOME

Increasing national prosperity and population growth inevitably resulted in more building. Redistribution of wealth from the poorer to the richer produced more great houses on large estates, ever grander and more elaborately furnished, with paintings, carvings, tapestries and liveried servants; successful yeomen farmers and merchants had larger, more comfortable houses, with pretty glass windows, more chimneys, painted plasterwork, more furniture, brass and pewter; there were also more and more two-room or one-room cottages (not always with chimneys), mudfloor huts and slum hovels, where a labourer's 'estate' might run to a few pots and pans, wooden dishes and no beds or tables, only boards and stools.

As to the great houses: from the 1560s, Flemish influence was considerable, affecting all the arts, especially architecture, where it produced what one might call Renaissance Gothic, characterized by elaborate pattern and a taste for the picturesque and even the grotesque. Owners and builders cobbled together different designs – there was little sense of a need for an 'architect' (a new and rare word). Probably the finest early Elizabethan mansion, relatively restrained in design and harmoniously proportioned, was Longleat (chiefly the work of Sir John Thynne in the 1570s), itself a significant influence on the greatest Elizabethan architect-designer, Robert Smythson, who was responsible in varying degree for many great Elizabethan show houses, especially in the Midlands, such as Wollaton Hall and Worksop Manor in Nottinghamshire (1580s) and Bess of Hardwick's 'Hardwick Hall, more window than wall' (1590s). All were mighty 'lighthouses', lofty, extravagant, with huge windows (cold, cold, surely). Jacobean great houses – the most notable being Audley End (1603–16) and Hatfield House (1607–11) – continued the 'Flemish' style: high halls, ogee-capped towers, great windows, elaborate ornamentation, strapwork, romantic silhouettes. It is not until Inigo Jones (colleague with his coeval, Ben Jonson, on James's Court masques, and an architect of international quality) that we find true High Renaissance classicism, with the Banqueting House, Whitehall Palace (1619–22) and the Queen's House, Greenwich Palace (1616–35), that announce a new aesthetic and culture.

For the middle range of houses, one might look at such buildings as, in Cheshire, Little Moreton Hall and Churche's Mansion in Nantwich, or the High House in Stafford, or Sherar's Mansion in Shrewsbury, built for the gentry and successful businessmen, half-timbered, with massive chimney-stacks, high gables, 'jettied' (i.e. overhanging) upper storeys, often with bays and (top-heavy) galleries, the country houses often on an E-plan or H-plan, the town houses narrow and deep. Modest cottages, such as Izaak Walton's Staffordshire cottage, were built in large numbers; of the wretched huts and tenements, little remains. In later years, chiefly as a result of the shortage and consequent high price of timber, more building was done in brick (especially in East Anglia) and stone (as in the north and the Cotswolds).

Living conditions varied in proportion to income. The poor might rely on 'pottage' (a vegetable porridge) and 'white meat' – cheese, milk, whey – and garden greens; bread for them might be 'horse bread' (ground peas, etc., usually fed to horses) or maslin bread, from rye; white manchet bread was not for them. Continual rent-increases gave little room for manoeuvre; of the small husbandmen, Richard Baxter wrote, 'If their sow pig or their hens breed chickens, they cannot afford to eat them, but must sell them to make their rent. They cannot afford to eat the eggs that their hens lay, nor the apples and pears that grow on their trees (save some that are not vendible), but must make money of all.' The more prosperous, the 'middling sort' (such as Justice Shallow in *Henry IV, Part Two*), however, lived increasingly well.

In any event, housewives were kept busy, both in person and through their maids. Apart from supervising the kitchen garden and poultry, they were also responsible for housecleaning (sweeping stone or earth floors, changing floor-rushes, cleaning chamber-pots), cooking, laundering (having first made the soap and starch), churning butter, making cheese, pickles and preserves, salting meat, brewing ale and beer, weaving, knitting, and home doctoring. Think of all the labour, of all the vats, pans, tubs, stoppered jars, troughs, pails, sieves, churns, presses, barrels, spits, baskets, brushes, ladles . . .

> Though husbandry seemeth to bring in the gains,
> Yet huswifery labours seem equal in pains.
> Some respite to husbands the weather may send,
> But housewives' affairs have never an end.

Thomas Tusser, *Five Hundred Points of Good Husbandrie* (1580)

BUILDING AND FURNISHING

The greatest part of our building in the cities and good towns of England consisteth only of timber, for as yet few of the houses of the commonality (except here and there in the West Country towns) are made of stone, although they may, in my opinion, in diverse places be builded so good cheap of one as of the other. In old time the houses of the Britons were slightly set up, with a few posts and many raddles [rails or wattles], the like whereof almost is to be seen in the fenny countries and northern parts unto this day, where for lack of wood they are enforced to continue this ancient manner of building. It is not in vain therefore in speaking of building to make distinction between the plain and woody soils: for as in these our houses are commonly strong and well-timbered, so that in many places there are not above four, six or nine inches between stud [rail] and stud, so, in the open champion countries they are enforced for want of stuff to use no studs at all, but only frank-posts, resons [supporting beams], beams, prickposts [spikes], ground-sills, transoms and such principals, with here and there a girding [supporting girder], whereunto they fasten their splints or raddles, and then cast it all over with thick clay to keep out the wind, which otherwise would annoy them. . . . In like sort as every country house is thus apparelled on the outside, so is it inwardly divided into sundry rooms above and beneath;

and where plenty of wood is, they cover them with tiles, otherwise with straw, sedge or reed, except some quarry of slate be near hand, from whence they have for their money as much as may suffice them. . . .

In plastering likewise of our fairest houses over our heads, we use to lay first a layer or two of white mortar tempered with hair, upon laths, which are nailed one by another (or sometimes upon reed or wicker, more dangerous for fire, and made fast here and there with sap-laths, for falling down) and finally cover all with the aforesaid plaster, which, beside the delectable whiteness of the stuff itself, is laid on so even and smoothly, as nothing, in my judgement, can be done with more exactness. The walls of our houses on the inner sides in like sort be either hanged with tapestry, arras work or painted cloths, wherein either divers histories ['a pretty slight drollery, or the story of the Prodigal, or the German hunting,' suggested Falstaff], or herbs, beasts, knots and suchlike are stained, or else they are sealed with oak of our own, or wainscot brought hither out of the east countries, whereby the rooms are not a little commended, made warm and much more close than otherwise they would be. . . .

Of old time, our country houses, instead of glass, did use much lattice, and that made either of wicker or fine rifts of oak in chequer wise. . . . Only the clearest glass is most esteemed: for we have divers sorts, some brought out of Burgundy, some out of Normandy, much out of Flanders, beside that which is made in England . . .

The furniture of our houses also exceedeth, and is grown in manner even to passing delicacy; and herein I do not speak of the nobility and gentry only, but likewise of the lowest sort in most places of our south country that have anything at all to take to. Certes, in noblemen's houses it is not rare to see abundance of arras, rich hangings of tapestry, silver vessel, and so much other plate as may furnish sundry cupboards, to the sum oftentimes of a thousand or two thousand pounds at the least, whereby the value of this and the rest of their stuff doth grow to be almost inestimable. Likewise in the houses of knights, gentlemen, merchantmen and some other wealthy citizens, it is not geason [uncommon] to behold generally their great provision of tapestry, Turkey work [(imitation) Turkish tapestry], pewter, brass, fine linen, and thereto costly cupboards of plate, worth five or six hundred, or a thousand pounds, to be deemed by estimation . . .

There are old men yet dwelling in the village where I remain, which have noted three things to be marvellously altered in England within their sound remembrance. One is, the multitude of chimneys lately erected, whereas in their young days there were not above two or three, if so many, in most uplandish towns of the realm (the religious houses, and manor places of their lords always excepted, and peradventure some great personages), but each one made his fire against a reredos in the hall, where he dined and dressed his meat.

The second is the great amendment (although not general) of lodging, for, said they, our fathers (yea, and we ourselves also) have lain full oft upon straw pallets, covered only with a sheet, under coverlets made of dagswain or hopharlots [coarse material] (I use their own terms), and a good round log under their heads instead of a bolster or pillow. If it were so that our fathers or the goodman of the house had within seven years after his marriage purchased a mattress or flockbed, and thereto a sack of chaff to rest his head upon, he thought himself to be as well lodged as the lord of the town, that peradventure lay seldom in a bed of down or whole feathers, so well were they contented. Pillows, said they, were thought meet only for women in childbed. As for servants, if they had any sheet above them, it was well, for seldom had they any under their bodies, to keep them from the pricking straws that ran oft through the canvas of the pallet, and razed their hardened hides.

The third thing they tell of, is the exchange of vessel, as of treen [wooden] platters into pewter, and wooden spoons into silver or tin.

*

By encroaching and joining of house to house, and laying land to land . . . the inhabitants of many places of our country are devoured and eaten up and their houses either altogether pulled down or suffered to decay by little and little, although sometime a poor man peradventure doth dwell in one of them, who, not being able to repair it, suffereth it to fall down, and thereto thinketh himself very friendly dealt withal if he may have an acre of ground assigned unto him whereon to keep a cow, or wherein to set cabbages, radishes, parsnips, carrots, melons, pompions [pumpkins] or suchlike stuff, by which he and his poor household liveth as by their principal food, sith they can do no better. And as for wheaten bread, they eat it when they can reach unto the price of it, contenting themselves in the meantime with bread made of oats or barley: a poor estate, God wot! Howbeit, what care our great encroachers? But in divers places where rich men dwelled sometime in good tenements, there be no houses at all, but hopyards and sheds for poles, or peradventure gardens, as we may see in Castle Hedingham, and divers other places. But to proceed.

It is so, that our soil being divided into champion ground and woodland, the houses of the first lie uniformly builded in every town together, with streets and lanes; whereas in the woodland countries (except here and there in great market towns) they stand scattered abroad, each one dwelling in the midst of his own occupying. And as in many and most great market towns there are commonly three hundred or four hundred families or mansions, and two thousand communicants, or peradventure more, so in the other, whether they be woodland or champion, we find not often above forty, fifty or three score households, and two or three hundred communicants, whereof the greatest part nevertheless are very poor folks, oftentimes without all manner of occupying, sith the ground of the parish is gotten up into a few men's hands, yea, sometimes into the tenure of one, two or three, whereby the rest are compelled, either to be hired servants unto the other, or else to beg their bread in misery from door to door.

William Harrison, *The Description of England* (1587)

GARDENS AND ORCHARDS

From Henry IV till the latter end of Henry VII, and beginning of Henry VIII, there was little or no use of [vegetables] in England, but they remained either unknown, or supposed as food more meet for hogs and savage beasts to feed upon, than mankind. Whereas in my time their use is not only resumed among the poor commons – I mean of melons, pompions, gourds, cucumbers, radishes, skirrets [water parsnips), parsnips, carrots, cabbages, navews [rape or turnips], turnips and all kinds of salad herbs – but also fed upon as dainty dishes at the tables of delicate merchants, gentlemen and the nobility, who make their provision yearly for new seeds out of strange countries, from whence they have them abundantly. Neither do they now stay with such of these fruits as are wholesome in their kinds, but adventure further upon such as are very dangerous and hurtful, as the verangenes [aubergines], mushrooms, etc.; as if nature had ordained all for the belly, or that all things were to be eaten, for whose mischievous operation the Lord in some measure hath given and provided a remedy. . . .

HOUSE AND HOME

If you look into our gardens annexed to our houses, how wonderfully is their beauty increased, not only with flowers, which Columella calleth *Terrena Sydera*, saying, *Pingit et in varios terrestria sydera flores*, and variety of curious and costly workmanship, but also with rare and medicinable herbs sought up in the land within these forty years: so that in comparison of this present, the ancient gardens were but dunghills and laystalls [manureheaps] to such as did possess them. How art also helpeth nature, in the daily colouring, doubling and enlarging the proportion of our flowers, it is incredible to report; for so curious and cunning are our gardeners now in these days, that they presume to do in manner what they list in nature, and moderate her course in things as if they were her superiors. It is a world to see how many strange herbs, plants and annual fruits are daily brought unto us from the Indies, Americas, Taprobane, Canary Isles and all parts of the world . . .

And even as it fareth with our gardens, so doth it with our orchards, which were never furnished with so good fruit nor with such variety as at this present. For beside that we have most delicate apples, plums, pears, walnuts, filberts, etc., and those of sundry sorts, planted within these forty years past, in comparison of which most of the old trees are nothing worth, so have we no less store of strange fruit, as apricots, almonds, peaches, figs, corn-trees [cornelian cherries] in noblemen's orchards. I have seen capers, oranges and lemons, and heard of wild olives growing here, beside other strange trees, brought from far, whose names I know not . . .

William Harrison, *The Description of England* (1587)

A COOK

The kitchen is his hell, and he the devil in it, where his meat and he fry together. His revenues are showered down from the fat of the land, and he interlards his own grease among, to help the drippings. Choleric he is not by nature so much as his art, and it is a shrewd temptation that the chopping-knife is so near. His weapons ofter offensive are a mess of hot broth and scalding water, and woe be to him that comes in his way. In the kitchen he will domineer and rule the roast in spite of his master, and curses in the very dialect of his calling. . . . He is never a good Christian till a hissing pot of ale hath slaked him, like water cast in a firebrand,

and for that time he is tame and dispossessed. His cunning is not small in architecture, for he builds strange fabrics in paste [pastry], towers and castles, which are offered to the assault of valiant teeth, and like Darius's palace in one banquet demolished. He is a pitiless murderer of innocents, and he mangles poor fowls with unheard-of tortures; and it is thought the martyrs' persecutions were devised from hence: sure we are, St Lawrence's gridiron came out of his kitchen.

John Earle, *Micro-cosmographie* (1628)

VOLUNTARY FEASTS

In number of dishes and changes of meat, the nobility of England (whose cooks are for the most part musical-headed Frenchmen and strangers) do most exceed, sith there is no day in manner that passeth over their heads wherein they have not only beef, mutton, veal, lamb, kid, pork, coney [rabbit], capon, pig or so many of these as the season yieldeth, but also some portion of the red or fallow deer, beside great variety of fish and wildfowl, and thereto sundry other delicates wherein the sweet hand of the seafaring Portingale is not wanting. So that for a man to dine with one of them and to taste of every dish that standeth before him (which few use to do, but each one feedeth upon that him best liketh for the time) is rather to yield unto a conspiracy with a great deal of meat for the speedy suppression of natural health than to satisfy himself with a competent repast to sustain his body withal. But as this large feeding is not seen in their guests, no more is it in their own persons, for sith they have daily much resort unto their tables (and many times unlooked for) and thereto retain great numbers of servants, it is very requisite and expedient in them to be somewhat plentiful in this behalf.

The chief part likewise of their daily provision is brought in before them (commonly in silver vessels if they be of the degree of barons, bishops and upwards) and placed on their tables, whereof when they have taken what it pleaseth them, the rest is reserved, and afterward sent down to their serving men and waiters, who feed thereon in like sort with convenient moderation, their reversion also being bestowed upon the poor, which lie ready at their gates in great numbers to receive the same. . . .

The gentlemen and merchants keep much about one rate, and each of them contenteth himself with four, five or six dishes, when they have but small resort, or peradventure with one, or two or three at the most, when they have no strangers to accompany them at their tables. And yet their servants have their ordinary diet assigned, besides such as is left at their masters' boards and not appointed to be brought thither the second time, which nevertheless is often seen, generally in venison, lamb or some especial dish, whereon the merchantman himself liketh to feed when it is cold, or peradventure for sundry causes incident to the feeder is better so than if it were warm or hot. . . . In such cases also jellies of all colours, mixed with a variety of the representation of sundry flowers, herbs, trees, forms of beasts, fish, fowls and fruits, and thereunto marchpane wrought with no small curiosity, tarts of divers hues, foreign and home bred, suckets [crystallized fruit], codinacs [quince marmalade], marmalades, marchpane, sugar-bread [confectionery], florentines [meat pies], wildfowl, venison of all sorts, and sundry outlandish confections do generally bear the sway, besides infinite devices of our own, not possible for me to remember. Of the potato and such venerous [aphrodisiac] roots as are brought out of Spain, Portugal and the Indies to furnish up our banquets, I speak not, wherein our mures [mulberries] of no less force, and to be had about Crosby Ravenswath, do now begin to have place.

But among all these, the kind of meat which is obtained with most difficulty and cost is commonly taken for the most delicate, and thereupon each guest will soonest desire to feed. And as all estates do exceed herein, I mean for strangeness and number of costly dishes, so these forget not to use the like excess in wine, insomuch as there is no kind to be had (neither anywhere more store of all sorts than in England, although we have none growing with us but yearly to the proportion of 20,000 or 30,000 ton and upwards, notwithstanding the daily restraints of the same brought over unto us), whereof at great meetings there is not some store to be had. Neither do I mean this of small wines only, as claret, white, red, French, etc., which amount to about fifty-six sorts, according to the number of regions from whence they come; but also of the thirty kinds of Italian, Grecian, Spanish, Canarian, etc.; whereof vernage [strong sweet wine], cate pument [fine apple?], raspis [raspberry], muscadel, rumney [sweet Greek wine], bastard lire [sweet Spanish wine], osey [sweet Alsatian wine], caprike, clary [wine with honey and spices] and malmsey [sweet Spanish wine] are not least of all accounted of, because of their strength and valour. . . .

The artificer and husbandman make greatest account of such meat as they may soonest come by, and have it quickliest ready. Their food also consisteth principally in beef, and such meat as the butcher selleth, that is to say, mutton, veal, lamb, pork, etc., whereof he findeth great store in the markets adjoining, beside souse [pickled meat], brawn, bacon, fruit, pies of fruit, fowls of sundry sort, cheese, butter, eggs, etc.; as the other wanteth [lacks] it not at home by his own provision, which is at the best hand and commonly least charge. In feasting also, this latter sort do exceed after their manner, especially at bridals, purifications of women, and such odd meetings, where it is incredible to tell what meat is consumed and spent, each one bringing such a dish, or so many, as his wife and he do consult upon, but always with this consideration, that the liefer [more beloved] friend shall have the better provision. This also is commonly seen at these banquets, that the goodman of the house is not charged with anything saving bread, drink, sauce, houseroom and fire. But the artificers in cities and good towns do deal far otherwise; for, albeit that some of them do suffer their jaws to go oft before their claws, and divers of them, by making good cheer, do hinder themselves and other men, yet the wiser sort can handle the matter well enough in these junketings, and therefore their frugality deserveth commendation. To conclude, both the artificer and the husbandman are sufficiently liberal, and very friendly at their tables; and when they meet, they are so merry without malice, and plain without inward French or Italian craft and subtlety, that it would do a man good to be in company among them. Herein only are the inferior sort somewhat to be blamed, that being thus assembled, their talk is now and then such as savoureth of scurrility and ribaldry, a thing naturally incident to carters and clowns [rustics], who think themselves not to be merry and welcome if their foolish veins in this behalf be never so little restrained. . . .

With us the nobility, gentry and students do ordinarily go to dinner at eleven before noon, and to supper at five, or between five and six at afternoon. The merchants dine and sup seldom before twelve at noon and six at night, especially in London. The husbandmen dine also at high noon as they call it, and sup at seven or eight; but out of the term in our universities the scholars dine at ten. As for the poorest sort, they generally dine and sup when they may, so that to talk of their order of repast, it were but a needless matter.

William Harrison, *The Description of England* (1587)

HOUSE AND HOME

A CITIZEN FAMILY DINNER, WITH GUESTS

[FROM AN ENGLISH-FRENCH CONVERSATION MANUAL]

Father   Wife, shall we go to dinner? Shall we dine?

Wife   When it will please you, my lover, all is ready. The meat marreth; where have you tarried so long? You come not now from the church, that I know well, for it is twelve strucken.

Father   Go to. Let us go to dinner. Let us sit.

Wife   Go cause the folk to sit which are in the hall, and I go to the kitchen to cause to serve the board.

Father   Make speed then, I pray you, for truly I am hungry.

Masters, you be all welcome; I am sorry that I make you tarry so long.

Guests   No force, sir, we do warm us in the meanwhile. Come near to the fire, come warm you.

Father   Truly I am more hungry than a-cold. Go, let us wash hands. . . .

Page, call the children for to bless the board: ring the bell. . . .

Boy   What is your pleasure, mother?

Wife   Where are you? Why went you not to meet your father and your uncle? I will tell your master: I will cause you to be beaten. Go quickly say grace, and take your sister by the hand. Take off your cap, and make curtsy.

Boy   Well, mother, I go thither. You are welcome, father, and all your company.

Father   Where have you been, wanton? One must always call and seek you when one should say grace. Pray unto God. . . .

[AFTER GRACE, THE MEAL BEGINS]

Father   What, is not the children's table covered yet? What dost thou there, great lubber? Why goest thou not and serve the children?

Servant   They be two or three about it, sir.

Father   Who?

Servant   Their lackey and their chamberlain.

Master lackey, truly you shall be whipped today. You do lick here the dishes in the kitchen, and taste if the sauce is salted, and serve not your little master. Who hath drawn the lard out of these rabbits?

Lackey	It is not I.
Servant	You lie. Go your ways, you are lickerish [greedy]. O Lord, he hath supped up all the broth of this mince pie! I would not be in thy skin for twenty crowns of gold. . . .
Father	William, give here some bread. Take a ladder, and see what wanteth on the board. You will never learn to serve, why do you not lead it with a trencher plate and not with the hand? I have told you above an hundred times; you learn nothing; it is a great shame. Hold, give this platter of porridge unto the children, and give them some spoons. Peter, take up my knife which is fallen under the table.
Guest [to boy]	You do nothing but play the wanton little fellow. I will tell your father. Why do you not eat your porridge whilst they be hot? You are not hungry.
Boy	They are yet too hot. I have burned my tongue and my lips.
Guest	If they be too hot, blow them.
Father	Are those your good manners to blow your porridge at the board? Where have you learned that – at your village? . . .
Wife	Husband, I pray you pull in pieces that capon, and help your neighbour: truly, he eateth nothing.
Father	Tarry a little, wife. I have not yet tasted of these cabbages.
Wife	You cannot eat of them, for they be too much peppered and salted.
Father	Ah, what pity is that! It is the meat that I love best, and it is marred. They say commonly in England that God sendeth us meat, and the Devil cooks.
Wife	My lover, taste a little of these turnips. . . . If you will eat of a good meat, eat of that leg of mutton stuffed with garlic.
Father	Give me rather of that capon boiled with leeks, for I should smell of garlic three days after. . . . Cut that turkeycock in pieces, but let it be cold, for it is better cold than hot. Sir, shall I be your carver? . . . Will you have this hen's wing?
Guest	As for me, I love the white of the hen – and you love the rump.
Father	You are a scoffer, as I perceive. Peter, fill me some wine.
Peter	What wine shall it please you to drink?
Father	It is all one to me. Give me claret wine; put water in it, for it is too strong to drink without water. Pour still. Hold up, it is enough. . . . Mistress, shall I give you some crust of this pie?

Wife	As it will please you; I am well, God be thanked.
Father	Me thinketh it is too much baked.
Wife	No, forsooth, but it is well; but it is a great pity that the liquor is so run out.
Father	It is the fault of the baker. I would that he had it in his belly.
Guest	I would be sorry of it truly, for I should lose. . . .
Father	Wife, have we nothing else?
Wife	Yea, husband. Are the blackbirds roasted, the larks and the woodcock? Set here this partridge larded.
Father	Cousin, if you will eat of a good morsel, cut some of these loins of the hare, dressed with a black sauce.
Guest	Uncle, here is too much meat, methinketh we be at a wedding! . . .
Father	Elizabeth, take all away; give us the fruit. . . . Lay here those roasted pears, and the scraped cheese. Set those apples lower, they be pippins, as it seemeth to me. Did you ever see fairer pippins?
Guest	I hold a penny that it cometh out of Normandy.
Father	No, no, it is grown in England. These tarts be cold, and the egg pie also. Mistress, will you have some cake? Truly, it is but dough; I would the baker had been baked when he did heat the oven. . . . Roland, shall we have a song?
Roland	Yea, sir. Where be your books of music – for they be the best corrected?
Father	They be in my chest. Katherine, take the key of my closet, you shall find them in a little till at the left hand.
	Behold, there be fair songs at four parts.
Roland	Who shall sing with me?
Father	You shall have company enough: David shall make the base, John the tenor and James the treble. Begin. . . .

[SINGING FOLLOWS, AND THEN GRACE]

Guest	It is time to depart, for they have rung twice to evening prayers.
Father	Have you so great haste? Let us warm us first, and then we will go together.

Claudius Hollyband (De Sainliens), *The French Schoolemaister* (1573)

SHAKESPEARE'S ENGLAND

GARDENING TIPS

The daily experience is to the gardener as a schoolmaster to instruct him, how much it availeth and hindereth, that seeds to be sown, plants to be set, yea, scions to be grafted (in this or that time) having herein regard, not to the time especially of the year, as the sun altereth the same, but also the moon's increase and wane, yea, to the sign she occupieth, and places both above and under the earth.

To the aspects also of the other planets, whose beams and influence both quicken, comfort, preserve and maintain, or else nip, wither, dry, consume and destroy by sundry means the tender seeds, plants, yea and grafts, and these after their property, and virtue natural or accidental. . . .

The yearly almanacs do marvellously help the gardeners in the election for times for sowing, planting and grassing, but especially in observing the moon, about the bestowing of plants, as when the moon increasing occupieth Taurus and Aquarius. But if it be for the setting of young trees, let the same be done in the last quarter of the moon, she then being in Taurus and in a conjunction with Venus, for so these speedier take root in the earth, and the gardener planting in either Taurus and Aquarius or Virgo and Pisces must as carefully take heed always that the moon is not evil-aspected of Saturn and Mars.

In the planting also of young trees, let the same be done from the middle of October unto the middle of March. In the sowing of seeds in a well-dressed earth, let the moon run at those times in Taurus, Cancer, Virgo, Libra and Capricornus.

But this diligently learn, that the seeds and plants increase the better if any of these signs be ascending in the east-angle, and that Mars neither behold the ascendant or the moon by any aspect, but shall be weakly standing in a weak place of the figure at that time.

SOME USEFUL PLANTS TABULATED

Beet looseth the belly, provoketh urine, purgeth the body of evil humours; it helpeth the smelling, the pain of the ears and of the gums, it procureth hair to grow and killeth lice, nits and dandry [dandruff?]; it healeth whelks [pimples], blisters of scalding and burning, gripings of the belly, stayeth a loose belly, helpeth the obstructions or stoppings of the liver, the corrupted spleen and the shingles.

The discommodities of the beet: it gripeth and biteth the stomach, and increaseth evil humours.

Beet softeneth the belly, cureth the biting of a scorpion, the beating pain of the temples; it profiteth the oil on the milt [spleen], it restraineth the terms [menstrual flow].

Borage procureth gladsomeness, it helpeth the giddiness and swimming of the head, the trembling and beating of the heart, it increaseth memory and removeth melancholy, and the king's evil [scrofula] it doth only comfort.

Bugloss prevaileth for the roughness of the throat and cough, it procureth gladsomeness, it purgeth red choler, it expelleth the noisome humours of the lungs, it removeth the swellings of the feet; it preserveth a good memory, it comforteth the heart, and engendereth good blood. . . .

Blessed thistle causeth urine, helpeth the megrim [migraine], restoreth memory and hearing, helpeth the diseases of the lungs, purgeth phlegm of the stomach and the blood, helpeth consumption of the lungs, gripings, provoketh sweat, breaketh the stone, and helpeth the monthly terms. It comforteth the brain and sight, purgeth the blood in the eyes, stoppeth the bleeding at the nose, purgeth the uvula and ceaseth the spitting of phlegm.

Blessed thistle helpeth a weak stomach, procureth appetite, abateth heat, consumeth evil blood, provoketh sweat, strengtheneth the palsy members, recovereth the lungs exulcerated; it profiteth against the dropsy, helpeth the plague, imposthumes, cancers and falling sickness, it is a present remedy against the plague, the fever of the stomach, and the quartain; it cureth green wounds, pushes [boils], swellings of the plague, any burning, the colic, scabs, a stinking breath; it helpeth women's privities; it helpeth stitches, pleurisies and infants encumbered with the falling sickness.

Thomas Hill, *The Gardeners Labyrinth* (1577–1652)

DOCTOR, DOCTOR

A worthy physician is the enemy of sickness, in purging nature from corruption. His action is most in feeling of pulses, and his discourses chiefly of the nature of diseases. He is a great searcher-out of simples [medicinal herbs], and accordingly makes his composition. He persuades abstinence and patience for the benefit of health, while purging and bleeding are the chief courses of his counsel. The apothecary [dispensing chemist] and chirurgeon [surgeon] are his two chief attendants, with whom conferring, upon time he grows temperate in his cures. Surfeits and wantonness are great agents for his employment, when by the secret of his skill out of others' weakness he gathers his own strength. In sum, he is a necessary member for an unnecessary malady, to find a disease and cure the diseased.

An unlearned and so unworthy physician is a kind of horse-leech, whose cure is most in drawing of blood, and a desperate purge, either to cure or kill, as it hits. His discourse is most of the cures that he hath done, and them afar off; and not a receipt [prescription] under a hundred pounds, though it be not worth three halfpence. Upon the market-day he is much haunted with urinals [specimen jars], where, if he find anything (although he know nothing), yet he will say somewhat, which if it hit to some purpose with a few fustian words, he will seem a piece of strange stuff. He is never without old merry tales and stale jests to make old folks laugh, and comfits [sweets] or plums in his pocket to please little children; yea, and he will be talking of complexions [psychological dispositions], though he know nothing of their dispositions; and if his medicine do a feat, he is a made man among fools. . . .

Nicholas Breton, *The Good and the Badde* (1616)

THE LAST HOME

Now, this bell tolling softly for another, says to me: Thou must die.

MEDITATION

Perchance he for whom this [passing] bell tolls may be so ill, as that he knows not it tolls for him; and perchance I may think myself so much better than I am [in my sickness], as that they who are about me, and see my state, may have caused it to toll for me, and I know not that. The church is catholic, universal, so are all her actions; all that she does belongs to all. When she baptises a child, that action concerns me; for that child is thereby connected to that head which is my head too, and ingrafted into that body whereof I am a member. And when she buries a man, that action concerns me: all mankind is of one author, and is one volume; when one man dies, one chapter is not torn out of the book, but translated into a better language; and every chapter must be so translated. God employs several translators; some pieces are translated by age, some by sickness, some by war, some by justice; but God's hand is in every translation, and his hand shall bind up all our scattered leaves again, for that library where every book shall lie open to one another. As therefore the bell that rings to a sermon calls not upon the preacher only, but upon the congregation to come, so this bell calls us all; but how much more me, who am brought so near the door by sickness. There was a contention as far as a suit (in which both piety and dignity, religion and estimation, were mingled), which of the religious orders should ring to prayers first in the morning; and it was determined, that they should ring first that rose earliest. If we understand aright the dignity of this bell that tolls for our evening prayer, we would be glad to make it ours by rising early, in that application, that it might be ours as well as his, whose indeed it is. The bell doth toll for him that thinks it doth; and though it intermit again, yet from that minute that that occasion wrought upon him, he is united to God. Who casts not his eye to the sun when it rises? But who takes off his eye from a comet when that breaks out? Who bends not his ear to any bell which upon any occasion rings? But who can remove it from that bell which is passing a piece of himself out of this world? No man is an island, entire of itself; every man is a piece of the continent, a part of the main. If a clod be washed away by the sea, Europe is the less, as well as if a promontory were, as well as if a manor of thy friend's or of thine own were; any man's death diminishes me, because I am involved in mankind, and therefore never send to know for whom the bell tolls; it tolls for thee. Neither can we call this a begging of misery, or a borrowing of misery, as though we were not miserable enough of ourselves, but must fetch in more from the next house, in taking upon us the misery of our neighbours. Truly it were an excusable covetousness if we did, for affliction is a treasure, and scarce any man hath enough of it. No man hath affliction enough that is not matured and ripened by it, and made fit for God by that affliction. If a man carry treasure in bullion, or in a wedge of gold, and have none coined into current moneys, his treasure will not defray him as he travels. Tribulation is treasure in the nature of it, but it is not current money in the use of it, except we get nearer and nearer our home, heaven, by it. Another man may be sick too, and sick to death, and this affliction may lie in his bowels, as gold in a mine, and be of no use to him; but this bell, that tells me of his affliction, digs out and applies that gold to me, if by this consideration of another's danger I take mine own into contemplation, and so secure myself, by making my course to my God, who is our only security.

John Donne, *Devotions upon Emergent Occasions* (1624)

4

COUNTRY LIFE

Between the acres of the rye.
Shakespeare, *As You Like It* (1599)

Most people lived and worked in the country, but the great differences in soil and conditions meant that farming itself varied widely. The north and west, generally higher, cooler, wetter and with poorer soil, was largely pastoral, with grass and fodder crops; fields were mostly smaller, with more hedges, settlements were smaller and more scattered, and manorial control featured less. South and east of a York–Weymouth line there was more arable and mixed farming, especially in the Midlands, with larger fields, more compact settlements and great social inequality, with more rich and more poor.

In the 1560s, most villages and towns were still surrounded by huge, hedgeless open fields many acres in size, divided into half-acre strips, their owners' holdings widely distributed to ensure equal access to good land. Farming practice mostly involved crop-rotation, with one-third planted with rye (or, later, wheat), one-third with barley or oats for silage, and one-third fallow. Common land was available for grazing, woody wasteland provided small timber, beechmast or acorns for pigs, and straw and ferns for thatching and animal bedding. All this was vital for the poor. The common open-field system, known as 'champion', was being replaced by farming 'in several', where strips were redistributed, consolidated and hedged off. 'More profit is quieter found/Where pastures in several be/Of one silly acre of ground/Than champion maketh of three,' wrote Thomas Tusser – but the change benefited the wealthier more than the poor. Some yeomen and farmers acquired large holdings; many men were small husbandmen or landless labourers. Hours were long: up to fourteen hours a day in the lighter half of the year, twelve in the darker. A 1552 Act banned Sunday labour and listed twenty-three feastday holidays, with eleven more days at Whitsun, Easter and Christmas; a traditional, religious calendar of festivals still shaped most people's work and leisure (see the introduction to 'Arts and Pleasures').

Population growth pushed up food prices and land rents, but wages remained low, so that cottagers and small husbandmen did badly as larger, commercial farmers sought greater productivity and profit. Major means of achieving these included engrossment (the purchase and reorganization of stripland), the enclosure of common grazing and waste land (with serious consequences for the poor), and the transfer of arable to grazing land, with fewer workers; many people were driven out of work, or to poorer land, or to the towns. 'Convertible husbandry', alternating tillage and pasturage, replaced the three-year cycle. More land was put into cultivation (draining marshy land, cutting down woodland, turning game reserves to agriculture), and soil was improved, particularly with new fodder crops. Despite occasional periods of dearth (with bad harvests provoked by bad weather – as complained of in *A Midsummer Night's Dream*), England steadily became self-sufficient in food necessities. One should also note the developing rural industries, usually linked with clothing – weaving, clothmaking, lacemaking – carried on in villages and cottages.

Vital to most rural areas were the market towns (over eight hundred in all), operating as trading, service and social centres; alehouses greatly increased in numbers – the use of hops encouraging a shift from ale to beer – providing drink, food, accommodation and entertainment for the poor. Villages were largely under the control of manorial courts that directed land usage and agricultural practice, and supervised such matters as clean water provision, sanitation and road maintenance, working through parish officials. With changes in working practices and population displacements came increasing social tensions: there were demonstrations against enclosures and removal of common rights; conversely, complaints against intrusions on private land, against vagrancy and the dependent poor; revenge arson attacks; accusations of witchcraft. Parish officers increased their efforts against alehouse disorders, church absenteeism, sexual irregularity, and customary sports, dances and festivities. All combined to undermine, to a limited degree, traditional ways and values, in a long, continuous cultural shift.

> I wonder now and then
> To see the wise and learnèd men
> With countenance grim, and many a frown,
> Cries, 'Masters, pluck the maypole down!'
> To hear this news, the milkmaid cries,
> To see the sight, the ploughman dies.

Humphrey King, *An Halfe-penny Worth of Wit* (1613)

A COUNTRY GENTLEMAN: HENRY HASTINGS (1551–1650)

Mr Hastings, by his quality, being the son, brother and uncle to the Earls of Huntingdon, and his way of living, had the first place amongst us. He was peradventure an original in our age, or rather the copy of our nobility in ancient days in hunting and not warlike times. He was low, very strong and very active, of a reddish flaxen hair, his clothes always green cloth, and never all worth when new five pounds. His house was perfectly of the old fashion, in the midst of a large park well stocked with deer, and near the house rabbits to serve his kitchen, many fish-ponds, and great store of wood and timber; a bowling-green in it, long but narrow, full of high ridges, it being never levelled since it was ploughed; they used round sand bowls, and it had a banqueting house like a stand, a large one built in a tree. He kept all manner of sport hounds that ran buck, fox, hare, otter and badger, and hawks long and short winged; he had all sorts of nets for fishing; he had a walk in the New Forest and the manor of Christ Church. This last supplied him with red deer, sea and river fish; and indeed all his neighbours' grounds and royalties were free to him, who bestowed all his time in such sports, but what he borrowed to caress his neighbours' wives and daughters, there being not a woman in all his walks of the degree of a yeoman's wife or under, and under the age of forty, but it was extremely her fault if he were not intimately acquainted with her. This made him very popular, always speaking kindly to the husband, brother or father, who was to boot very welcome to his house, whenever he came.

There he found beef pudding and small beer in great plenty, a house not so neatly kept as to shame him or his dirty shoes, the great hall strewed with marrow-bones, full of hawks' perches, hounds, spaniels and terriers, the upper sides of the hall hung with the fox-skins of this and the last year's skinning, here and there a polecat intermixed, guns and keepers' and huntsmen's poles in abundance. The parlour was a large, long room as properly furnished; on a great hearth paved with brick lay some terriers and the choicest hounds and spaniels; seldom but two of the great chairs had litters of young cats in them which were not to be disturbed, he having always three or four of them attending him at dinner, and a little white round stick of fourteen inches long lying by his trencher that he might defend such meat as he had no mind to part with to them. The windows, which were very large, served for places to lay his arrows, crossbows, stonebows [catapults for shooting stones] and other suchlike accoutrements; the corners of the room full of the best chose hawking and hunting poles; an oyster-table at the lower end, which was of constant use twice a day all the year round, for he never failed to eat oysters before dinner and supper through all seasons. The neighbouring town of Poole supplied him with them. The upper part of this room had two small tables and a desk, on the one side of which was a church Bible, on the other the Book of Martyrs; on the tables were hawks' hoods, bells and suchlike, two or three old green hats with their crowns thrust in so as to hold ten or a dozen eggs, which were of a pheasant kind of poultry he took much care of and fed himself, tables [backgammon], dice, cards and boxes were not wanting. In the hole of the desk were store of tobacco-pipes that had been used. One one side of this end of the room was the door of a closet, wherein stood the strong beer and the wine, which never came thence but in single glasses, that being the rule of the house exactly observed, for he never exceeded in drink nor permitted it. On the other side was a door into an old chapel not used for devotion; the pulpit, as the safest place, was never wanting of a cold chine of beef, pasty of venison, gammon of bacon, or great apple-pie, with thick crust extremely baked. His table cost him not much, though it was very good to eat at, his sports supplying all but beef and mutton, except Friday, when he had the best sea-fish as well as other fish he could get, and was the day that his neighbours of best quality most visited him. He never wanted a London pudding, and always sang it in with 'my part lies therein-a'. He drank a glass of wine or two at meals, very often syrup of gillyflower in his sack, and had always a tun glass without feet stood by him holding a pint of small beer, which he often stirred with a great sprig of rosemary.

He was well-natured, but soon angry, calling his servants bastards and cuckoldy knaves, in one of which he often spoke truth to his own knowledge, and sometimes in both, though of the same man. He lived to a hundred, never lost his eyesight, but always writ and read without spectacles, and got to horse without help. Until past fourscore he rode to the death of a stag as well as any.

Anthony Ashley Cooper, Earl of Shaftesbury, *Memoirs* (written *c.* 1680)

A FARMER

Is a concealed commodity. His worth or value is not known till he be half rotten, and then he is worth nothing. He hath religion enough to say, 'God bless his Majesty; God send peace, and fair weather,' so that one may glean harvest out of him to be his time of happiness; but the tithe-sheaf goes against his conscience, for he had rather spend the value upon his reapers and ploughmen than bestow anything to the maintenance of a parson. He is sufficiently book-read, nay, a profound Doctor, if he can search into the diseases of cattle; and to foretell rain by tokens makes him a miraculous astronomer. To speak good English is more than he much regards, and for him not to contemn [disdain] all arts and languages were to condemn his own education. The pride of his housekeeping is a mess of cream, a pig, or a green goose; and if his servants can uncontrolled find the highway to the cupboard, it wins the name of a bountiful yeoman.

Doubtless he would murmur against the [Roman] tribunes' law by which none might occupy more than five hundred acres, for he murmurs against himself because he cannot purchase more. To purchase arms (if he emulates gentry) sets upon him like an ague: it breaks his sleep, takes away his stomach, and he can never be quiet till the herald hath given him the harrows, the cuckoo or some ridiculous emblem for his armoury. The bringing up and marriage of his eldest son is an ambition which afflicts him so soon as the boy is born, and the hope to see his son superior, or placed above him, drives him to dote upon the boy in his cradle. To peruse the statutes and prefer them before the Bible makes him purchase the credit of a shrewd fellow, and then he brings all adversaries to composition [to settle, on terms]; and if at length he can discover himself in large legacies beyond expectation, he hath his desire. Meantime, he makes the prevention of a dearth his title to be thought a good commonwealth's man. And therefore he preserves a chandler's treasure of bacon, links [sausage] and puddings in the chimney corner.

He is quickly and contentedly put into the fashion, if his clothes be made against Whitsuntide or Christmas day; and then outwardly he contemns appearance. He therefore cannot choose but hate a Spaniard likewise, and he thinks that hatred only makes him a loyal subject: for benevolence and subsidies be more unseasonable to him than his quarter's rent. Briefly, being a good housekeeper, he is an honest man; and so he thinks of no rising higher but rising early in the morning; and being up, he hath no end of motion, but wanders in his woods and pastures so continually that when he sleeps or sits, he wanders also. After this, he turns into his element, by being too venturous hot and cold: then he is fit for nothing but a chequered grave. Howsoever, some may think him convenient to make an everlasting bridge, because his best foundation hath been (perhaps) upon woolpacks.

John Stephens, *Essayes and Characters* (1615)

WOMAN'S WORK IS NEVER DONE: THE FARMER'S WIFE

First, in the morning when thou art waked and purpose to rise, lift up thy hand and bless thee and make a sign of the Holy Cross. *In nomine patris et filii et spiritus sancti. Amen*: in the name of the Father, the Son and the Holy Ghost. And if thou say a *Pater Noster*, an *Ave* and a *Credo*, and remember thy maker, thou shalt speed much the better. And when thou art up and ready, then first sweep thy house, dress up thy dishboard, and set all things in good order within thy house. Milk thy ki[n]e, suckle thy calves, sile up [strain] thy milk, take up thy children and array them, and provide for thy husband's breakfast, dinner, supper, and for thy children and servants; and take thy part with them. And . . . ordain corn and malt to the mill to bake and brew withal when need is. And mete [measure] it to the mill and from the mill, and see that thou have thy measure again besides the toll, or else the miller dealeth not truly with thee, or else thy corn is not dry as it should be. Thou must make butter and cheese when thou may. Serve thy swine both morning and evening, and give thy pullen [poultry] meat in the morning. And when time of year cometh, thou must take heed of how thy hens, ducks and geese do lay, and to gather up their eggs, and when they wax broody to set them there as no beasts, swine nor other vermin hurt them. And thou must know that all whole-footed fowl will sit a month and all cloven-footed fowl will sit but three weeks, except a peahen and such other great fowls as cranes, bustards and such other. And when they have brought forth their birds, to see that they be well kept from the gleyd [kites], crows, fullymarts [polecats] and other vermin.

And in the beginning of March, or a little before, is time for a wife to make her garden and to get as many good seeds and herbs as she can, and specially such as be good for the pot and for to eat. And as oft as need shall require, it must be weeded, for else the weed will overgrow the herbs. And also in March is time to sow flax and hemp, for I have heard old housewives say that better is March hurds than April flax, the reason appeareth. But how it should be sown, weeded, pulled, rippled [combed], watered, washed, dried, beaten, braked [crushed], tawed [softened], hackled [broken up], spun, wound, wrapped and woven, it needed not for me to show, for they be wise enough. And thereof may they make sheets, boardcloths [tablecloths], towels, shirts, smocks and such other necessaries. And therefore let thy distaff be always ready for a pastime, that thou be not idle . . .

It may fortune sometime that thou shalt have so many things to do that thou shalt not well know where is best to begin. Then take heed which thing should be the greatest loss if it were not done and in what space it would be done; and then think what is the greatest loss, and there begin . . .

It is a wife's occupation to winnow all manner of corns, to make malt, wash and wring, to make hay, to shear corn, and in time of need to help her husband to fill the muckwain or dungcart, drive the plough, to load hay, corn and such other. Also to go or ride to the market to sell butter, cheese, milk, eggs, chickens, capons, hens, pigs, geese and all manner of corn. And also to buy all manner of necessary things belonging to a household, and to make true reckoning and account to her husband what she hath received and what she hath paid. And if the husband go to the market to buy or sell (as they often do), he then to show his wife in like manner. For if one of them should use to deceive the other, he deceiveth himself, and he is not like to thrive, and therefore they must be true either to other.

Sir Anthony Fitzherbert, *The Book of Husbandry* (1523)

SHEEP EAT MEN

Sheep have eat up our meadows and our downs,
Our corn, our wood, whole villages and towns.
Yea, they have eat up many wealthy men,
Besides widows and orphan childeren,
Besides our statutes and our iron laws
Which they have swallowed down into their maws.
   Till now I thought the proverb did but jest,
   Which said a black sheep was a biting beast.

Thomas Bustard, *Chrestoleros* (1598)

PREPARING FOR THE SHEEPFARMERS' FEAST

Young Shepherd.   Let me see: every 'leven wether tods [eleven sheep make one tod, i.e. twenty-eight pounds of wool]; every tod yields pound and odd shilling; fifteen hundred shorn, what comes the wool to? . . . I cannot do't without counters. Let me see: what am I to buy for our sheep-shearing feast? Three pound of sugar, five pound of currants, rice – what will this sister of mine do with rice? But my father hath made her mistress of the feast, and she lays it on. She hath made me four and twenty nosegays for the shearers – three-man songmen all, and very good ones; but they are most of them means [tenors] and basses; but one Puritan amongst them, and he sings psalms to hornpipes. I must have saffron to colour the warden [winter pear] pies; mace; dates – none, that's out of my note; nutmegs, seven; a race [root] or two of ginger, but that I may beg; four pound of prunes, and as many of raisins o'th'sun.

Shakespeare, *The Winter's Tale* (1611)

COUNTRY LIFE

ROGUES AT COUNTRY FAIRS

Let my pen gallop over a few lines and it shall bring you without spurring swiftlier into Gloucestershire than if you rode upon Pacolet [a flying horse ridden by dwarf Pacolet, in *Valentine and Orson*]. There if you please to alight near Tewkesbury at a place called Deerhurst Fair, being kept there upon the two Holy Rood Days [3 May, 14 September], you shall see more rogues than ever were whipped at a cart's arse through London, and more beggars than ever came dropping out of Ireland. If you look upon them you would think you lived in Henry VI's time, and that Jack Cade and his rebellious ragamuffins were there mustering. Dunkirk [a pirates' base] cannot show such sharks. The wild Irish are but flocks of wild geese to them. And these swarms of locusts come to this lousy fair from all parts of the land within an hundred miles' compass. To describe the booths is lost labour, for let the hangman show but his wardrobe and there is not a rag difference between them. None here stands crying 'What do you lack?' for you can ask for nothing that is good here but it is lacking. The buyers and sellers are both alike, tawny sunburnt rascals, and they flock in such troops that it shows as if Hell were broke loose. The shopkeepers are thieves and the chapmen rogues, beggars and whores, so that to bring a purse full of money hither were madness, for it is sure to be cut.

But would you know what wares these merchants of eelskins utter? Only *duds* for the *quarons* (that is to say, 'clothes' for the 'body') which they have pilfered from hedges [laundry left to dry] or houses. And this filthy fair begins before day and endeth before nine in the same morning, at which breaking up they do not presently [immediately] march away with their bags and their baggages; but he who is chosen Lord of the Fair, who is commonly the lustiest rogue in the whole bunch, leads his tattered footmen and footwomen from alehouse to alehouse, where, being armed all in ale of proof and their *bene booze* the 'strong liquor' causing them to have *nase nabs* 'drunken cockscombs', up fling they the cans, down go the booths, about fly broken jugs. Here lies a rogue bleeding, there is a *mort* [woman beggar] cursing, here a *doxy* [whore] stabbing with her knife. And thus this fair which begins merrily ends madly, for knaves set it up and *queans* [whores] pull it down.

Thomas Dekker, *English Villainies Discovered* (1608)

ALEHOUSE AND ALEWIFE

If these houses have a box-bush, or an old post, it is enough to show their profession. But if they be graced with a sign complete, it's a sign of good custom. In these houses you shall see the history of Judith, Susanna, Daniel in the lions' den, or Dives and Lazarus painted upon the wall. It may be reckoned a wonder to see or find the house empty, for either the parson, churchwarden or clerk, or all, are doing some church or court business in this place. They thrive best where there are fewest. It is the host's chiefest pride to be speaking of such a gentleman, or such a gallant, that was here, and will be again ere long. Hot weather and thunder, and want of company, are the hostess's grief, for then her ale sours. Your drink is usually very young, two days old; her chiefest wealth is seen if she can have one brewing under another. If either the hostess or her daughter or maid will kiss handsomely at parting, it is a good shoeing-horn or birdlime to draw the company hither again the sooner. She must be courteous to all, though not by nature yet by her profession; for she must entertain all, good and bad, tag and rag, cut and long-tail. She suspects tinkers and poor soldiers most, not that they will not drink soundly, but that they will not pay lustily. She must keep touch with three sorts of men: that is, the maltman, the baker and the justice's clerks. She is merry, and half mad, upon Shrove Tuesday, May days, feast days and morris dances; a good ring of bells in the parish helps her to many a tester; she prays the parson may not be a Puritan; a bagpiper and a puppet-play brings her in birds that are flush, and she defies a wine tavern as an upstart outlandish fellow, and supsects the wine to be poisoned. Her ale, if new, looks like a misty morning, all thick. Well, if her ale be strong, her reckoning right, her house clean, her fire good, her face fair, and the town great or rich, she shall seldom or never sit without chirping birds to bear her company, and at the next churching or christening, she is sure to be rid of two or three dozen of cakes and ale by gossiping neighbours.

Donald Lupton, *London and the Countrey carbonadoed* (1632)

HARVEST HOME

As we were returning to our inn, we happened to meet some country people celebrating their Harvest Home. Their last load of corn they crown with flowers, having beside an image richly dressed, by which perhaps they would signify Ceres; this they keep moving about, while men and women, men and maidservants, riding through the streets in the cart, shout as loud as they can till they arrive at the barn. The farmers do not bind up their corn in sheaves . . . but directly as they have reaped or mowed it, put it into carts and convey it to their barns.

Paul Hentzner, *Travels in England* (1598; pub. 1757)

MORRIS DANCERS

Ho! Who comes here all along with bagpiping and drumming?
O, 'tis the morris dance I see a-coming.
  Come ladies out, come quickly!
And see about how trim they dance and trickly.
  Hey! there again! how the bells they shake it!
  Hey ho! now for our town and take it!
  Soft awhile, not away so fast! They melt them.
  Piper, be hanged, knave! see'st thou not the dancers how they
  swelt [sweat] them?
Stand out awhile! You come too far, I say, in.
There give the hobby-horse more room to play in!

Thomas Morley, *Madrigals to Four Voyces* (1594)

MAY-GAMES AND MISRULE: A PURITAN VIEW

Against May, Whitsunday or other time, all the young men and maids, old men and wives, run gadding overnight to the woods, groves, hills and mountains, where they spend all the night in pleasant pastimes, and in the morning they return, bringing with them birch and branches of trees, to deck their assemblies withal, and no marvel, for there is a great lord present among them, as superintendent and lord over their pastimes and sports, namely, Satan prince of hell. But the chiefest jewel they bring from thence is their Maypole, which they bring home with great veneration, as thus. They have twenty or forty yoke of oxen, every ox having a sweet nosegay of flowers placed on the tip of his horns, and these oxen draw home this Maypole (this stinking idol, rather) which is covered all over with flowers and herbs bound round about with strings from the top to the bottom, and sometimes painted with variable colours, with two or three hundred men, women and children following it with great devotion. And thus being reared up, with handkerchiefs and flags hovering on the top, they straw the ground round about, bind green boughs about it, set up summer halls, bowers and arbours hard by it. And then fall they to dance about it like as the heathen people did at the dedication of the idols, whereof this is a perfect pattern, or rather the thing itself. I have heard it credibly reported (and that, viva voce) by men of great gravity and reputation, that of forty, threescore or a hundred maids going to the wood overnight, there have scarcely the third part of them returned home again undefiled. These be the fruits which these cursed pastimes bring forth.

First, all the wild-heads of the parish, conventing together, choose them a Grand Captain (of all mischief) whom they ennoble with the title of my Lord of Misrule, and him they crown with great solemnity, and adopt for their king. This king anointed, chooseth forth twenty, forty, threescore or a hundred lusty guts like to himself to wait upon his lordly majesty, and to guard his noble person. Then every one of these his men he investeth with his liveries, of green, yellow or some other light wanton colour. And as though that were not (bawdy) gaudy enough I should say, they bedeck themselves with scarves, ribbons and laces hanged all over with gold rings, precious stones and other jewels; this done, they tie about either leg xx [20] or xl [40] bells, with rich handkerchiefs in their hands, and sometimes laid across their shoulders and necks, borrowed for the most part from their pretty Mopsies and loving Besses, for bussing [kissing] them in the dark. Thus, all things set in order, then have they their hobby-horses, dragons and other antiques, together with their bawdy pipers and thundering drummers to strike up the devils' dance withal; then march these heathen company towards the church and churchyard, their pipers piping, their drummers thundering, their stumps dancing, their bells jingling, their handkerchiefs swinging about their heads like madmen, their hobby-horses and other monsters skirmishing amongst the rout. And in this sort they go to the church, I say, and into the church (though the minister be at prayer or preaching) dancing and swinging their handkerchiefs over their heads, in the church, like devils incarnate, with such a confused noise that no man can hear his own voice. Then the foolish people, they look, they stare, they laugh, they fleer [grimace], and mount upon forms and pews to see these goodly pageants solemnised in this sort. Then after this, about the church they go again and again, and so forth into the churchyard, where they have commonly their summer halls, their bowers, arbours and banqueting houses set up, wherein they feast, banquet and dance all that day, and, peradventure, all the night too. And thus these terrestrial furies spend the Sabbath day.

Philip Stubbes, *The Anatomy of Abuses* (1583)

HUNTING THE HARE

And when thou hast on foot the purblind hare,
Mark the poor wretch, to overshoot his troubles
How he outruns the wind, and with what care
He cranks and crosses with a thousand doubles:
    The many musets [escape-holes] through the which he goes
    Are like a labyrinth to amaze his foes.

Sometime he runs among a flock of sheep,
To make the cunning hounds mistake their smell,
And sometime where earth-delving coneys [rabbits] keep,
To stop the loud pursuers in their yell,
    And sometime sorteth with a herd of deer:
    Danger deviseth shifts; wit waits on fear.

For there his smell with others being mingled,
The hot scent-smelling hounds are driven to doubt,
Ceasing their clamour cry till they have singled
With much ado the cold fault cleanly out.
    Thus do they spend their mouths; echo replies,
    As if another chase were in the skies.

By this, poor Wat, far off upon a hill,
Stands on his hinder legs with listening ear,
To hearken if his foes pursue him still.
Anon their loud alarums he doth hear;

And now his grief may be compared well
To one sore sick that hears the passing-bell.

Then shalt thou see the dew-bedabbled wretch
Turn, and return, indenting with the way;
Each envious briar his weary legs doth scratch,
Each shadow makes him stop, each murmur stay;
  For misery is trodden on by many,
  And being low, never relieved by any.

Shakespeare, Venus and Adonis (1593)

THE YEAR ROUND

JANUARY.

It is now January, and Time begins to turn the wheel of his revolution, the woods begin to lose the beauty of their spreading boughs, and the proud oak must stoop to the axe. The squirrel now surveyeth the nut and the maple, and the hedgehog now rolls up himself like a football. An apple and a nutmeg make a gossip's cup, and the ale and the faggot are the victualler's merchandise. The northern black dust [coal] is the during fuel, and the fruit of the grape heats the stomach of the aged. Down beds and quilted caps are now in the pride of their service, and the cook and the pantler [bread-controller] are men of no mean office. The ox and the fat wether now furnish the market, and the coney is so ferreted, that she cannot keep in her burrow; the currier [decoy-light] and the lime-rod are the death of the fowl, and the falcon's bells ring the death of the mallard. The trotting gelding makes a way through the mire, and the hare and his hound put the huntsman to his horn. The barren doe subscribes to the dish, and the smallest seed makes sauce to the greatest flesh; the dead grass is the horse's ordinary, and the meal of the beans makes him go through with his travail. Fishermen now have a cold trade, and travellers a foul journey; the cook-room now is not the worst place in the ship, and the shepherd hath a bleak seat on the mountain. The blackbird leaveth not a berry on the thorn, and the garden earth is turned up for her roots. The water-floods run over the proud banks, and the gaping oyster leaves his shell in the streets, while the proud peacock leaps into the pie. Muscovy [Russian] commodities are now much in request, and the water spaniel is a necessary servant. The load horse to the mill hath his full back burden, and the thresher in the barn tries the strength of his flail. The woodcock and the pheasant pay their lives for their feed, and the hare after a course makes his hearse in a pie; the shoulder of a hog is a shoeing horn to good drink, and a cold alms makes a beggar shrug. To conclude, I hold it a time of little comfort, the rich man's charge and the poor man's misery. Farewell.

FEBRUARY.

It is now February, and the sun is gotten up a cockstride of his climbing, the valleys now are painted white, and the brooks are full of water; the frog goes to seek out the paddock [another frog], and the crow and the rook begin to mislike their old mates; forward coneys begin now to kindle, and the fat grounds are not without lambs. The gardener falls to sorting of his seeds, and the husbandman falls afresh to scouring of his ploughshare. The term travellers make the shoemaker's harvest, and the chandler's cheese makes the chalk walk apace [increases the score or debt chalked up]. The fishmonger sorts his ware against Lent, and a lambskin is good for a lame arm. The waters now alter the nature of their softness, and the soft earth is made stony hard; the air is sharp and piercing, and the winds blow cold. The taverns and the inns seldom lack guests, and the ostler knows how to gain by his hay. The hunting horse is at the heels of the hound, while the ambling nag carrieth the physician and his footcloth. The blood of youth begins to spring, and the honour of art is gotten by exercise. The trees a little begin to bud, and the sap begins to rise up out of the root. Physic now hath work among weak bodies, and the apothecary's drugs are very gainful. There is hope of a better time not far off, for this in itself is little comfortable; and for the small pleasure that I find in it, I will thus briefly conclude of it: it is the poor man's pickpurse and the miser's cut-throat, the enemy to pleasure and the time of patience. Farewell.

MARCH.

It is now March, and the northern wind drieth up the southern dirt. The tender lips are now masked for fear of chapping, and the fair hands must not be ungloved. Now riseth the sun a pretty step to his fair height, and Saint Valentine calls the birds together, where Nature is pleased in the variety of love. The fishes and the frogs fall to their manner of generation, and the adder dies to bring forth her young. The air is sharp, but the sun is comfortable, and the hay begins to lengthen. The forward gardens give the fine sallets [salads, greens], and a nosegay of violets is a present for a lady. Now beginneth Nature as it were to wake out of her sleep, and send the traveller to survey the walks of the world. The sucking rabbit is good for weak stomachs, and the diet for the rheum doth many a good air; the farrier is now the horse's physician, and the fat dog feeds the falcon in the mew. The tree begins to bud, and the grass to peep abroad, while the thrush with the blackbird make a charm [song] in the young springs. The milkmaid with her best beloved talk away weariness to the market, and in an honest meaning kind words do no hurt. The football now trieth the legs of strength, and merry matches continue good fellowship. It is a time of much work, and tedious to discourse of; but in all I find it, I thus conclude in it: I hold it the servant of Nature and the schoolmaster of Art, the hope of labour and the subject of reason. Farewell.

APRIL.

It is now April, and the nightingale begins to tune her throat against May. The sunny showers perfume the air, and the bees begin to go abroad for honey; the dew, as in pearls, hangs upon the tops of the grass, while the turtles [doves] sit billing upon the little green boughs; the trout begins to play in the brooks, and the salmon leaves the sea to play in the fresh waters. The garden-backs are full of gay flowers, and the thorn and the plum send forth their fair blossoms; the March colt begins to play, and the cosset [hand-reared] lamb is learned to butt. The poets now make their studies in the woods, and the youth of the country makes ready for the morris dance. The little fishes lie nibbling at a bait, and the porpoise plays in the pride of the tide; the shepherd's pipe now entertains the princess of Arcadia, and the healthful soldier hath a pleasant march. The lark and the lamb look up at the sun, and the labourer is abroad by the dawning of the day. Sheep's eyes in lambs' heads [coy looks in young women] tell kind hearts strange tales, while faith and troth make the true-lovers' knot; the aged hairs find a fresh life, and the youthful cheeks are as red as a cherry. It were a world to set down the worth of this month, but in sum I thus conclude: I hold it the Heaven's blessing and the earth's comfort. Farewell.

COUNTRY LIFE

MAY.

It is now May, and the sweetness of the air refresheth every spirit; the sunny beams bring forth fair blossoms, and the dripping clouds water Flora's great garden. The male deer puts out the velvet head [first soft horns] and the pagged [swollen] doe is near her fawning. The sparrowhawk now is drawn out of the mew, and the fowler makes ready his whistle for the quail; the lark sets the morning watch, and the evening the nightingale. The barges, like bowers, keep the streams of the sweet rivers, and the mackerel with the shad are taken prisoners in the sea. The tall young oak is cut down for the maypole; the scythe and the sickle are the mower's furniture, and fair weather makes the labourer merry. The physician now prescribes the cold whey, and the apothecary gathers the dew for a medicine. Butter and sage make the wholesome breakfast, but fresh cheese and cream are meat for a dainty mouth; and the strawberry and the peascod want no price in the market. The chicken and the duck are fattened for the market, and many a gosling never lives to be a goose. It is the month wherein Nature hath her full of mirth, and the senses are filled with delights. I conclude, it is from the Heavens a grace, and to the earth a gladness. Farewell.

JUNE.

It is now June and the haymakers are mustered to make an army for the field, where, not always in order, they march under the Bag and the Bottle, when betwixt the Fork and the Rake [implements of male and female reapers] there is seen great force of arms. Now doth the broad oak comfort the weary labourer, while under his shady boughs he sits singing to his bread and cheese; the haycock is the poor man's lodging, and the fresh river is his gracious neighbour. Now the falcon and the tassel try their wings at the partridge, and the fat buck fills the great pasty. The trees are all in their rich array, but the seely [innocent] sheep is turned out of his coat. The roses and sweet herbs put the distiller to his cunning, while the green apples on the tree are ready for the great-bellied wives. Now begins the hare to gather up her heels, and the fox looks about him for fear of the hound. The hook and the sickle are making ready for harvest; the meadow grounds gape for rain, and the corn in the ear begins to harden. The little lads make pipes of straw, and they that cannot dance will yet be hopping. The air now groweth somewhat warm, and the cool winds are very comfortable; the sailor now makes merry passage, and the nimble foot-man [runner] runs with pleasure. In brief, I thus conclude, I hold it a sweet season, the senses' perfume and the spirit's comfort. Farewell.

JULY.

It is now July, and the sun is gotten up to his height, whose heat parcheth the earth and burns up the grass on the mountains. Now begins the cannon of heaven to rattle, and when the fire is put to the charge, it breaketh out among the clouds; the stones of congealed water cut off the ears of the corn, and the black storms affright the faint-hearted. The stag and the buck are now in pride of their time, and the hardness of their heads makes them fit for the horn. Now hath the sparrowhawk the partridge in the foot, and the ferret doth tickle the coney in the burrow. Now doth the farmer make ready his team, and the carter with his whip hath no small pride in his whistle. Now do the reapers try their backs and their arms, and the lusty youths pitch the sheaves into the cart. The old partridge calls her covey in the morning, and in the evening the shepherd falls to folding of his flock; the sparrows make a charm upon the green bushes, till the fowler come and take them by the dozens. The smelt [small fish] now begins to be in season, and the lamprey out of the river leaps into a pie. The soldier now hath a hot march, and the lawyer sweats in his lined gown; the pedlar now makes a long walk, and the aqua vitae bottle sets his face on a fiery heat. In sum, I thus conclude of it, I hold it a profitable season, the labourer's gain and the rich man's wealth. Farewell.

AUGUST.

It is now August, and the sun is somewhat towards his declination, yet such is his heat as hardeneth the soft clay, dries up the standing ponds, withereth the sappy leaves and scorcheth the skin of the naked. Now begin the gleaners to follow the corn cart, and a little bread to a great deal of drink makes the travailer's dinner. The melon and the cucumber is now in request, and oil and vinegar give attendance on the sallet herbs. The alehouse is more frequented than the tavern, and a fresh river is more comfortable than a fiery furnace; the bath is now much visited by diseased bodies, and in the fair rivers swimming is a sweet exercise. The bow and the bowl pick many a purse [through gambling on games], and the cocks with their heels [at a cockfight] spurn away many a man's wealth. The pipe and the tabor is now lustily set on work, and the lad and the lass will have no lead on their heels. The new wheat makes the gossip's cake, and the bride cup is carried above the heads of the whole parish; the frumenty [wheat boiled in milk and seasoned] cup welcomes home the harvest cart, and the garland of flowers crowns the captain of the reapers. Oh, 'tis the merry time, wherein honest neighbours make good cheer, and God is glorified in his blessings on the earth. In sum, for that I find, I thus conclude, I hold it the world's welfare, and the earth's warming-pan. Farewell.

SEPTEMBER.

It is now September, and the sun begins to fall much from his height, the meadows are left bare by the mouths of hungry cattle, and the hogs are turned into the cornfields. The winds begin to knock the apples' heads together on the trees, and the fallings are gathered to fill the pies for the householder. The sailors fall to work to get afore the wind, and if they spy a storm it puts them to prayer; the soldier now begins to shrug at the weather, and, the camp dissolved, the companies are put to garrison. The lawyer now begins his harvest, and the client pays for words by weight. The inns now begin to provide for guests, and the night-eaters in the stable pinch the traveller in his bed. Paper, pen and ink are much in request, and the Quarter Sessions take order with the way-layers [highway robbers]. Coals and wood make towards the chimney, and ale and sack are in account with good fellows. The butcher now knocks down the great beeves, and the poulterers' feathers make toward the upholsterer. Wallfleet oysters are the fishwives' wealth, and pippins fine are the costermongers' rich merchandise. The flail and the fan fall to work in the barn, and the cornmarket is full of the bakers; the porkets [piglets] now are driven to the woods, and the home-fed pigs make pork for the market. In brief, I thus conclude of it, I hold it the Winter's forewarning and the Summer's farewell. Adieu.

OCTOBER.

It is now October, and the lofty winds make bare the trees of their leaves, while the hogs in the woods grow fat with the fallen acorns; the forward deer begin to go to rut, and the barren doe groweth good meat. The basket-makers now gather their rods, and the fishers lay their leaps [traps] in the deep; the load horses go apace to the mill, and the meat-market is seldom without people. The hare on the hill makes the greyhound a fair course, and the fox in the woods calls the hounds to a full cry. The multitude of people raiseth the price of wares, and the smooth tongue will sell much; the sailor now bestirreth his stumps, while the merchant liveth in fear of the weather. The great feasts are now at hand for the City, but the poor must not beg, for fear of the stocks; a fire and a pair of cards keep the guests in the ordinary [tavern or eating-house], and tobacco is held very precious for the rheum. The coaches now begin to rattle in the street, but the cry of the poor is unpleasing to the rich. Muffs and cuffs are now in request, and the shuttlecock with the battledore is a pretty house-exercise; tennis and balloon are sports of some charge, and a quick bandy [game] is the court-keeper's commodity; dancing and fencing are now in some use, and kind hearts and true lovers lie close, to keep off cold. The titmouse now keeps in the hollow tree, and the blackbird sits close in the bottom of a hedge. In brief, for the little pleasure I find in it, I thus conclude of it; I hold it a messenger of all news, and a second service to a cold dinner. Farewell.

NOVEMBER.
It is now November, and according to the old proverb,

> Let the thresher take his flail,
> And the ship no more sail,

for the high winds and the rough seas will try the ribs of the ship, and the hearts of the sailors. Now come the country people all wet to the market, and the toiling carriers are pitifully moiled [muddied]. The young heron and the shoveller are now too fat for the great feast, and the woodcock begins to make toward the cockshoot [net]; the warreners [rabbiters] now begin to ply their harvest, and the butcher, after a good bargain, drinks a health to the grazier. The cook and the comfitmaker [confectioner] make ready for Christmas, and the minstrels in the country beat their boys for false fingering. Scholars before breakfast have a cold stomach to their book, and a Master without Art is fit for an ABC. A red herring and a cup of sack make war in a weak stomach, and the poor man's fast is better than the glutton's surfeit. Trenchers and dishes are now necessary servants, and a lock to the cupboard keeps a bit for a need. Now begins the goshawk to weed the wood of the pheasant, and the mallard loves not to hear the bells of the falcon. The winds now are cold and the air chill, and the poor die through want of charity. Butter and cheese begin to raise their prices, and kitchen stuff is a commodity that every man is not acquainted with. In sum, with a conceit of the chilly cold of it, I thus conclude in it: I hold it the discomfort of Nature, and Reason's patience. Farewell.

DECEMBER.

It is now December, and he that walks the streets shall find dirt on his shoes, except he go all in boots. Now doth the lawyer make an end of his harvest, and the client of his purse. Now capons and hens, besides turkeys, geese and ducks, besides beef and mutton, must all die for the great feast, for in twelve days a multitude of people will not be fed with a little. Now plums and spice, sugar and honey, square it among pies and broth, and 'Gossip, I drink to you' and 'You are welcome, and I thank you,' and 'How do you' and 'I pray you be merry.' Now are the tailors and the tiremakers [dressmakers] full of work against the holidays, and music now must be in tune or else never. The youth must sing and dance and the aged sit by the fire. It is the law of Nature and no contradiction in Reason. The ass that hath borne all the year must now take a little rest, and the lean ox must feed till he be fat. The footmen now shall have many a foul step, and the ostler shall have work enough about the heels of horses, while the tapster, if he take not heed, will lie drunk in the cellar. The prices of meat will rise apace, and the apparel of the proud will make the tailor rich. Dice and cards will benefit the butler; and if the cook do not lack wit, he will sweetly lick his fingers. Starchers and launderers will have their hands full of work, and periwigs and painting will not be a little set by.

> Strange stuffs will be well sold,
> Strange tales well told,
> Strange sights much sought,
> Strange things much bought,
> And what else, as falls out.

To conclude, I hold it the costly purveyor of excess, and the after breeder of necessity, the practice of folly and the purgatory of Reason. Farewell.

Nicholas Breton, *Fantastickes* (1626)

COUNTRY SPRING AND WINTER

I

When daisies pied and violets blue
And ladysmocks all silver-white
And cuckoo-buds of yellow hue
Do paint the meadows with delight,
The cuckoo then, on every tree,
Mocks married men, for thus sings he:
   'Cuckoo,
Cuckoo, cuckoo.' O word of fear,
Unpleasing to a married ear.

When shepherds pipe on oaten straws,
And merry larks are ploughmen's clocks,
When turtles tread, and rooks, and daws,
And maidens bleach their summer smocks,
The cuckoo then, on every tree,
Mocks married men, for thus sings he:
   'Cuckoo,
Cuckoo, cuckoo,' O word of fear,
Unpleasing to a married ear.

II

When icicles hang by the wall,
And Dick the shepherd blows his nail,
And Tom bears logs into the hall,
And milk comes frozen home in pail,
When blood is nipped, and ways be foul,
Then nightly sings the staring owl:
   'Too-whoo,
Too-whit, too-whoo,' a merry note,
While greasy Joan doth keel the pot.

COUNTRY LIFE

When all aloud the wind doth blow,
And coughing drowns the parson's saw,
And birds sit brooding in the snow,
And Marion's nose looks red and raw,
When roasted crabs [apples] hiss in the bowl,
Then nightly sings the staring owl:
    'Too-whoo,
Too-whit, too-whoo,' a merry note,
While greasy Joan doth keel the pot.

Shakespeare, *Love's Labour's Lost* (1594–5)

5

EDUCATION

They have been at a great feast of languages and stolen the scraps.
Shakespeare, *Love's Labour's Lost* (1594–5)

'Education, education, education.' From the beginning of the sixteenth century the importance of education for the social, cultural and economic strength of the nation had been recognized. At first, the aristocracy thought it sufficient for 'the sons of gentlemen to blow the horn, to ride well, and elegantly to carry and train a hawk,' but the early humanists, such as More, Colet and Pace, pressed the case for education as a general benefit, producing intellectually alert, religiously informed, useful citizens, promoting national prosperity and order, advancing the talented and fitting them for public office; the aristocracy soon enough recognized the threat from ambitious scholarship-boys, and by 1531 Sir Thomas Elyot's *The Governour* was urging the value of education for the governing classes.

The dissolution of the monasteries closed down some education, but some new schools were started, a practice continued by Edward VI. It was in Elizabeth's reign that education really boomed – 136 endowed grammar schools were founded, followed by 83 more in James I's time – and the purpose, theory, practice and consequences of education were widely discussed. By the turn of the century about one-third of the male population nationally was literate, while in London the literacy rate was over 70 per cent. Reading increasingly became part of the experience of ordinary people, necessary for such as apprentices, tradesmen and husbandmen, as well as for Bible study; the sales of almanacs, ballads and popular romances indicate the growth of literacy generally.

EDUCATION

The gentry and rising citizens could have private tutors; otherwise children started at their local 'petty' school at the age of four or five, learning to read, by a combination of look-and-say and phonics; writing was usually taught by peripatetic scriveners. From the ages of seven or eight to about fourteen, the boys went to grammar school, to be taught to read and write Latin and study Latin literature (including some history, biography and moral essays, as well as poetry and drama); a few schools also taught Greek and arithmetic. The overriding emphasis was on composition and rhetoric, learning by imitation of approved models. Not everyone could afford the fees, while the poorer often needed their sons' labour in the fields or home-working, so their education might be limited.

The gentry and middling sort saw the social value in education, and more and more went on, at about fifteen years of age, to Oxford or Cambridge (when the Queen visited Cambridge in 1564 there were some 1,200 undergraduates; by 1620, there were some 3,000). Again, costs effectively acted as a filter on entry (though some went as 'sizars' or servant-students). Living-conditions and work could be rigorous: undergraduates often lived three or four to a 'set' of rooms, with a college fellow occupying the 'high bed' and the others sharing truckle beds. Dawn rising was followed by compulsory chapel, before lectures and the first real meal at 10 a.m., then work, and later, chapel and supper; college gates closed at 8 or 9 p.m. Students followed a BA course of sixteen terms; at Oxford one would have studied (Latin) grammar, literature, rhetoric, logic, arithmetic and music, while at Cambridge philosophy replaced grammar, arithmetic and music. A major element was participation in formal debates and disputations. In later years the traditional classical authors (Aristotle, Virgil, Cicero) were supplemented by more recent writers: the logic and rhetoric of Ramus, the political philosophy of Machiavelli, the astronomy of Copernicus might figure, as well as lectures on modern history, languages and navigation. About one-third of students left without a degree (only needed for entry to the church – and there was great need for educated clergy – or the learned professions): some Catholics avoided the oath involved in taking the degree; some went on to the Inns of Court; for most, the value of university attendance lay in the making of contacts, the acquisition of common values, the development of a sense of cultural cohesion among the governing class (and an increasing sense of difference from the rest). Nevertheless, a frequent character in plays and satires was the discontented under- or un-employed graduate.

Education took two other forms. One was apprenticeship – a seven-year period begun at about the age of fifteen, being trained in a trade or skill, living with and working for a master before acquiring the freedom of a guild; a significant number of younger sons of gentry undertook apprenticeships. For the wealthy and ambitious there was also travel (often accompanied by a tutor) in Europe, to learn other countries' political, legal and commercial practices, their languages and characteristics, and make useful political and commercial contacts.

OF STUDIES

Studies serve for delight, for ornament, and for ability. Their chief use for delight is in privateness and retiring; for ornament, is in discourse; and for ability, is in the judgement and execution of business. For expert men can execute, and perhaps judge of particulars, one by one; but the general counsels, and the plots and marshalling of affairs, come best from those that are learned. To spend too much time in studies is sloth; to use them too much for ornament is affectation; to make judgement wholly by their rules is the humour [affectation] of a scholar. They perfect nature, and are perfected by experience; for natural abilities are like natural plants, that need pruning by study; and studies themselves do give forth directions too much at large, except they be bounded in by experience. Crafty men contemn [despise] studies; simple men admire them; and wise men use them: for they teach not their own use; but that is a wisdom without them and above them, won by observation. Read not to contradict and confute, nor to believe and take for granted, nor to find talk and discourse, but to weigh and consider. Some books are to be tasted, others to be swallowed, and some few to be chewed and digested: that is, some books are to be read only in parts; others to be read, but not curiously [with minute attention]; and some few to be read wholly, and with diligence and attention. Some books also may be read by deputy, and extracts made of them by others; but that would be only in the less important arguments, and the meaner sort of books; else distilled books are like common distilled waters, flashy things. Reading maketh a full man; conference a ready man; and writing an exact man. And therefore, if a man write little, he had need have a great memory; if he confer little, he had need have a present wit; and if he read little, he had need have much cunning, to seem to know that, he doth not. Histories make men wise; poets witty; the mathematics subtle; natural philosophy deep; moral, grave; logic and rhetoric able to contend. *Abeunt studia in mores* [studies go to form character].

Francis Bacon, Essayes (1595–1625)

WHO SHOULD BE EDUCATED?

Whether all children be to be set to school or no without repressing the infinity of the multitude, it is a matter of great weight. . . . Whereof I say thus, that too many learned be too burdenous, that too few be too bare, that wits well sorted be most civil, that the same misplaced be most unquiet and seditious. . . .

To have so many gaping for preferment as no gulf hath store enough to suffice, and to let them roam helpless whom nothing else can help, how can it be but that such shifters must needs shake the very strongest pillar in that state where they live loiter without living? . . .

As too many brings surfeits, so too few breeds consumptions. . . .

Again, wits misplaced [be] most unquiet and seditious, as anything else strained against nature. . . . An imperial wit, for want of education and ability, being placed in a mean calling will trouble the whole company if he have not his will. . . . He that beareth a tankard by meanness of degree and was born for a cockhorse by sharpness of wit will keep a canvass at the conduits till he be master of his company. Such a stirring thing it is to have wits misplaced and their degrees mis-lotted by the iniquity of fortune, which the equity of fortune did seem to mean unto them. . . .

Some doubt may rise here between the rich and the poor, whether all rich and none poor or but some in both may and ought to be set to learning. . . . If all rich be excluded ability will snuff, if all poor be restrained then will towardness [aptitude] repine. If ability set out some rich by private purses for private preferment, towardness will commend some poor to public provision for public service. . . . The middle sort of parents which neither welter in too much wealth nor wrestle with too much want seemeth fittest of all, if the children's capacity be answerable to their parents' state and quality.

Richard Mulcaster, *Positions* (1581)

SCHOOL RULES

The school-time should begin at six. . . . The best means that ever I could find to make them rise early, to prevent all . . . fear of whipping, is this: by letting the little ones to have their places in their forms daily, according to their coming after six of the clock. So many as are there at six, to have their places as they had them by election on the day before. All whom come after six, every one to sit as he cometh, and so to continue that day. . . . So greatly even children are provoked by the credit of their places.

Thus they are to continue until nine, signified by monitors, subdoctor or otherwise. Then at nine I find that order which is in Westminster [School] to be far the best: to let them to have a quarter of an hour at least, or more, for intermission, either for breakfast, for all who are near unto the school can be there within the time limited, or else for the necessity of everyone, or their honest recreation, or to prepare their exercises against the master's coming in.

After, each of them to be in his place in an instant upon the knocking of the door or some other sign given by the subdoctor or monitors, in pain of loss of his place, or further punishment, as was noted before; so to continue until eleven of the clock, or somewhat after, to countervail the time of the intermission at nine.

To be again all ready and in their places at one, in an instant; to continue until three or half an hour after; then to have another quarter of an hour or more, as at nine, for drinking and necessities. So to continue till half an hour after five, thereby in that half hour to countervail the time at three. Then to end so as was showed, with reading a piece of chapter [from the Bible] and with singing two staves of a psalm; lastly with prayer to be used by the master. . . .

Education

I would indeed have their recreations as well looked into as their learning; as you may perceive plainly by their intermissions at nine and at three. Besides those and all other their intermissions, it is very requisite also that they should have weekly one part of an afternoon for recreation, as a reward of their diligence, obedience and profiting; and that to be appointed at the master's discretion, either the Thursday after the usual custom, or according to the best opportunity of the place. . . .

All recreations and sports for scholars would be meet for gentlemen. Clownish sports, or perilous, or yet playing for money are no way to be admitted. The [re]creations of the studious are as well to be looked unto as the study of the rest, that none take hurt by his study, either for mind or body, or any way else.

Yet here of the other side, very great care is to be had in the moderating of their recreation. For schools, generally, do not take more hindrance by any one thing than by over-often leave to play. Experience teacheth that this draweth their minds utterly away from their books, that they cannot take pains for longing after play and talking of it; as also, devising means to procure others to get leave to play, so that ordinarily when they are but in hope thereof they will do things very negligently, and after the most play they are evermore for the worst. . . .

For inflicting punishments we ought to come thereunto unwillingly, and even enforced; and therefore to proceed by degrees: . . .

1. To use reproofs; and those sometimes more sharp according to the nature of the offender and his fault.
2. To punish by loss of place to him who doth better, according to our discretion.
3. To punish by a note, which may be called the black bill. . . . The manner of it may be thus. To keep a note in writing, or, which may more easily be done, to keep a remembrance of all whom you observe very negligent, stubborn, lewd, or any way disobedient, to restrain them from all liberty of play. And therefore to give them all to know so much beforehand, that whosoever asketh leave to play, or upon what occasion soever, yet we intend always to except all such. . . .
4. Sometimes in greater faults, to give three or four jerks with a birch, or with a small red willow where birch cannot be had. Or for terror in some notorious fault, half a dozen stripes or more, soundly laid on,

according to the discretion of the master. . . . In this correction with the rod, special provision must be had for sundry things.

I. That when you are to correct any stubborn or unbroken boy, you may be sure with him to hold him fast; as they are enforced to do, who are to shoe or to tame an unbroken colt. To this end, appoint three or four of your scholars, whom you know to be honest, and strong enough, or more if need be, to lay hands upon him together, to hold him fast, over some form, so that he cannot stir hand nor foot. . . .

II. To be wary for smiting them over the backs, in any case, or in such sort as in any way to hurt or endanger them. To the end to prevent all mischiefs, for our own comfort, and to cut off all occasions from quarrelling parents or evil reports of the school. . . .

III. That the master do not in any case abase himself to strive or struggle with any boy to take him up, but to appoint other of the strongest to do it. . . .

IV. That the masters and ushers also do by all means avoid all furious anger, threatening, chafing, fretting, reviling: for these things will diminish authority. . . .

Finally, as God hath sanctified the rod and correction, to cure the evils of their conditions, to drive out that folly which is bound up in their hearts, to save their souls from hell, to give them wisdom: so it is to be used as God's instrument to these purposes. To spare them in these cases is to hate them. To love them is to correct them betime. Do it under God, and for Him to these ends and with these cautions, and you shall never hurt them: you have the Lord for your warrant.

John Brinsley, *Ludus Literarius, or the Grammar Schoole* (1612)

LEARNING A LESSON

Before Master Downhall came to be our master in Christ school, an ancient citizen of no great learning was our schoolmaster; whose manner was to give us out several lessons in the evening, and in the next morning to examine us thereupon, by making all the boys in the first form to come from their seats and stand on the outskirts of their desks towards the middle of the school, and so the second form and so the rest in order, whiles himself walked up and down by them and hearing them construe their lesson one after another, and then giving one of the words to one, and another to another (as he thought fit) for parsing of it. Now when the two highest forms were dispatched, some of them whom we called prompters would come and sit in our seats of the lower forms, and so being at our elbows would put into our mouths answers to our master's questions, as he walked up and down by us: and so by our prompters' help we made shift to escape correction, but understood little to profit by it, having this circular motion, like the millhorse that travels all day yet in the end finds himself not a yard further than when he began.

I being thus supported by my prompter, it fell out one day that one of the eldest scholars and one of the highest form fell out with me on occasion of some boys'-play abroad, and in his anger, to do me the greatest hurt he could (which then he thought to be, to fall under the rod) he dealt with all the prompters, that none of them should help me, and so (as he thought) I must necessarily be beaten. When I found myself at this strait, I gathered all my wits together (as we say) and listened the more carefully to my fellows that instruct before me, and having also some easy word to my lot for parsing I made hard shrift to escape for that time. And when I observed my adversary's displeasure to continue against me, so as I could have no help from my prompters, I doubled my diligence and attention to our master's construing our next lesson to us, and observing carefully how in construction one word followed and depended upon another, which with heedful observing two or three lessons more, opened the way to . . . me . . . so as I needed no prompter.

R. Willis, *Mount Tabor* (pub. 1639)

QUICK AND SLOW LEARNERS

This will I say, that even the wisest of our great beaters [among schoolmasters] do as oft punish nature as they do correct faults. Yea, many times, the better nature is the sorer punished. For, if one, by quickness of wit, take his lesson readily, another, by hardness of wit, taketh it not so speedily: the first is always commended, the other is commonly punished; when a wise schoolmaster should rather discreetly consider the right disposition of both their natures, and not so much weigh what either of them is able to do now, as what either of them is likely to do hereafter. For this I know, not only by reading of books in my study, but also by experience of life abroad in the world, that those which be commonly the wisest, the best learned, and best men also when they be old, were never commonly the quickest of wit when they were young. The causes why, amongst other, which be many, that move me thus to think, be these few, which I will reckon. Quick wits commonly be apt to take, unapt to keep; soon hot and desirous of this and that, as cold and soon weary of the same again; more quick to enter speedily than able to pierce far; even like other sharp tools, whose edges be very soon turned. Such wits delight themselves in easy and pleasant studies, and never pass far forward in high and hard sciences. And therefore the quickest wits commonly may prove the best poets, but not the wisest orators: ready of tongue to speak boldly, not deep of judgement, either for good counsel or wise writing. Also, for manners and life, quick wits commonly be, in desire newfangled, in purpose unconstant; light to promise anything, ready to forget everything, both benefit and injury; and thereby neither fast to friend nor fearful to foe; inquisitive of every trifle, not secret in greatest affairs; bold with any person; busy in every matter; soothing such as be present, nipping any that is absent; of nature also, always flattering their betters, envying their equals, despising their inferiors; and, by quickness of wit, very quick and ready to like none so well as themselves.

Roger Ascham, *The Scholemaster* (1570)

EDUCATING GIRLS

And to prove they are to be trained, I find four special reasons, whereof any one, much more all, may persuade any their most adversary, much more me, which am for them tooth and nail. The first is the manner and custom of my country, which allowing them to learn will be loth to be contraried by any of her countrymen. The second is the duty which we owe unto them, whereby we are charged in conscience not to leave them lame in that which is for them. The third is their own towardness, which God by nature would never have given them to remain idle or to small purpose. The fourth is the excellent effects in that sex when they have had the help of good bringing up

EDUCATION

. . .I do think the same time [of starting education] fit for both [sexes], not determinable by years but by ripeness of wit to conceive without tiring, and strength of body to travail without wearying. For though the girls seem commonly to have a quicker ripening in wit than boys have, for all that seeming yet it is not so. Their natural weakness which cannot hold long, delivers very soon, and yet there be as prating boys as there be prating wenches. Besides their brains be not so much charged, neither with weight nor with multitude of matters as boys' heads be, and therefore like empty casks they make the greater noise. As those men which seem to be very quick-witted by some sudden pretty answer, or some sharp reply, be not always most burdened, neither with letters nor learning. . . . As for bodies, the maidens be more weak, most commonly even by nature, as of a moonish influence, and all our whole kind is weak of the mother side, which when she was first made even then weakened the man's side. Therefore great regard must be had to them, no less, nay, rather more, than to boys in that time. . . .

Where the question is how much a woman ought to learn, the answer may be, so much as may be needful. If that also come in doubt, the return may be, either so much as her parents conceive of her in hope, if her parentage be mean, or provide for her in state, if her birth bear a sail. . . . This *how much* consisteth either in perfecting of those forenamed four, reading well, writing fair, singing sweet, playing fine, beyond all cry and above all comparison, that pure excellency in things but ordinary may cause extraordinary liking; or else in skill of languages annexed to these four, that more good gifts may work wonder. . . . I fear no workmanship in women to give them geometry and her sister sciences, to make them mathematicals, though I mean them music; nor yet bars to plead at, to leave them the laws; nor urinals to look on to lend them some physic though the skill of herbs hath been the study of nobility, by the Persian story, and much commended in women; nor pulpits to preach in, to utter their divinity . . . The time how long they are to learn, which time is commonly till they be about thirteen or fourteen years old, wherein as the matter which they must deal withal cannot be very much in so little time, so the perfecting thereof requireth much travail.

Richard Mulcaster, *Positions* (1581)

A SCHOOL FOR SCANDAL
OR, WILLIAM LEARNING QUICKLY

Mrs Page.   Sir Hugh, my husband says my son profits nothing in the world at his book. I pray you, ask him some questions in his accidence [Latin grammar].

Sir Hugh Evans [Welsh parson].   Come hither, William; hold up your head; come.

Mrs Page.   Come on, sirrah; hold up your head; answer your master; be not afraid.

Evans.   William, how many numbers is in nouns?

William.   Two.

Mrs Quickly [servant].   Truly, I thought there had been one number more, because they say, 'Od's nouns' [God's wounds].

Evans.   Peace your tattlings. What is 'fair', William?

William.   *Pulcher.*

Quickly.   Polecats [prostitutes]! There are fairer things than polecats, sure.

Evans.   You are a very simplicity 'oman; I pray you, peace. What is *lapis* [stone; laps, female genitals], William?

William.   A stone [testicle].

Evans.   And what is 'a stone', William?

William.   A pebble.

Evans.   No, it is *lapis*; I pray you, remember in your prain.

William.   *Lapis.*

Evans.   That is a good William. What is he, William, that doth lend articles?

William.   Articles are borrowed of the pronoun, and be thus declined: *singulariter, nominativo: hic, haec, hoc* [this].

Evans.   *Nominativo*, hig, hag, hog. Pray you, mark: *genitivo, hujus* [of this; genitals, hugeous]. Well, what is your accusative case?

William.   *Accusativo, hinc.*

Evans.   I pray you, have your remembrance, child. *Accusativo*, hung, hang, hog.

Quickly.   'Hang-hog' is Latin for bacon, I warrant you.

Evans.   Leave your prabbles, 'oman. What is the focative [vocative/fuckative] case [body], William?

William.   O! *vocativo*, O! [female genitals, sexual cry]

EDUCATION

Evans.	Remember, William: focative is caret [missing].
Quickly.	And that's a good root [carrot; penis].
Evans.	'Oman, forbear.
Mrs Page.	Peace.
Evans.	What is your genitive case plural, William?
William.	Genitive case?
Evans.	Ay.
William.	Genitive: *horum, harum, horum* [of these; whore 'em].
Quickly.	Vengeance of Jenny's case [genitals], fie on her! Never name her, child, if she be a whore.
Evans.	For shame, 'oman.
Quickly.	You do ill to teach the child such words. He teaches him to hick and to hack [ride whores], which they'll do fast enough of themselves; and to call *horum* [whore 'em]: fie on you!
Evans.	'Oman, art thou lunatics? Hast thou no under-standings [erections] for thy cases [genitals], and the numbers of the genders [acts of engendering]? Thou art as foolish Christian creatures as I would desires [sexually!].
Mrs Page.	Prithee, hold thy peace.
Evans.	Show me now, William, some declensions of your pronouns.
William.	Forsooth, I have forgot.
Evans.	It is, *qui, quae, quod*; if you forget your *qui*'s [keys, penis], *quae*'s, and your *quod*'s [cods, testicles], you must be preeches [breeched, beaten]. Go your ways and play; go.

Shakespeare, *The Merry Wives of Windsor* (1599?)

LANGUAGE, STYLE AND SOCIETY

We may conclude, wheresoever manners and fashion are corrupted, language is. It imitates the public riot. The excess of feasts and apparel are the notes of a sick state, and the wantonness of language, of a sick mind. . . .

Speech is the only benefit man hath to express his excellency of mind above other creatures, it is the instrument of society. Therefore Mercury, who is president of language, is called *Deorum hominumque interpres* [the interpreter of gods and men]. In all speech, words and sense are as the body and the soul. The sense is as the life and soul of language, without which all words are dead. Sense is wrought out of experience, the knowledge of human life and actions, or of the liberal arts. . . . Words are the people's; yet there is a choice of them to be made. For *verborum delectus origo est eloquentiae* [delight in words is the origin of eloquence]. They are to be chose according to the persons we make speak or the things we speak of. Some are of the camp, some of the sheepcote, some of the pulpit, some of the bar, etc. And herein is seen their elegance and propriety when we use them fitly and draw them forth to their just strength and nature by way of translation, or metaphor. . . .

Custom is the most certain mistress of language, as the public stamp makes the current money. But we must not be too frequent with the mint, every day coining; nor fetch words from the extreme and utmost ages, since the chief virtue of a style is perspicuity, and nothing so vicious in it as to need an interpreter. Words borrowed of antiquity do lend a kind of majesty to style and are not without their delight sometimes, for they have the authority of years and out of their intermission do win to themselves a kind of grace like newness. But the eldest of the present and newest of the past language is the best. For what was the ancient language, which some men so dote upon, but the ancient custom? Yet when I name custom, I understand not the vulgar custom, for that were a precept no less dangerous to language than life, if we should speak or live after the manners of the vulgar; but that I call custom of speech which is the consent of the learned, as the custom of life which is the consent of the good. . . .

Language most shows a man: speak that I may see thee. It springs out of the most retired and inmost parts of us, and is the image of the parent of it, the mind. No glass renders a man's form or likeness so true as his speech.

Ben Jonson, *Timber, or Discoveries* (pub. 1640)

THE UNIVERSITIES

The manner to live in these universities is not as in some other of foreign countries we see daily to happen, where the students are enforced for want of such houses [college accommodation] to dwell in common inns and taverns, without all order and discipline. . . .

In most of our colleges there are also great numbers of students, of which many are found by the revenues of the houses, and others by the purveyances and help of their rich friends; whereby in some one college you shall have two hundred scholars, in others an hundred and fifty, in divers an hundred and forty, and in the rest, less numbers, as the capacity of the said houses is able to receive. So that at this present, of one sort and another, there are about three thousand students nourished in them both. . . . They were erected by their founders at the first only for poor men's sons, whose parents were not able to bring them up unto learning; but now they have the least benefit of them, by reason the rich do encroach upon them. And so far hath this inconvenience spread itself, that it is in my time an hard matter for a poor man's child to come by a fellowship (though he be never so good a scholar, and worthy a scholar) . . .

Such bribage is made, that poor men's children are commonly shut out, and the richer sort received (who in time past thought it dishonour to live as it were upon alms), and yet, being placed, most of them study little other than histories [stories], tables [backgammon], dice and trifles, as men that make not the living by their study the end of their purposes, which is a lamentable hearing. Besides this, being for the most part either gentlemen, or rich men's sons, they oft bring the universities into much slander. For, standing upon their reputation and liberty, they ruffle and roist it out, exceeding in apparel, and banting [fooling about with] riotous company (which draweth them from their books unto another trade), and for excuse, when they are charged with breach of all good order, think it sufficient to say, that they be gentlemen, which grieveth many not a little.

The first degree is that of the general sophisters, from whence, when they have learned more sufficiently the rules of logic, rhetoric, and obtained thereto competent skill in philosophy and in the mathematicals, they ascend higher unto the estate of bachelors of art, after four years of their entrance into their sophistry. From thence also giving their minds to more perfect knowledge in some or all the other liberal sciences, and the tongues, they rise at the last (to wit, the other three or four years) to be called masters of art.

After forty years of age the most part of students [fellows] do commonly give over their wonted diligence, and live like drone bees on the fat of the colleges, withholding better wits from the possession of their places, yet doing little good in their own vocation and calling. I could rehearse a number if I listed, of this sort, as well in the one university as the other. But this shall suffice instead of a larger report, that long continuance in those places is either a sign of lack of friends, or of learning, or of good and upright life, as Bishop Fox sometime noted, who thought it sacrilege for a man to tarry any longer at Oxford than he had a desire to profit.

William Harrison, *Description of England* (1587)

A POOR SERVANT-STUDENT (THOMAS NASHE)

Pierce-penniless, exceeding poor scholar, that hath made clean shoes in both universities, and been a pitiful batteler [poorly provisioned] all thy lifetime, full often heard with this lamentable cry at the buttery-hatch, 'Ho, Lancelot, a cue [tiny portion] of bread and a cue of beer,' never passing beyond the confines of a farthing, nor once munching commons [standard rations] but only on Gaudy [feast] days.

Thomas Middleton, *The Blacke Booke* (1604)

TWO UNDERGRADUATES

A plodding student is a kind of alchemist or persecutor of nature, that would change the dull lead of his brain into finer metal, with success many times as unprosperous, or at least not quitting the cost, to wit, of his own oil and candles. He has a strange forced appetite to learning, and to achieve it brings nothing but patience and a body. His study is not great but continual, and consists much in the sitting up after midnight in a rug gown and a nightcap, to the vanquishing perhaps of some six lines; yet what he has, he has perfect, for he reads it so long to understand it till he gets it without book. He may with much industry make a breach into logic, and arrive at some ability in an argument; but for politer studies, he dare not skirmish with them, and for poetry accounts it impregnable. . . . He is a great discomforter of young students, by telling them what travail it has cost him, and how often his brain turned at philosophy, and makes others fear studying as a cause of duncery.

A young gentleman of the university is one that comes there to wear a gown, and to say hereafter he has been at the university. His father sent him thither, because he heard there were the best fencing and dancing schools; from these he has his education, from his tutor the oversight. The first element of his knowledge is to be shown the colleges, and initiated in a tavern by the way, which hereafter he will learn of himself. The two marks of his seniority is the bare velvet of his gown and his proficiency at tennis, where when he can once play a set, he is a freshman no more. His study has commonly handsome shelves, his books neat silk strings, which he shows to his father's man, and is loth to untie or take down, for fear of misplacing. Upon foul days, for recreation, he retires thither, and looks over the pretty book his tutor reads to him, which is commonly some short history or a piece of *Euphormio* [a modern Latin satire]; for which his tutor gives him money to spend the next day. His main loitering is at the library, where he studies arms and books of honour, and turns a gentleman-critic in pedigrees. Of all things he endures not to be mistaken for a scholar, and hates a black suit though it be of satin. His companion is ordinarily some stale fellow, that has been notorious for an ingle to gold hatbands [sexual playmate for gentlemen], whom he admires at first, afterward scorns. If he have spirit or wit, he may light of better company and may learn some flashes of wit, which may do him knight's service in the country hereafter. But he is now gone to the Inns of Court, where he studies to forget what he learned before: his acquaintance and the fashion.

John Earle, *Micro-cosmographie* (1628)

A MERE SCHOLAR

Is an intelligible ass, or a silly fellow in black, that speaks sentences more familiarly than sense. The antiquity of his university is his creed, and the excellency of his college (though but for a match at football) an article of his faith. He speaks Latin better than his mother tongue, and is a stranger in no part of the world but his own country. He does usually tell great stories of himself to small purpose, for they are commonly ridiculous, be they true or false. His ambition is, that he either is or shall be a graduate: but if ever he get a fellowship, he has then no fellow. In spite of all logic he dare swear and maintain it, that a cuckold and a townsman are *termini convertibiles* [interchangeable terms], though his mother's husbandman be an alderman. He was never begotten (as it seems) without much wrangling, for his whole life is spent in *pro* and *contra*. His tongue goes always before his wit, like a gentleman usher, but somewhat faster. That he is a complete gallant in all points, cap à pied, witness his horsemanship and the wearing of his weapons. He is commonly longwinded, able to speak more with ease than any man can endure to hear with patience. University jests are his universal discourse, and his news the demeanour of the proctors. His phrase, the apparel of his mind, is made of divers shreds like a cushion, and when it goes plainest it hath a rash outside and fustian linings. The current of his speech is closed with an *ergo*; and whatever be the question, the truth is on his side. 'Tis a wrong to his reputation to be ignorant of anything; and yet he knows not that he knows nothing. . . . That learning which he hath, was in his nonage [youth] put in backward like a clyster [enema], and now 'tis ware mislaid in a pedlar's pack: 'a has it, but knows not where it is. In a word, he is the index of a man, and the title page of a scholar; or a Puritan in morality: much in profession, nothing in practice.

Sir Thomas Overbury, *Characters* (1614–16)

STUDENT DAYS REMEMBERED

Justice Shallow. I dare say my cousin William is become a good scholar; he is at Oxford still, is he not?

Silence. Indeed, sir, to my cost.

Shallow. 'A must, then, to the Inns o' Court shortly. I was once of Clement's Inn; where I think they will talk of mad Shallow yet.

Silence. You were called 'lusty Shallow' then, cousin.

Shallow. By the mass, I was called anything; and I would have done anything indeed too, and roundly too. There was I, and little John Doit of Staffordshire, and black George Barnes, and Francis Pickbone, and Will Squele a Cotsole [Cotswold] man – you had not four such swinge-bucklers [bold fellows] in all the Inns of Court again. And I may say to you, we knew where the bonarobas [smart whores] were, and had the best of them all at commandment. Then was Jack Falstaff, now Sir John, a boy, and page to Sir Thomas Mowbray . . . Jesu, Jesu, the mad days that I have spent! . . .

EDUCATION

Falstaff.   Lord, lord, how subject we old men are to this vice of lying! This same starved Justice hath done nothing but prate to me of the wildness of his youth and the feats he hath done about Turnbull Street [brothel area]; and every third word a lie, duer paid to the hearer than the Turk's tribute. I do remember him at Clement's Inn, like a man made after supper of a cheese-paring. When 'a was naked, he was for all the world like a forked radish, with a head fantastically carved upon it with a knife. 'A was so forlorn that his dimensions to any thick sight were invisible. 'A was the very genius of famine; yet lecherous as a monkey, and the whores called him mandrake.

Shakespeare, *King Henry IV, Part II* (1598)

OF TRAVEL

Travel, in the younger sort, is a part of education; in the elder, a part of experience. He that travelleth into a country before he hath some entrance into the language, goeth to school, and not to travel. That young men travel under some tutor or grave servant, I allow well, so that he be such a one that hath the language and hath been in the country before; whereby he may be able to tell them what things are worthy to be seen in the country where they go, what acquaintances they are to seek; what exercises or discipline the place yieldeth. For else young men shall go hooded, and look abroad little. . . .

The things to be seen and observed are: the courts of princes, specially when they give audience to ambassadors; the courts of justice, where they sit and hear causes, and so of consistories ecclesiastic; the churches and monasteries, with the monuments which are therein extant; the walls and fortifications of cities and towns, and so the havens and harbours; antiquities and ruins; libraries; colleges; disputations and lectures, where any are; shipping and navies; houses and gardens of state and pleasure, near great cities; armouries; arsenals; magazines [depots]; exchanges; burses; warehouses; exercises of horsemanship, fencing, training of soldiers, and the like; comedies, such whereunto the better sort of persons do resort; treasuries of jewels and robes; cabinets and rarities; and, to conclude, whatsoever is memorable in the places where they go.

After all which the tutors or servants ought to make diligent enquiry. As for triumphs, masques, feasts, weddings, funerals, capital executions, and such shows, men need not to be put in mind of them; yet are they not to be neglected. . . .

As for the acquaintance which is to be sought in travel: that which is most of all profitable is acquaintance with the secretaries and employed men of ambassadors; for so in travelling in one country he shall suck the experience of many. Let him also see and visit eminent persons in all kinds, which are of great name abroad, that he may be able to tell how the life agreeth with the fame. For quarrels, they are with care and discretion to be avoided: they are commonly for mistresses, healths, place and words. And let a man beware how he keepeth company with choleric and quarrelsome persons, for they will engage him into their own quarrels.

Francis Bacon, *Essayes* (1597–1625)

LEARNING BY TRAVEL: 'EAST, WEST, . . .'

The first traveller was Cain, and he was called a vagabond runagate on the face of the earth. Travel (like the travail [frame] wherein smiths put wild horses when they shoe them) is good for nothing but to tame and bring men under. . . .

He that is a traveller must have the back of an ass to bear all, a tongue like the tail of a dog to flatter all, the mouth of a hog to eat what is set before him, the ear of a merchant to hear all and say nothing. . . .

So let others tell you strange accidents, treasons, poisonings, close packings [secret plottings] in France, Spain and Italy; it is no harm for you to hear of them, but come not near them.

What is there in France to be learned more than in England, but falsehood in fellowship, perfect slovenry, to love no man but for my pleasure, to swear 'Ah par la mort Dieu' when a man's hams are scabbed? For the idle traveller, I mean not for the soldier, I have known some that have continued there by the space of half a dozen years, and when they come home they have hid a little wearish [sickly] lean face under a broad French hat, kept a terrible coil [disturbance] with the dust in the street in their long cloaks of grey paper, and spoke English strangely. Nought else have they profited by their travel, save learnt to distinguish of the true Bordeaux grape, and know a cup of neat Gascoigne wine from wine of Orleans. Yea, and peradventure this also, to esteem of the pox as a pimple, to wear a velvet patch on their face, and walk melancholy with their arms folded.

From Spain what bringeth our traveller? A skull-crowned hat of the fashion of an old deep porringer [bowl], a diminutive alderman's ruff with short strings like the droppings of a man's nose, a close-bellied doublet coming down like a peak behind as far as the crupper and cut off before by the breastbone, like a partlet or neckerchief, a wide pair of gaskins [baggy breeches] which ungathered would make a couple of women's riding kirtles, huge hangers [sword straps] that have half a cow-hide in them, a rapier that is lineally descended from half a dozen dukes at the least. Let his cloak be as long or as short as you will: if long, it is faced with Turkey grogram [coarse silk] ravelled; if short, it hath a cape like a calf's tongue and is not so deep in his whole length, nor hath so much cloth in it, I will justify, as only the standing cape of a Dutchman's cloak. . . . A soldier and a braggart he is (that's concluded). He jetteth [swaggers] strutting, dancing on his toes with his hands under his sides. If you talk with him, he makes a dishcloth of his own country in comparison of Spain, but if you urge him more particularly wherein it exceeds, he can give no instance but 'in Spain they have better bread than any we have'; when, poor hungry slaves, they may crumble it into water well enough and make misers [bread sops] with it, for they have not a good morsel of meat except it be salt pilchards to eat it with all the year long, and, which is more, they are poor beggars and lie in foul straw every night.

Italy, the paradise of the earth and the epicure's heaven, how doth it form our young master? It makes him to kiss his hand like an ape, cringe his neck like a starveling, and play at heypass, repass come aloft [gesture absurdly, like a conjuror], when he salutes a man. From thence he brings the art of atheism, the art of epicurising, the art of whoring, the art of poisoning, the art of sodomitry. The only good thing they have to keep us from utterly condemning it is, that it maketh a man an excellent courtier, a curious carpet knight; which is, by interpretation, a fine close lecher, a glorious hypocrite. It is now a privy note amongst the better sort of men, when they would set a singular mark or brand on a notorious villain, to say he hath been in Italy.

With the Dane and the Dutchman I will not encounter, for they are simple honest men, that, with Danaus's daughters [who were condemned to collect water in sieves for ever], do nothing but fill bottomless tubs and will be drunk and snort in the midst of dinner. . . .

Believe me, no air, no bread, no fire, no water doth a man any good out of his own country. Cold fruits never prosper in a hot soil, nor hot in a cold. Let no man for any transitory pleasure sell away the inheritance he hath of breathing in the place where he was born.

Thomas Nashe, The Unfortunate Traveller (1594)

6

BELIEFS

Elizabethans generally assumed a coherent cosmos, where spirits
(angels, daemons and others), the stars and planets turning on their
invisible, musical (but inaudible) spheres, the animal, vegetable
and mineral orders, the human body and society existed in
hierarchical order – a 'chain of being' – and correspondence (so
that the supreme seraphim, the sun, lion, rose, gold, reason, king
and father were correspondent, heading their respective orders);
the macrocosm (the universe) was repeated in the microcosm, the
'little world of man' for which it existed (King Lear thought the
thunder manifested divine anger at human disorder). Thus, the
universe was fundamentally orderly and beneficent; but since the
Fall, death, sin and disorder had entered the world, producing the
difficult, unreliable and moribund existence generally experienced.
The turn of the century was marked by scepticism, melancholy
and political, social and intellectual strife, as the very nature of
existence was questioned in a new, scientistic spirit, millenarians
expected Armageddon, faith fragmented as Catholics, Protestants
and heterodoxical sects fought in the collapse of Christendom, and
a new relativism and individualism spread.

The 'new philosophy' that, as John Donne observed, 'calls all in
doubt', worked through scientific experimentation, assuming a
material universe – Tourneur's D'Amville, in *The Atheist's Tragedy*
(1611) thought thunder 'a mere effect of nature'. Traditional neo-
Aristotelean thinking worked inductively from unexamined general
principles, assuming a purposeful universe in which change enabled
creation to achieve an intended potential (so, theoretically, all metals
had it in them to become gold). Four elements (earth, air, fire, water)
could be analysed by four qualities (hot, cold, wet, dry) and related
to the four humours (melancholy, sanguine, choler, phlegm), all of

which could be permutated to explain all physical and psychological conditions. Others, following the Renaissance Italian Neoplatonists, believed in occult powers (daemons and spirits) driving the world through forces that could be controlled by magicians (like Prospero in *The Tempest*), through alchemy, astrology, numerology and magic. Operating at a lower, more 'popular' level were witches, who leagued with devils, hobgoblins and fairies, and were discredited by both rationalists and Puritans, who associated them with paganism and Catholicism.

It would hardly be possible to exaggerate the central importance of Christianity, in its various forms, in these times: it shook monarchies, divided nations and families, and harrowed men's minds with fear and wonder; it shaped everyone's way of thinking; it was a matter of actual as well as spiritual life and death, with fire, noose or axe for some, and persecution, fines and punishment for many. After half a century of violent oscillation between Catholicism and Protestantism, the country was in desperate need of settlement. Following the Act of Supremacy and Uniformity (1559), the position of the Church under its 'supreme governor' was a moderate Protestantism, with Catholic-sympathetic clergy removed but Puritans discouraged, somewhat Calvinistic in doctrine, emphasizing individual salvation and Scripture-reading more than predestination, but conservative in practice, with bishops and vestments (constant sources of dangerous dispute). Despite remains of popular, traditional neo-pagan superstition and custom, and of Catholic communities (persisting patchily in Lancashire, the north-east and the west Midlands), England by the turn of the century was a Protestant country. While an unenthusiastic orthodoxy prevailed generally, a fair number took their religion very earnestly; everyone had to attend their parish church on Sundays, and take Communion three times a year, or be fined; the Church courts were active.

Catholics had been put in a difficult position by the Pope's 1570 excommunication of Elizabeth and the later 'fatwa' on her life; not trusted, they could be severely punished for recusancy. The Jesuit mission to England, begun in 1579, seemed a real threat to national security, and the Gunpowder Plot of 1605 (even if, as has been suggested, partly a 'sting' engineered by Burghley) made matters worse. Religious tensions worsened: while Catholics' hopes of James were disappointed, the more Puritan-minded became increasingly discontented, many even emigrating (particularly to, and in search of, the New World); but the pressure remained, and intensified. As Donne wrote:

> . . . On a huge hill,
> Cragged, and steep, Truth stands, and he that will
> Reach her, about must, and about must go . . .

Third Satire (1594–5; pub. 1633)

DIVINE LAW AND ORDER
(OR, WHY THERE SHOULD BE BISHOPS)

This world's first creation, and the preservation since of things created, what is it but only so far forth a manifestation by execution, what the Eternal Law of God is concerning things natural? And as it cometh to pass in a kingdom rightly ordered, that after a law is once published it presently takes effect far and wide, all states framing themselves thereunto, even so let us think it fareth in the natural course of the world. Since the time that God did first proclaim the edicts of his law upon it, heaven and earth have hearkened unto his voice, and their labour hath been to do his will: *He made a Law for the Rain*, He gave his *Decree unto the Sea that the Waters should not pass his commandment*. Now if nature should intermit her course, and leave altogether, though it were but for a while, the observation of her own laws; if those principal and mother elements of the world whereof all things in this lower world are made, should lose the qualities which now they have; if the frame of that heavenly arch erected over our heads should loosen and dissolve itself; if celestial spheres should forget their wonted motions and by irregular volubility [rotation] turn themselves any way as it might happen; if the Prince of the lights of heaven, which now as a giant doth run his unwearied course, should as it were through a languishing faintness begin to stand and rest himself; if the moon should wander from her beaten way, the times and seasons of the year blend themselves by disordered and confused mixture, the winds breathe out their last gasp, the clouds yield no rain, the earth be defeated of heavenly influence, the fruits of the earth pine away as children at the withered breasts of their mother no longer able to yield them relief; what would become of Man himself, whom all these things now do all serve? See we not plainly that obedience of creatures unto the Law of nature is the stay of the whole world?

Bishop Richard Hooker, *Of the Laws of Ecclesiastical Polity* (1594)

NOTHING IS PERMANENT

I need not call in new philosophy, that denies a settledness, an acquiescence in the very body of the earth, but makes the earth to move in that place where we thought the sun had moved. I need not that help, that the earth itself is in motion, to prove this, that nothing upon earth is permanent. The assertion will stand of itself, till some man assign me some instance, something that a man may rely upon, and find permanent. Consider the greatest bodies upon earth, the monarchies, objects which one would think Destiny might stand and stare at, but not shake; consider the smallest bodies upon earth, the hairs of our head, objects which one think Destiny would not observe nor could not discern; and yet Destiny (to speak to a natural man) and God (to speak to a Christian) is no more troubled to make a monarchy ruinous than to make a hair grey. Nay, nothing need to be done to either, by God or Destiny: a monarchy will ruin, as a hair will grow grey, of itself. In the elements themselves, of which all sub-elementary things are composed, there is no acquiescence, but a vicissitudinary transmutation into one another: air condensed becomes water, a more solid body, and air rarefied becomes fire, a body more disputable and inapparent. It is so in the condition of men, too: a merchant condensed, kneaded and packed up in a great estate, becomes a lord; and a merchant rarefied, blown up by a perfidious factor [steward], or by a riotous son, evaporates into air, into nothing, and is not seen. And if there were anything permanent and durable in this world, yet we got nothing by it, because howsoever that it might last in itself, yet we could not last to enjoy it; if our goods were not amongst moveables, yet we ourselves are; if they could stay with us, yet we cannot stay with them.

John Donne, *A Sermon preached at the Funerals of Sir William Cockayne* (1626)

THE CHURCH OF ENGLAND

I think it good also to remember that the names usually given unto such as feed the flock remain in like sort as in times past, so that these words, parson, vicar, curate and such are not yet abolished more than the Canon Law itself, which is daily pleaded, as I have said elsewhere; although the statutes of the realm have greatly infringed the large scope, and brought the exercise of the same into some narrower limits. There is nothing read in our churches but the canonical scriptures, whereby it cometh to pass that the psalter is said over once in thirty days, the New Testament four times, and the Old Testament once in the year. And hereunto if the curate be adjudged by the bishop or his deputies sufficiently instructed in the holy scriptures, and therewithal able to teach, he permitteth him to make some exposition or exhortation in his parish unto amendment of life. And for so much as our churches and universities have been so spoiled in time of error, as there cannot yet be had such number of able pastors as may suffice for every parish to have one, there are (beside four sermons appointed by public order in the year) certain sermons or homilies devised by sundry learned men, confirmed for sound doctrine by consent of the divines, and public authority of the Prince, and those appointed to be read by the curates of mean understanding (which homilies do comprehend the principal parts of Christian doctrine, as of original sin, of justification by faith, of charity, and suchlike) upon the sabbath days unto the congregation.

And after a certain number of psalms read, which are limited according to the dates of the month, for morning and evening prayer, we have two lessons, whereof the first is taken out of the Old Testament, the second out of the New; and of these latter, that in the morning is out of the Gospels, the other in the afternoon of some one of the epistles. After morning prayer we have also the Litany and Suffrages, an invocation in mine opinion not devised without the assistance of the spirit of God, although many curious [pedantic] mindsick persons condemn it as superstitious, and savouring of conjuration and sorcery.

This being done, we proceed unto the Communion, if any communicants be to receive the eucharist; if not, we read the Decalogue, Epistle and Gospel, with the Nicene Creed (of some in derision called, 'The Dry Communion') and then proceed unto an homily or sermon, which hath a psalm before and after it, and finally unto the baptism of such infants as on every Sabbath day (if occasion so require) are brought unto the churches; and thus is the forenoon bestowed. In the afternoon likewise we meet again, and, after the psalms and lessons ended, we have commonly a sermon, or at the least our youth catechised by the space of an hour. And thus do we spend the Sabbath day in good and godly exercises, all done in our vulgar tongue, that each one present may hear and understand the same, which also in cathedral and collegiate churches is so ordered that the psalms only are sung by note, the rest being read (as in common parish churches) by the minister with a loud voice, saving that in the administration of the Communion the choir singeth the answers, the Creed, and sundry other things appointed, but in so plain, I say, and distinct manner, that each one present may understand what they sing, every word having but one note, though the whole harmony consist of many parts, and those very cunningly set by the skilful in that science. . . .

As for our churches, bells and times of morning and evening prayer remain as in times past, saving that all images, shrines, tabernacles, rood-lofts and monuments of idolatry are removed, taken down and defaced; only the stories in glass windows excepted, which for want of sufficient store of new stuff and by reason of extreme charge that should grow by the alteration of the same into white panes throughout the realm, are not altogether abolished in most places at once but by little and little suffered to decay, that white glass may be provided and set up in their rooms. Finally, whereas there was wont to be a great partition between the choir and the body of the church, now it is either very small or none at all, and, to say the truth, altogether needless, sith the minister saith his service commonly in the body of the church, with his face toward the people, in a little tabernacle of wainscot provided for the purpose; by which means the ignorant do not only learn divers of the psalms and usual prayers by heart, but also such as can read do pray together with him; so that the whole congregation at one instant do pour out their petitions unto the living God for the whole estate of his church in most earnest and fervent manner.

Our holy and festival days are very well reduced also unto a less number, for whereas not long since we had under the Pope four score and fifteen called festival, and thirty *Profesti*, beside the Sundays, they are all brought unto seven and twenty, and with them the superfluous numbers of the idle wakes, guilds, fraternities, church-ales, help-ales, and soul-ales, also called dirge-ales, with the heathenish rioting at bride-ales, are well diminished and laid aside. And no great matter were it the feasts of all our apostles, evangelists and martyrs, with that of all saints, were brought to the holy days that follow upon Christmas, Easter and Whitsuntide; and those of the Virgin Mary, with the rest, utterly removed from the calendars, as neither necessary nor commendable in a reformed church. . . .

Not a few find fault with our threadbare gowns, as if not our patrons but our wives were causes of our woe. But if it were known to all, that I know to have been performed of late in Essex – where a minister taking a benefice (of less than twenty pounds in the Queen's books so far as I remember) was enforced to pay to his patron twenty quarters of oats, ten quarters of wheat, and sixteen yearly of barley, which he called hawks' meat; and another let the like in farm to his patron for ten pounds by the year, which is well worth forty at the least – the cause of our threadbare gowns would easily appear, for such patrons do scrape the wool from our cloaks.

William Harrison, *Description of England* (1587)

WHAT SHALL WE DO TO BE SAVED?

If we come to reason, we may rather wonder that any shall be saved, then so few shall be saved. For we have all the lets and hindrances that may be, both within us and without us. We have, as they say, the sun, moon and seven stars against us. We have all the devils in hell against us, with all their horns, heads, marvellous strength, infinite wiles, cunning devices, deep sleights and methodical temptations. Here runs a sore stream against us. Then we have this present evil world against us, with her innumerable baits, snares, nets, gins and grins to catch us, fetter us and entangle us. Here have we profits and pleasures, riches and honour, wealth and preferment, ambition and covetousness. Here comes in a camp royal of spiritual and invisible enemies. Lastly, we have our flesh, that is, our corrupted nature against us: we have our selves against our selves. For we ourselves are as great enemies to our salvation as either the world or the devil. For our understanding reason, will and affections are altogether against us. Our concupiscences and lusts do minister strength to Satan's temptations. They are all in league with Satan against us. They take part with him in everything against us and our salvation. They fight all under his standard, and receive their pay of him. This then goeth hard on our side, that the devil hath an inward party against us; and we carry always within us our greatest enemy, which is ever ready, night and day, to betray us into the hands of Satan, yea, to unbolt the door and let him in to cut our throats. Here then we see an huge army of dreadful enemies, and a very legion of devils, lying in ambush against our souls. Are we not, therefore, poor wretches, in a most pitiful case, which are thus betrayed and besieged on every side? All things then considered, may we not justly marvel that any shall be saved? For who seeth not, who knoweth not, that thousand thousands are carried headlong to destruction, either with the temptations of the world, the flesh or the devil? But yet further. I will show, by another very manifest, apparent reason, that the number of God's elect upon the face of the earth are very few in comparison; which may thus be considered.

First let there be taken away from amongst us all Papists, atheists and heretics. Secondly, let there be shoaled out all vicious and notorious evil livers, as, swearers, drunkards, whoremongers, worldlings, deceivers, cozeners, proud men, rioters, gamesters, and all the profane multitude. Thirdly, let there be refused and sorted out all hypocrites, carnal Protestants, vain professors, backsliders, decliners and cold Christians. Let all these, I say, be separated; and then tell me, how many sound, sincere, faithful and zealous worshippers of God will be found amongst us. I suppose we should not need the art of arithmetic to number them. For I think there would be very few, in every village, town and city. I doubt they would walk very thinly in the streets, so as a man might easily tell them as they go. Our Lord Jesus asketh a question in the Gospel of St Luke, saying, 'Do you think, when the son of man cometh, that he shall find faith on the earth?' To the which we may answer: surely very little.

Arthur Dent, *The Plaine-Mans Path-way to Heaven* (1601)

IMPERFECT PRAYER

When we consider with a religious seriousness the manifold weaknesses of the strongest devotions in time of prayer, it is a sad consideration. I throw myself down in my chamber, and I call in, and invite God and his angels thither, and when they are there, I neglect God and his angels, for the noise of a fly, for the rattling of a coach, for the whining of a door.

FARMWORKERS REAPING. (*Holinshed, Chronicles, 1577*). *Men do the reaping, women and lads do the stacking; the master or bailiff supervises.*

WOMAN SPINNING, MAN HUNTING. *Many countrywomen engaged in clothworking, often for a second income. The man stag-hunting on horseback is of higher social status.* (Roxburghe Ballads)

O R,

The Man-Woman:

Being a Medicine to cure the Coltish Difeafe of
the Staggers in the Mafculine-Feminines
of our Times.

Expreft in a briefe Declamation.

Non omnes poffumus omnes.

Miftris, will you be trim'd or truff'd?

London printed for I. T. and are to be fold at Chrift Church gate. 1620.

WOMEN AT MEN'S BARBERS. *The title-page of* Hic Mulier, *or,* The Man-
Woman, *1620, comments on women's masculine fashions, a worrying
sign of social disorder.*

FINE COURTSHIP. *This couple's elegant clothes suggest their status as at least wealthy yeomanry; her bared breasts indicate her unmarried condition.*

THE WEDDING NIGHT. *The newly-weds are put in their curtained four-poster by their encouraging friends and relatives.* (The Dying Mans good Counsel, *early seventeenth century*)

THE SONNETEERS' BELOVED. *The picture was used in various books to illustrate the clichés of love poetry: her breasts are globes, her lips pink coral, her teeth pearls,* 'roses and lilies her cheeks disclose', *her eyes are suns darting arrows of desire, her eyebrows are bows, her hair nets hearts, and Cupid sits in her brow. (Charles Sorel,* The Extravagant Shepherd, *1652)*

VILLAGE STREET SCENE. *An open drain and sewer occupies the middle of the street, with dunghills and a scavenging pig. The man in the doorway has cuckold's horns, while his wife (the picture of a dog eating from her kitchen stewpot suggests her sluttishness) empties the chamber-pot over the mocking neighbours. The three on the right are engaged on a skimmington-ride, used to mock cuckolds and unfaithful wives.* (Roxburghe Ballads)

WORKSOP MANOR, NOTTINGHAMSHIRE. *Probably designed by Robert Smythson. High, wide and handsome, a lighthouse on a hill, it was completed in 1586 for the sixth Earl of Shrewsbury, Earl Marshal of England and husband of Bess of Hardwick; it burned down in 1761.*

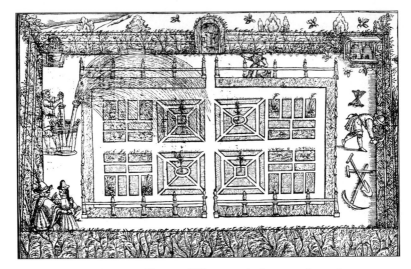

WATERING THE GARDEN. *Thomas Hill suggests the use of a water pump or 'great Squirt' so that 'the water in the breaking may fall as drops of rain'; a beehive is seen in one corner, and love's sting in another.*

FAMILY AT TABLE. *Parents and elder children sit, while the younger stand. Even the parents are on stools, not on (expensive) chairs. Only spoons are used: forks were only just coming in to use.* (Roxburghe Ballads)

SCHOOLROOM: THE THREE RS. *A smaller, quieter establishment: the dividers suggest that mathematics is taught here as well as writing; there are knives to trim the quill pens.* (Roxburghe Ballads)

ANTI-CATHOLIC PROPAGANDA. *The Pope's seven-headed beast and vomited toads derive from the Book of the Revelation of St John, as he infects friar, priest and gentleman.* (Roxburghe Ballads)

TESTING FOR A WITCH. *The true witch cannot sink, even when tied up; here, the sow is her familiar.* (Witches Apprehended, Examined and Executed, *1613*)

QUEEN ELIZABETH RECEIVING AMBASSADORS. *Elizabeth receives Dutch ambassadors in the rush-matted Privy Chamber. The Earl of Leicester and the Lord Admiral lounge by the window under the birdcage, while, impossibly, Mary, Queen of Scots looks on, and three Maids of Honour perch on a cushion.* (Dutch, sixteenth century)

ENTERTAINMENTS AT ELVETHAM. *Spectacular entertainments were provided by the Earl of Hertford when the Queen visited Elvetham House in Hampshire in 1591, including an artificial lake, pavilions, three islands and an imitation ship, with cannon, fireworks, music, masques, feasts and sports.* (John Nichols, Progresses of Queen Elizabeth, *1823*)

LONDON BRIDGE. *The only bridge, lined with houses and shops. The severed heads are drawn out of scale, so as not to be overlooked; thirty-four were counted in 1592. The drawbridge is visible to the left, between the houses; the piers of the 60-ft high arches had protective timber structures, called 'starlings', at the base.* (C.J. Visscher, 1616)

A COURT LADY. *From high heels to bouffant (and probably false) hair, high forehead, exposed breasts, pearl necklace, lacy collar and sleeves, padded shoulder 'wings', feather fan, apron and farthingale, the tip-top of fashion.* (Roxburghe Ballads)

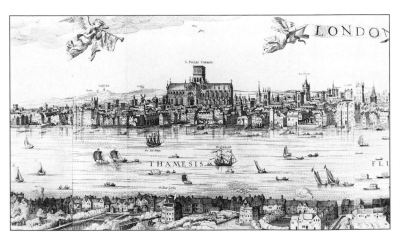

LONDON: THE SOUTH BANK *(C.J. Visscher). Printed in 1616, it shows the London of a few years earlier: the Bear Garden (with an excited dog) and the first Globe Theatre are shown, though this theatre (where most of Shakespeare's plays were performed) burned down in 1613, and the second Globe was built in 1614.*

CHEAPSIDE, LONDON. *St Paul's is shown before its steeple collapsed in 1561. On the left is the 'Crown Sild' gallery for watching processions, then the belfry of Bow Church and a row of goldsmiths' shops. In the centre is the Standard water conduit and, further along, Edward I's Great Cross.*

A LONDON BROTHEL. *Possibly the notorious Hollands Leaguer in Paris Gardens, on the south bank. (Dutch, early seventeenth century)*

A Rod *for* Run-awayes.

In which flight of theirs, if they looke backe, they may

behold many fearefull Iudgements of God, fundry wayes pronounced vpon this City, and on feuerall perfons, both
flying from it, and ftaying in it.

Expreffed in many dreadfull Examples of fudden Death, falne vpon both young and
old, within this City, and the Suburbes, in the Fields, and open Streets, to the
terrour of all thofe who liue, and to the warning of thofe who are to
dye, to be ready when God Almighty fhall bee pleafed
to call them.

With additions of fome new Accidents.

Written by T H O. D.

> L'ord, haue mercy
>
> on London.
>
> I follow.
>
> We fly
>
> Wee dye.
>
> Keep out.

Printed at London for *John Trundle*, and are to be fold at his Shop in Smithfield. 1625.

THE LONDON PLAGUE. *Dekker writes of Londoners fleeing the plague in the City, only to be driven away by terrified country people. (Thomas Dekker,* A Rod for Run-awayes, *1625)*

A GROUP OF BEGGARS. *Two upright men, a doxy and two kinchen or kitchen.* (Roxburghe Ballads)

WHIPPING TO THE GALLOWS. *This may be a vagabond or petty criminal being whipped through the streets; he may be one of the thousand who each year died on the gallows. (Holinshed,* Chronicles, *1577)*

A SKIRMISH WITH ESKIMOS. *Martin Frobisher was one of many who led expeditions seeking a north-west passage to the Pacific and the riches of the Orient. Here, Eskimos who had previously traded with his crew have turned hostile.*

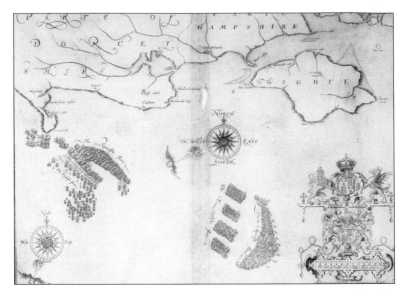

THE SPANISH ARMADA, 1588. *The Armada proceeds up Channel, after the skirmish near Portland. On the left, Admiral Howard attempts to relieve Frobisher's ships which have been cut off; on the right, later, the English fleet is grouped into four squadrons, while the Spanish fleet is in half-moon formation. (An engraving by Augustine Ryther)*

SWEARING FEALTY. *Hugh O'Neill leads Irish chieftains to swear fealty to the Queen, in the person of Sir Henry Sidney, Lord Deputy of Ireland. (John Derricke, The Image of Irelande, 1581)*

BELIEFS

I talk on, in the same posture of praying, eyes lifted up, knees bowed down, as though I prayed to God; and if God or his angels should ask me, when I thought last of God in that prayer, I cannot tell. Sometimes I find that I had forgot what I was about, but when I began to forget it, I cannot tell. A memory of yesterday's pleasures, a fear of tomorrow's dangers, a straw under my knee, a noise in mine ear, a light in mine eye, an anything, a nothing, a fancy, a chimera in my brain, troubles me in my prayer. So certainly is there nothing, nothing in spiritual things, perfect in this world.

John Donne, *A Sermon Preached at the Funerals of Sir William Cockayne*
(1626)

FESTIVAL DAYS

GOOD FRIDAY

It is now Good Friday, and a general fast must be kept among all Christians, in remembrance of Christ's Passion. Flesh and fish must be banished all stomachs, strong or weak. Now begins the farewell to thin fare, and the fishmongers may shut up their shops till the holy days be past. The butchers now must wash their boards, make clean their aprons, sharpen their knives, and sort their pricks, and cut out their meat for Easter-eve market. Now must the poulterers make ready their rabbits and their fowl, the cooks have their ovens clean, and all for pies and tarts against the merry feast. Now the maids bestir them about their houses, and launderers about their linen, the tailors about apparel, and all for this holy time. Now young lambs, young rabbits and young chickens die for fine appetites, and now the minstrel tunes his instruments, to have them ready for the young people. But with the aged and religious, there is nothing but sorrow and mourning, confession, contrition, and absolution, and I know not what. Few that are merry, but children that break up school, and wenches that are upon the marriage. In sum, it is such an odd day in itself, that I will only make this conclusion of it: it is the bridle of nature, and the examiner of reason.

EASTER DAY

It is now Easter, and Jack of Lent [a figure for mockery] is turned out of doors. The fishermen now hang up their nets to dry, while the calf and the lamb walk toward the kitchen and the pastry. The velvet heads of the forest [young bucks] fall at the loose of the crossbow. The salmon-trout plays with the fly, and the March rabbit runs dead into the dish. The Indian commodities pay the merchant's adventure, and Barbary sugar puts honey out of countenance. The Holy Feast is kept for the faithful, and a known Jew hath no place among Christians. The earth now begins to paint her upper garment, and the trees put out their young buds. The little kids chew their cuds, and the swallow feeds on the flies in the air. The stork cleanseth the brooks of the frogs, and the sparrowhawk prepares her wing for the partridge. The little fawn is stolen from the doe, and the male deer begins to herd. The spirit of youth is inclined to mirth, and the conscionable [scrupulous] scholar will not break a holy day. The minstrel calls the maid from her dinner, and the lover's eyes do troll like tennis balls. There is mirth and joy, when there is health and liberty, and he that hath money will be no mean man in his mansion. The air is wholesome and the sky comfortable, the flowers odoriferous and the fruits pleasant. I conclude, it is a day of much delightfulness: the sun's dancing day, and the earth's holy-day.

CHRISTMAS DAY

It is now Christmas, and not a cup of drink must pass without a carol; the beasts, fowl and fish come to a general execution, and the corn is ground to dust for the bakehouse and the pastry. Cards and dice purge many a purse, and the youth show their agility in shoeing of the wild mare. Now 'Good cheer' and 'welcome' and 'God be with you' and 'I thank you' and 'Against the new year' provide for the presents. The Lord of Misrule is no mean man for his time, and the guests of the high table must lack no wine. The lusty bloods must look about them like men, and piping and dancing puts away much melancholy. Stolen venison is sweet, and a fat coney is worth money. Pitfalls are now set for small birds, and a woodcock hangs himself in a gin [trap]. A good fire heats all the house, and a full alms-basket makes the beggars' prayers. The maskers and mummers make the merry sport, but if they lose their money, their drum goes dead. Swearers and swaggerers are sent away to the alehouse, and unruly wenches go in danger of judgement. Musicians now make their instruments speak out, and a good song is worth the hearing. In sum, it is a holy time, a duty in Christians for the remembrance of Christ, and custom among friends for the maintenance of good fellowship. In brief, I thus conclude of it: I hold it a memory of the Heaven's love and the world's peace, the mirth of the honest and the meeting of the friendly.

Nicholas Breton, *Fantastickes* (1626)

THE BURNING BABE

As I in hoary winter's night stood shivering in the snow,
Surprised I was with sudden heat which made my heart to glow;
And lifting up a fearful eye to view what fire was near,
A pretty babe all burning bright did in the air appear;
Who, scorchèd with excessive heat, such floods of tears did shed
As though his floods should quench his flames which with his tears
    were fed.
'Alas,' quoth he, 'but newly born, in fiery heats I fry,
Yet none approach to warm their hearts or feel my fire but I.
My faultless breast the furnace is, the fuel wounding thorns,
Love is the fire, and sighs the smoke, the ashes, shame and scorns,
The fuel justice layeth on, and mercy blows the coals,
The metal in this furnace wrought are men's defilèd souls,
For which, as now on fire I am to work them to their good,
So will I melt into a bath to wash them in my blood.'
With this he vanished out of sight and swiftly shrunk away,
And straight I callèd unto mind, that it was Christmas day.

Robert Southwell, S.J., *St Peter's Complaint* (1595)

HOLY WAR

(I)

Of their martyrs they brag no more now; for it is now come to pass, that for a few apostates and cobblers of theirs burnt, we have bishops, lords, knights, the old nobility, patterns of learning, piety and prudence, the flower of the youth, noble matrons, and of the inferior sort innumerable, either martyred at once or by consuming imprisonment dying daily. At the very writing hereof, the persecution rages most cruelly. The house where I am is sad; no other talk but of death, flight, prison, or spoil of their friends; nevertheless they proceed with courage. Very many, even at this present, being restored to the Church, now soldiers give up their names, while the old offer up their blood; by which holy hosts and oblations God will be pleased, and we shall no question by Him overcome.

Edmund Campion, S.J., A Letter, 1580

(II)

The effect of their [Jesuits'] labours is to bring the realm not only into a dangerous war against the forces of strangers . . . but into a war domestical and civil, wherein no blood is usually spared, nor mercy yielded, and wherein the vanqueror nor the vanquished have cause to triumph. . . . These are the most evident perils that necessarily should follow, if these kind of vermin were suffered to creep by stealth into the realm and to spread their poison into the same; howsoever, when they are taken, like hypocrites they colour and counterfeit the same with profession of devotion in religion.

William Cecil, Lord Burleigh, *The Execution of Justice in England* (1583)

(III)

I have been a close prisoner since the 18th day of September, whereof 46 days together I lay upon a little straw in my boots, my hands continually manacled in irons, for one month together never taken off. After, they were twice or thrice taken off to shift me and to ease me for a day together; this was all the favour my keeper did show. The morrow after Simon and Jude's Day I was hanged at the wall from the ground, my manacles fast locked into a staple as high as I could reach upon a stool; the stool was taken away, there I hanged from a little after 8 o'clock in the morning till after 4 in the afternoon, without any ease or comfort at all, saving that Topcliffe [notorious government examiner] came in unto me and told me that the Spaniards were come into Southwark by our means: 'For, lo, do you not hear the drums' (for then the drums played in honour of my Lord Mayor). The next day after also I was hanged an hour or two: such is the malicious minds and practices of our adversaries. For my clothes, I have no other than my summer weed, wherein I was taken.

Father White, S.J., A Letter, 1591
[By permission, Stonyhurst College, *Anglia*, i.66]

BELIEFS

THE CHARACTER OF A CHURCH PAPIST

A Church Papist is one that parts his religion betwixt his conscience and his purse, and comes to church not to serve God, but the King. The face of the law makes him wear the mask of the Gospel, which he uses not as a means to save his soul, but charges [fines for non-attendance]. He loves Popery well, but is loth to lose by it; and though he be somewhat scared with the bulls of Rome, yet they are far off, and he is struck with more terror at the apparitor [who brought offenders before the ecclesiastical courts]. Once a month he presents himself at the church, to keep off the churchwarden, and brings in his body to save his bail. He kneels with the congregation, but prays by himself, and asks God's forgiveness for coming thither. If he be forced to stay out a sermon, he pulls his hat over his eyes, and frowns out the hour, and when he comes home, thinks to make amends for this fault by abusing the preacher. His main policy is to shift off the communion, for which he is never unfurnished of a quarrel, and will be sure to be out of charity at Easter, and indeed he lies not, for he has a quarrel to the sacrament. He would make a bad martyr and good traveller, for his conscience is so large he could never wander out of it; and in Constantinople would be circumcised with a reservation. His wife is more zealous and therefore more costly, and he bates her in tires [reduces her dress allowance, by] what she stands him in religion [costs him in fines]. But we leave him hatching plots against the state, and expecting [Cardinal] Spinola.

John Earle, *Micro-cosmographie* (1628)

THE SUPERSTITIOUS MAN

This man doth not stir forth till his breast be crossed, and his face sprinkled. If but an hare cross him the way, he returns; or if his journey began unawares on the dismal day; or if he stumbled at the threshold. If he see a snake unkilled, he fears a mischief; if the salt fall towards him, he looks pale and red, and is not quiet till one of the waiters have poured wine on his lap; and when he sneezeth, thinks them not his friends that uncover not [do not remove their hats]. In the morning he listens whether the crow cry even or odd, and by that token presages the weather. If he hear but a raven croak from the next roof, he makes his will, or if a bittern fly over his head by night; but if his troubled fancy shall second his thoughts with the dream of a fair garden, or green rushes, or the salutations of a dead friend, he takes leave of the world and says he cannot live. He will never set to sea but on a Sunday; neither ever goes without an *Erra Pater* [popular astrological handbook] in his pocket. Saint Paul's Day and Saint Swithin's with the Twelve are his oracles [as weather forecasts], which he dares believe against his almanac. When he lies sick on his deathbed, no sin troubles him so much as that he did once eat flesh on a Friday, no repentance can expiate that; the rest need none. There is no dream of his without an interpretation, without a prediction; and if the event answer not his exposition, he expounds it according to the event. Every dark grove and pictured wall strikes with an aweful but carnal devotion. Old wives and stars are his counsellors; his night-spell is his guard, and charms, his physicians. He wears Paracelsian characters [written spells] for the toothache, and a little hallowed wax is his antidote for all evils.

Joseph Hall, *Characters of Vertues and Vices* (1608)

Better the Devil You Know

Certain players at Exeter, acting upon the stage the tragical story of Dr Faustus the conjuror; as a certain number of devils kept every one his circle there, and as Faustus was busy in his magical invocations, on a sudden they were all dashed, every one hearkening other in the ear, for they were all persuaded there was one devil too many amongst them; and so after a little pause desired the people to pardon them, they could go no further with this matter. The people also understanding the thing as it was, every man hastened to be first out of doors. The players, as I heard it, contrary to their custom spending the night in reading and in prayer, got them out of the town the next morning.

Anon., quoted in E.K. Chambers, *The Elizabethan Stage*, Vol. 3 (1923)

Six Kinds of Spirits

Fiery spirits or devils are such as commonly work by blazing stars, firedrakes (will-o'-the-wisps) or *ignes fatui* . . . likewise they counterfeit suns and moons, stars oftentimes, and sit on ship masts . . .

Aerial spirits or devils are such as keep quarter most part in the air, cause many tempests, thunder and lightnings, tear oaks, fire steeples, houses, strike men and beasts, make it rain stones (as in Livy's time), wool, frogs, etc., counterfeit armies in the air. . . . These can corrupt the air, and cause plagues, sickness, storms, shipwrecks, fires, inundations. . . . They are they which, Cardan thinks, desire so much carnal copulation with witches (incubae and succubae), transform bodies, and are so very cold if they be touched; and that serve magicians . . .

Waterdevils are those naiads or water-nymphs which have been heretofore conversant [dwelling] about waters and rivers. The water, as Paracelsus thinks, is their Chaos, wherein they live. Some call them fairies and say that Habundia is their queen; these cause inundations, many times shipwrecks, and deceive men divers ways, as succubae or otherwise, appearing most part (saith Tritemius) in women's shapes. Paracelsus hath several stories of them that have lived and been married to mortal men, and so continued for certain years with them, and after, upon some dislike, have forsaken them. . . . Olaus Magnus hath a long narration of one Hotherus, a king of Sweden, that having lost his company as he was hunting one day, met with these water-nymphs or fairies, and was feasted by them; and Hector Boethius, of Mackbeth and Banco, two Scottish lords, that as they were wandering in the woods had their fortunes told them by three strange women . .

Terrestrial devils are those Lares, Genii, Fauns, Satyrs, Wood-nymphs, Foliots, Fairies, Robin Goodfellows, Trolls, etc., which, as they are most conversant with men, so they do them most harm. . . . They are they that dance on heaths and greens, as Lavater thinks with Trithemius, and, Olaus Magnus adds, leave that green circle which we commonly find in plain fields, which others hold to proceed from a meteor falling, or some accidental rankness of the ground: so Nature sports herself. They are sometimes seen by old women and children. . . . A bigger kind there is of them, called with us Hobgoblins and Robin Goodfellows, that would in those superstitious times grind corn for a mess of milk, cut wood or do any manner of drudgery work. . . . Another sort of these there are which frequent forlorn houses, which the Italians call foliots, most part innocuous, Cardan holds. They will make strange noises in the night, howl sometimes pitifully, and then laugh again, cause great flame and sudden lights, fling stones, rattle chains, shave men, open doors and shut them, fling down platters, stools, chests, sometimes appear in the likeness of hares, crows, black dogs, etc. . . . These kind of devils many times appear to men, and affright them out of their wits, sometimes walking at noonday, sometimes at nights, counterfeiting dead men's ghosts. . . . Such sights are frequently seen, saith Lavater, in monasteries and about churchyards, marshes, great buildings, solitary places, or places notorious because of some murder, etc. . . . Sometimes they sit by the highway side, to give men falls, and make their horses stumble and start as they ride.

Subterranean devils are as common as the rest, and do as much harm . . . Their office, as Pictorius and Paracelsus think, is to keep treasure in the earth . . . besides, Cicogna avers that they are the frequent causes of those horrible earthquakes, which often swallow up not only houses, but whole islands and cities . . .

The last are conversant about the centre of the earth, to torture the souls of damned men to the Day of Judgement. . . .

Thus the Devil reigns, and in a thousand several shapes, as a roaring lion still seeks whom he may devour, by earth, sea, land, air, as yet unconfined, though some will have his proper place the air, all that space betwixt us and the moon for them that transgressed least, and hell for the wickedest of them.

Robert Burton, *The Anatomy of Melancholy* (1621–51)

THE MAKING OF FRIGHTS AND WITCHES

How were our children, old women and maids afraid to cross a churchyard, or a three-way leet [crossway], or to go for spoons into the kitchen without a candle? And no marvel. First, because the devil comes from a smoky black house, he; or a lewd friar was still at hand, with ugly horns on his head, fire in his mouth, a cow's tail in his breech, eyes like a basin, fangs like a dog, claws like a bear, a skin like a negro, and a voice roaring like a lion; then, 'boh!' or 'oh!' in the dark was enough to make their hair stand upright. And if that the bowl of curds and cream were not duly set out, for Robin Goodfellow the friar and Cis the dairymaid to meet at 'hinch pinch and laugh not' when the goodwife was abed, why then, either the pottage was burnt to next day in the pot, or the cheese would not curdle, or the butter would not come, or the ale in the fat [tub] would never have good head. But if a Peter-penny [annual penny tax paid to Rome, pre-Reformation] or an housel-egg [sacrament offering] were behind, or a patch of tithe unpaid to the Church (Jesu Maria!), then 'ware where you walk, for fear of bull-beggars [bogeymen], spirits, witches, urchins [goblins, possibly in hedgehog form], elves, hags [female spirits], fairies, satyrs, Pans, fauns, sylvans [wood-spirits], Kit with the candlestick, tritons, centaurs, dwarfs, giants, imps, calkers [magicians], conjurors, nymphs, changelings [fairies' offspring], screech-owls, incubus [male spirit], the spoorn [spectre], the mare [nightmare visitant], the man in the oak, hell-wean [devil's child], the firedrake, the puckle [bugbear sprite], Tom Thumb, hobgoblin, Tom-tumbler, Boneless, and the rest. And what girl, boy or old wizard would be so hardy to step over the threshold in the night for a halfpennyworth of mustard amongst this frightful crew, without half a dozen *Ave Maries*, two dozen crosses surely signed, and half a dozen *Pater Nosters*, and the commending himself to the tuition of Saint Uncumber, or else our blessed Lady?

These be the Pope's and his holy legates', and those of his holy mission and commission from hell, their frightful crew, their black guard, with which they work wonders amongst a faithless, senseless generation: these shout about them, attend them, and are of their guard and train wheresoever they go or walk, as Styx, Phlegeton [rivers of Hades] and the Eumenides do guard [Judge] Aeacus in hell. With these they work their wonders, making images to speak, vaults to sound, trunks to carry tales, churchyards to swarm, houses to rush, rumble and clatter with chains, highways, old graves, pits and woods to be haunted with lights, owls and pokers [pucks, demons]; and with these they a-dread and gaster [terrify] senseless old women, witless children and melancholic dotterels [fools] out of their wits.

These monster-swarms his Holiness and his helly crew have scraped and raked together out of old doting historiographers, wizardising augurs, imposturising soothsayers, dreaming poets, chimerical conceiters, and coiners of fables, such as puff up our young gallants with big looks and bombast phrases, as the book of *Lancelot du Lake, Guy of Warwick, The Mirrour of Knighthood, Amadis de Gaule* and suchlike their legends; out of these they conceit their monstrous shapes, ugly bugbears, hideous apparitions of ghosts; out of these they conform their charms, enchantments, periapts [amulets], amulets, characters [written spells], waistcoats and smocks of proof [protection] against hail, thunder, lightning, biting of mad dogs, gnawing of rats, against botches [tumours], biles [boils], crossbiting [fraud], sparrow-blasting [cursing, blighting], owl-hunting [bewitchment] and the like.

Out of these is shaped us the true idea of a witch, an old weather-beaten crone, having her chin and her knees meeting for age, walking like a bow leaning on a shaft, hollow-eyed, untoothed, furrowed on her face, having her lips trembling with the palsy, going mumbling in the streets, one that hath forgotten her Pater Noster and hath yet a shrewd tongue in her head, to call a drab, a drab. If she have learned of an old wife in a chimney's end 'Pax, max, fax', for a spell, or can say Sir John of Grantham's curse, for the miller's eels that were stolen – 'All you that have stolen miller's eels, Laudate dominum de coelis; and all they that have consented thereto, benedicamus Domino' – why then, ho, beware, look about you my neighbours. If any of you have a sheep sick of the giddies, or an hog of the mumps, or an horse of the staggers, or a knavish boy of the school, or an idle girl of the [spinning-]wheel, or a young drab of the sullens and hath not fat enough for her porridge, nor her father and mother butter enough for their bread; and she have a little help of the mother [hysteria], epilepsy or cramp, to teach her roll her eyes, wry her mouth, gnash her teeth, startle with her body, hold her arms and hands stiff, make antic faces, girn, mop and mow [grimace] like an ape, tumble like a hedgehog, and can mutter out two or three words of gibberish, as, 'obus, bobus'; and then withal old Mother Nobs hath called her by chance, 'idle young hussy', or bid the devil scratch her: then no doubt but Mother Nobs is the witch, the young girl is owl-blasted and possessed. And it goes hard but ye shall have some idle, addle, giddy, lymphatical [frenzied], illuminate [visionary] dotterel, who, being out of credit, learning, sobriety, honesty and wit, will take this holy advantage to raise the ruins of his desperate decayed name, and for his better glory will be-pray the juggling drab, and cast out Mopp the devil.

They that have their brains baited and their fancies distempered with the imaginations and apprehensions of witches, conjurors and fairies, and all that lymphatical chimera, I find it to be marshalled in one of these five ranks: children, fools, women, cowards, sick or black melancholic discomposed wits.

Samuel Harsnet, *A Declaration of Egregious Popish Impostures* (1603)

BELIEFS

TESTING FOR A WITCH

His friend understanding this, advised him to take them, or any one of them, to his mill dam, having first shut up the mill gates that the water might be at highest, and then, binding their arms across, stripping them into their smocks, and leaving their legs at liberty, throw them into the water. Yet lest they should not be witches and that their lives might not be in danger of drowning, let there be a rope tied about their middles, so long as it may reach from one side of your dam to the other, where on each side let one of your men stand, that if she chance to sink they may draw her up and preserve her. Then if she swim, take her up, and cause some women to search her, upon which, if they find any extraordinary marks about her, let her a second time be bound, and have her right thumb bound to her left toe, and her left thumb to her right toe, and your men with the same rope (if need be) to preserve her, and be thrown into the water, when, if she swim, you may build upon it that she is a witch. I have seen it often tried in the north country. . . .

At which his men presently recovered, bound her to their master's horse, and brought her home to his house, and shutting up his mill gates did as before the gentleman had advised him; when, being thrown in the first time, she sank some two feet in the water with a fall, but rose again, and floated upon the water like a plank. Then he commanded her to be taken out, and had women ready that searched her, and found under her left thigh a kind of teat, which after, the bastard son confessed, her spirits in several shapes, as cats, moles, etc., used to suck her.

Then was she the second time bound cross, her thumbs and toes according to the former direction, and then she sunk not at all, but, sitting upon the water, turned round about like a wheel, or as that which commonly we call a whirlpool, notwithstanding Master Enger's men standing on each side of the dam with a rope tossing her up and down to make her sink, but could not.

Anon., *Witches Apprehended, Examined and Executed* (1613)

A WITCHCRAFT CASE

[NEIGHBOURS' REPORTS]

Joan Flower, the mother, was a monstrous malicious woman, full of oaths, curses and imprecations irreligious, and, for anything they saw by her, a plain atheist; besides of late days her very countenance was estranged, her eyes were fiery and hollow, her speech fell [threatening] and envious, her demeanour strange and exotic, and her conversation sequestered [her conduct unsociable]; so that the whole course of her life gave great suspicion that she was a notorious witch; yea, some of her neighbours dared to affirm that she dealt with familiar spirits, and terrified them all with curses and threatening of revenge, if there were never so little cause of displeasure and unkindness.

Concerning Margaret, that she often resorted from the Belvoir Castle to her mother, bringing such provision as they thought was unbefitting for a servant to purloin, and coming at such unseasonable hours that they could not but conjecture some mischief between them, and that their extraordinary riot and expenses tended both to rob the Lady [the Countess of Rutland] and to maintain certain debauched and base company which frequented this Joan Flower's house, the mother, and especially her youngest daughter.

Concerning Phillip, that she was lewdly transported with the love of one Th[omas] Simpson, who presumed to say that she had bewitched him, for he had no power to leave her, and was as he supposed marvellously altered both in mind and body since her acquainted company.

FROM *THE EXAMINATION OF THE SAID JOAN WILLIMOT* . . .
[2ND MARCH, 1618]
This examinate saith, that she hath a spirit which she calleth Pretty, which was given unto her by William Berry of Langholm in Rutlandshire, whom she served three years; and that her master, when he gave it unto her, willed her to open her mouth and he would blow into her a fairy which should do her good; and that she opened her mouth, and he did blow into her mouth; and that presently after her blowing there came out of her mouth a spirit which stood upon the ground in the shape and form of a woman, which spirit did ask of her, her soul, which she then promised unto it, being willed thereunto by her master.

FROM *THE EXAMINATION OF ELLEN GREENE OF STATHORNE* . . .
[17TH MARCH]
She saith, that one Joan Willimot of Goadby came about six years since to her in the wolds, and persuaded this examinate to forsake God and betake her to the Devil, and she would give her two spirits, to which

she gave her consent, and thereupon the said Joan Willimot called two spirits, one in the likeness of a kitlin, and the other of a mouldiwarp [mole]. The first, the said Willimot called Puss, the other, Hiss, Hiss, and they presently came to her, and she departing left them with this examinate, and they leapt on her shoulder, and the kitlin sucked under her right ear on her neck, and the mouldiwarp on the left side in the same place. After they had sucked her, she sent the kitlin to a baker of that town, whose name she remembers not, who had called her witch and struck her, and bade her said spirit go and bewitch him to death. The mouldiwarp she then bade go to Anne Dawse of the same town and bewitch her to death, because she had called this said examinate witch, whore, jade, etc., and within one fortnight after they both died. . . .

About three years since, this examinate removed thence to Stathorne, where she now dwelt. Upon a difference between the said Willimot and the wife of John Patchet of the said Stathorne, yeoman, she said the said Willimot called her, this examinate, to go and touch the said John Patchet's wife and her child, which she did, touching the said John Patchet's wife in her bed, and the child in the grace-wife's [midwife's] arms, and then sent her said spirits to bewitch them to death, which they did, and so the woman lay languishing by the space of a month and more, for then she died; the child died the next day after she touched it.

And she further saith, that the said Joan Willimot had a spirit sucking on her under the left flank, in the likeness of a little white dog, which this examinate saith that she last saw the same sucking in barley-harvest last, being then at the house of the said Joan Willimot.

And for herself, this examinate further saith, that she gave her soul to the Devil to have these spirits at her command; for a confirmation whereof, she suffered them to suck her always as aforesaid about the change and fall of the moon.

FROM *THE EXAMINATION OF PHILLIP FLOWER* . . . [25TH FEBRUARY]

She confesseth and saith, that she hath a spirit sucking on her in the form of a white rat, which keepeth her left breast, and hath so done for three or four years, and concerning the agreement betwixt her spirit and herself, she confesseth and saith, that when it came first unto her, she gave her soul to it, and it promised to do her good, and cause Thomas Simpson to love her, if she would suffer it to suck her, which she agreed unto; and so the last time it sucked was on Tuesday at night [two nights before].

FROM *THE EXAMINATION OF MARGARET FLOWER, AT THE SAME TIME, ETC.*

She confesseth, that she hath two familiar spirits sucking on her, the one white, the other black spotted; the white sucked under her left breast, and the black spotted within the inward parts of her secrets. When she first entertained them she promised them her soul, and they covenanted to do all things which she commanded them, etc.

She further saith, that about the 30 of January last past, being Saturday, four devils appeared unto her in Lincoln Jail, at eleven or twelve o'clock at midnight. The one stood at her bed's feet, with a black head like an ape, and spake unto her; but what, she cannot well remember, at which she was very angry because he would speak no plainer, or let her understand his meaning. The other three were Rutterkin [her cat], Little Robin and Spirit; but she never mistrusted them, nor suspected herself, till then.

FROM *ANOTHER EXAMINATION OF THE SAID MARGARET FLOWER* . . . [4TH FEBRUARY]

Being asked what she knoweth concerning the bewitching of the Earl of Rutland, his wife and children, she saith, that it is true that herself, her mother and sister were all displeased with him, especially with the Countess, for turning her out of service, whereupon, some four years since, her mother commanded her to go up to the Castle and bring her the right hand glove of the Lord Henry Rosse, the Earl's eldest son; which glove she found on the [floor-]rushes in the nursery, and delivered the same to her mother, who put it into hot water, pricked it often with her knife, then took it out of the water, and rubbed it upon Peterkin, bidding him hie and go and do some hurt to Henry, Lord Rosse, whereupon he fell sick, and shortly after died, which, her mother hearing of, said it was well. But after she had rubbed the glove on the spirit Rutterkin, she threw it into the fire and burned it, etc.

CONCLUSION

Thus were they apprehended about Christmas, and carried to Lincoln Jail, after due examination, before sufficient Justices of the Peace and discreet magistrates, who wondered at their audacious wickedness; but Joan Flower the mother, before conviction (as they say) called for bread and butter, and wished it might never go through her if she were guilty of that whereupon she was examined; so, mumbling it in her mouth, never spake more words after, but fell down and died as she was carried to Lincoln Jail, with a horrible excruciation of soul and body, and was buried at Ancaster.

When the Earl heard of their apprehension, he hasted down with his brother, Sir George, and sometimes examining them himself, and sometimes sending them to others, at last left them to the trial of law, before the Judges of Assize at Lincoln; and so they were convicted of murder and executed accordingly, about the 11 of March, to the terror of all beholders, and example of such dissolute and abominable creatures . . .

Anon., *The Wonderful Discoverie of the Witchcrafts of Margaret and Phillip Flower* (1619)

ALCHEMY

(I) THE THEORY

Subtle ['alchemist'].   No egg but differs from a chicken more
Than metals in themselves.

Surly [doubter].   That cannot be.
The egg's ordained by nature to that end,
And is a chicken *in potentia*.

Subtle.   The same we say of lead and other metals,
Which would be gold if they had time.

Mammon [enthusiast].   And that
Our art doth further.

Subtle.   Aye, for 'twere absurd
To think that nature in the earth bred gold
Perfect, i'the instant. Something went before.
There must be remote matter . . .

                              It is, of the one part,
A humid exhalation, which we call
Materia liquida, or the unctuous water;
On the other part, a certain crass and viscous
Portion of earth; both which, concorporate,

Do make the elementary matter of gold,
Which is not yet *propria materia*,   [a distinct substance]
But common to all metals and all stones. . . .
Nor can this remote matter suddenly
Progress so from extreme to extreme
As to grow old, and leap o'er all the means.
Nature doth first beget the imperfect, then
Proceeds she to the perfect. Of that airy
And oil water, mercury is engendered,
Sulphur o'the fat and earthy part: the one
(Which is the last) supplying the place of male,
The other of the female, in all metals. . . .
And even in gold they are; for we do find
Seeds of them, by our fire, and gold in them:
And can produce the species of each metal
More perfect thence than nature doth in earth.

Ben Jonson, The Alchemist (1610)

(II) THE PRACTICE

Let every man that is besotted in this art . . . take heed also of all false and double bottoms in crucibles, of all hollow wands or rods of iron, wherewith some of these varlets do use to stir the metal and the medicine together; of all amalgams and powders, wherein any gold or silver shall be craftily conveyed; of Sol [sun, gold] and Luna [moon, silver] first rubified, and then projection [experimentation] made on it, as it were on Venus [copper] herself; but especially of a false back to the chimney or furnace, having a loose brick or stone closely jointed, that may be taken away in another room, by a false Simon [Magus, conjuror] that attendeth on the alchemist's 'hem' or some other watchword, who, after the medicine and the mercury put together in the crucible, entertaineth Balbinus [the sucker] with a walk and with the volubility of his tongue, until his confederate might have leisure to convey some gold or silver into the melting-pot.

Hugh Plat, The Jewell House of Art and Nature (1594)

BELIEFS

AMAZE YOUR FRIENDS WITH HOME MAGIC

TO MAKE ONE SEE FEARFUL SIGHTS IN HIS SLEEP:
And to do this, take the blood of a lapwing and therewith anoint the pulses of thy forehead before thy going to rest, and then after in thy sleep thou shalt see both marvellous and fearful sights, as Vitalis Medicus writeth. Also he writeth, that if a man eateth in the evening before his going to bed of the herb named nightshade, or mandrake, or henbane, shall after see in his sleep pleasant sights.

HOW TO KILL FLEAS DIVERS WAYS:
And first to gather all the fleas of thy chamber into one place, anoint a staff with the grease of a fox or hedgehog, and lay the staff again where you list in your chamber, and it shall so gather all the fleas by it. Also fill a dish with goat's blood, and set the same by the bed, and all the fleas will come to it round about. And the like will they do by the blood of the hedgehog.

HOW TO WALK ON THE WATER, A PROPER SECRET:
For to do this, take two little timbrels [small flat drums] and bind them under the soles of thy feet, and at a stave's end fasten another, and with these may you safely walk on the water unto the wonder of all such as shall see the same, if so be you often exercise the same with a certain boldness and lightness of the body.

HOW TO MAKE AN EGG FLY ABOUT, A MERRY CONCLUSION:
And to do this, take a goose egg, and after the opening and cleansing of it, take a bat that syeth [flies] in the evening, which put into the shell, then glue it fast about the top, and the bat will so fly away with it, which perhaps will be thought of some to fly about in the air of itself.

HOW TO FIND A PERSON DROWNED, THAT HATH BEEN SOUGHT FOR:
To do this, take a white loaf and cast the same into the water near the suspected place, and it will forthwith go directly over the dead body, and there still abide, by which you may well find the dead body.

TO PROVE IF A MAIDEN BE CLEAN:
Burn motherwort, and let her take the smoke at her nose, and if she be corrupt she shall piss, or else not. Otherwise take grey nettles while they be green, and let her piss on them; if she be no maiden they will wither forth[with], or else not.

Thomas Hill, *Naturall and Artificiall Conclusions* (1567)

THE FAIRIES' FAREWELL

A Proper New Ballad, Intituled the Fairies' Farewell, or God-a-Mercy Will: to be sung or whistled, to the tune of *The Meadow Brow* by the learned, by the unlearned to the tune of *Fortune*.

Farewell, rewards and fairies,
 Good housewives now may say;
For now foul sluts in dairies
 Do fare as well as they,
And though they sweep their hearths no less
 Than maids were wont to do,
Yet who of late for cleanliness
 Finds sixpence in her shoe?

Lament, lament, old abbeys, [dissolved by Henry VIII, 1534–9]
 The fairies lost command;
They did but change priests' babies,
 But some have changed your land;
And all your children sprung from thence
 Are now grown Puritans,
Who live as changelings ever since,   [or renegades]
 For love of your demesnes.

At morning and at evening both,
 You merry were and glad,
So little care of sleep or sloth
 These pretty ladies had;
When Tom came home from labour,
 Or Cis to milking rose,

BELIEFS

Then merrily went their tabor,
   And nimbly went their toes.

Witness those rings and roundelays
   Of theirs, which yet remain,
Were footed in Queen Mary's days
   On many a grassy plain;
But since of late Elizabeth,
   And later James, came in,
They never danced on any heath
   As when the time hath been.

By which we note the fairies
   Were of the old profession;
Their songs were Ave Maries,
   Their dances were procession.
But now, alas, they all are dead,
   Or gone beyond the seas,
Or further for religion fled,
   Or else they take their ease.

A tell-tale in their company
   They never could endure,
And whoso kept not secretly
   Their mirth was punished sure:
It was a just and Christian deed
   To pinch such black and blue.
Oh, how the commonwealth doth need
   Such justices as you.

Now they have left our quarters,
   A register they have,
Who can preserve their charters,
   A man both wise and grave:
A hundred of their merry pranks
   By one that I could name
Are kept in store; con twenty thanks
   To William for the same.

I marvel who his cloak would turn
   When Puck had led him round,
Or where those walking fires would burn   [will-o'the-wisps]
   Where Cureton would be found;
How Broker would appear to be,
   For whom this age doth mourn;
But that their spirits live in thee,
   In thee, old William Chourne.   [a family servant]

To William Chourne of Staffordshire
   Give laud and praises due,
Who every meal can mend your cheer
   With tales both old and true.
To William all give audience,
   And pray ye for his noddle,   [head]
For all the fairies' evidence
   Were lost, if that were addle.

Richard Corbett, pub. 1647

7

THE COURT

For all that the Court was the centre of power and influence, glamorous, a magnet for the ambitious, theoretically, the acme of civilization and, practically, for many, a great, gaudy fruit-machine for making money (from grants, monopolies, pensions and bribes), few spoke well of it: Sir Walter Raleigh wrote, 'it glows and shines like rotten wood', while Sir Walter Mildmay warned off his son from 'this glittering misery'.

In a limited sense, the Court was wherever the monarch was, and might be thought to be no more than a few score people in the Presence Chamber, the Privy Chamber and the private apartments. One might, however, extend one's sense of the Court to include the life of its attendants (over 1,500 people at all levels), the aristocrats in their great houses, Court preachers such as Donne at St Paul's, or the translators working on the King James Bible, or attendant lawyers nearby at the Inns of Court, the players in the smart Blackfriars theatre or the Court masques, and even the tailors and barbers tempting and titivating the would-be chic: the ripples of its influence extended far and wide.

At the centre of State business was the Secretary of State ('King there in effect', as James said); the Lord Chamberlain supervised Court activities, including entertainments (with a special eye on plays), the Lord Steward struggled to cope with general 'housekeeping' expenses, and the Master of the Horse saw to transport – particularly important when planning the great Royal Progress. There was no single building; the chief palace, Whitehall, sprawled (with its surrounding grounds) over some 23 acres, in an area roughly bounded (in today's geography) by Green Park to the west, Westminster Abbey and Hall to the south, the river to the east and Charing Cross and Northumberland Avenue to the north. Other palaces in or near London included the Tower, Bridewell, Eltham, Richmond, Greenwich, Nonsuch, Hampton Court, Windsor and Westminster and St James.

Autumn saw the Court relaxing at Windsor or Hampton Court; during the winter the monarch was usually at Whitehall, especially if Parliament was in session; in November, Elizabeth enjoyed the Accession Day Tilts, the jousting entertainments that were part of Renaissance neo-medievalism; Christmas and Twelfth Night occasioned further revels and plays. In James's Court, Ben Jonson and Inigo Jones extended the masque far beyond amusing fancy-dress dances into elaborate, allegorical cultural-political spectacles, celebrating the *mythos* of Stuart monarchy. Where Elizabeth's Court, after its early glamour, with exciting courtship visits from France, but later ruled by a notoriously frugal old lady, had become a trifle old-fashioned and dull, James's Court, with its subsidiary Courts associated with his queen and children, as well as a host of Scots friends, new councillors and arrivistes, was even more notoriously expensive, immoral and financially corrupt. Philip Gawdy wrote home: 'There were a number of witty and very choice knights made [on James's coronation]; but with them (like cockle amongst good corn) a scum of such as it would make a man sick to think of . . . sheep-reeves, yeomen's sons . . . pedlars' sons. . . . amongst the rest Thimblethorpe the attorney, that was called Nimblechops full of the pox, was knighted for seven pound ten shillings.'

In the spring, the Court moved to the preferred river palaces at Richmond or Greenwich, or to Nonsuch in Surrey. High summer often found the Court on progress, visiting important towns in the south, and the estates of the great and ambitious (Longleat, Wilton, Kenilworth, Elvetham, Penshurst): these were enormous enterprises, involving huge expense for the hosts to entertain and provide for the monarch and the royal household. They helped to keep the monarch in touch with (some of) the people, while reducing the cost of maintaining the residential palaces, desperately in need of cleansing. Elizabeth and James both enjoyed hunting – James, it was felt, to excess.

The cultural importance of the Court was enormous: poets, painters, musicians, designers – and dramatists – directed their attention to the Court, its factions and different tastes, so broadening and refining the culture of the whole. Where Elizabeth's Court was relatively homogenous, traditional and insular, the Jacobean Court, more divided in every way, opened up the country to different and more sophisticated continental influences, to the true High Renaissance: Inigo Jones's elegant Banqueting House at Whitehall would be an exemplar.

QUEEN ELIZABETH AT GREENWICH PALACE

We were admitted by an order Mr Rogers had procured from the Lord Chamberlain, into the Presence Chamber, hung with rich tapestry, and the floor, after the English fashion, strewed with hay, through which the Queen commonly passes in her way to Chapel. At the door stood a Gentleman dressed in velvet, with a gold chain, whose office was to introduce to the Queen any person of distinction that came to wait on her. It was Sunday, when there is usually the greatest attendance of nobility. In the same hall there were the Archbishop of Canterbury, the Bishop of London, a great number of Counsellors of State, officers of the Crown, and Gentlemen, who waited the Queen's coming out; which she did from her own apartment, when it was time to go to prayers, attended in the following manner.

First went Gentlemen, Barons, Earls, Knights of the Garter, all richly dressed and bare-headed; next came the Chancellor, bearing the Seals in a red silk purse, between two, one of which carried the Royal Sceptre, the other the Sword of State in a red scabbard studded with golden fleurs-de-lis, the point upwards. Next came the Queen, in the sixty-fifth year of her age, as we were told, very majestic; her face oblong, fair but wrinkled; her eyes small, yet black and pleasant; her nose a little hooked; her lips narrow, and her teeth black (a defect the English seem subject to, from their too great use of sugar); she had in her ears two pearls, with very rich drops; she wore false hair, and that red; upon her head she had a small crown, reported to be made of some of the gold of the celebrated

Luneburg table. Her bosom was uncovered, as all the English ladies have it till they marry; and she had on a necklace of exceeding fine jewels; her hands were small, her fingers long, and her stature neither tall nor low; her air was stately, her manner of speaking mild and obliging. That day she was dressed in white silk, bordered with pearls the size of beans, and over it a mantle of black silk, shot with silver threads; her train was very long, and the end of it borne by a Marchioness; instead of a chain she had an oblong collar of gold and jewels.

As she went along in all this state and magnificence, she spoke very graciously, first to one, then to another, whether foreign ministers, or those who attended for different reasons, in English, French and Italian; for besides being well skilled in Greek, Latin and the languages I have mentioned, she is mistress of Spanish, Scotch and Dutch. Whoever speaks to her, it is kneeling; now and then she raises some with her hand. While we were there, William Slawata, a Bohemian baron, had letters to present to her; and she, after pulling off her glove, gave him her right hand to kiss, sparkling with rings and jewels, a mark of particular favour. Wherever she turned her face, as she was going along, everybody fell down on their knees.

The Ladies of the Court followed next to her, very handsome and well-shaped, and for the most part dressed in white; she was guarded on each side by the Gentlemen Pensioners, fifty in number, with gilt battle-axes. In the antechapel next the hall where we were, petitions were presented to her, and she received them most graciously, which occasioned the acclamation of 'Long live Queen Elizabeth!' She answered it with, 'I thank you, my good people.' In the chapel was excellent music; as soon as it and the service was over, which scarce exceeded half an hour, the Queen returned in the same state and order, and prepared to go to dinner. But while she was still at prayers, we saw her table set out with the following solemnity.

A Gentleman entered the room bearing a rod, and along with him another who had a tablecloth, which, after they had both kneeled three times with the utmost veneration, he spread upon the table; and after kneeling again, they both retired. Then came two others, one with the rod again, the other with a salt-cellar, a plate, and bread; when they had kneeled as the others had done, and placed what was brought upon the table, they too retired with the same ceremonies performed by the first. At last came an unmarried Lady (we were told she was a Countess) and along with her a married one, bearing a tasting-knife; the former was dressed in white silk, who, when she had prostrated herself three times, in the most graceful manner approached the table, and rubbed the plates with bread and salt, with as much awe as if the Queen had been present. When they had waited there a little while, the Yeomen of the Guard entered, bare-headed, clothed in scarlet with a golden rose upon the backs, bringing in at each turn a course of twenty-four dishes, served in plate, most of it gilt; these dishes were received by a Gentleman in the same order they were brought, and placed upon the table, while the lady taster gave to each of the Guard a mouthful to eat of the particular dish he had brought, for fear of any poison. During the time that this Guard, which consists of the tallest and stoutest men that can be found in all England, being carefully selected for this service, were bringing dinner, twelve trumpets and two kettledrums made the hall ring for half an hour together. At the end of all this ceremonial, a number of unmarried Ladies appeared, who with particular solemnity lifted the meat off the table and conveyed it into the Queen's inner and more private chamber, where, after she had chosen for herself, the rest goes to the Ladies of the Court.

The Queen dines and sups alone with very few attendants; and it is very seldom that anybody, foreign or native, is admitted at that time, and then only at the intercession of somebody in power.

Paul Hentzner, *Travels in England* (1598; pub. 1757)

SUCH SWEET THUNDER

She did oft ask the ladies around her chamber if they loved to think of marriage, and the wise ones did conceal well their liking hereto, as knowing the Queen's judgement in this matter. Sir Matthew Arundel's fair cousin, not knowing so deeply as her fellows, was asked one day hereof, and simply said she had thought much about marriage, if her father did consent to the man she loved. 'You seem honest, i'faith,' said the Queen, 'I will sue for you to your father.' The damsel was not displeased hereat; and when Sir Robert came to Court, the Queen asked him hereon, and pressed his consenting, if the match was discreet. Sir Robert, much astonished at this news, said he never heard his daughter had liking to any man, and wanted to gain knowledge of her affection, but would give free consent to what was most pleasing to her Highness's will and advice. 'Then I will do the rest,' saith the Queen. The lady was called in, and the Queen told her her father had given his free consent. 'Then,' replied the lady, 'I shall be happy, and please your Grace.' 'So thou shalt, but not to be fool and marry. I have his consent given to me, and I vow thou shalt never get it into thy possession. So go to thy business, I see thou art a bold one to own thy foolishness so readily.' . . .

I need not praise her frugality; but I will tell a story that fell out when I was a boy. She did love rich clothing, but often chid those that bought more finery than became their state. It happened that Lady M. Howard was possessed of a rich border powdered with gold and pearls, and a velvet suit belonging thereto, which moved many to envy; nor did it please the Queen, who thought it exceeded her own. One day the Queen did send privately, and got the lady's rich vesture, which she put on herself, and came forth the chamber among the ladies. The kirtle and border was far too short for her Majesty's height; and she asked everyone how they liked her new-fancied suit. At length, she asked the owner herself, if it was not made too short and ill-becoming – which the poor lady did presently consent to. 'Why then, if it become not me, as being too short, I am minded it shall never become thee, as being too fine; so it fitteth neither well.' This sharp rebuke abashed the lady, and she never adorned her herewith any more. . . .

When she smiled, it was a pure sunshine, that everyone did choose to bake in, if they could; but anon came a storm from a sudden gathering of clouds, and the thunder fell in wondrous manner on all alike.

Sir John Harington, Nugae Antiquae (pub. 1769)

GOSSIP

Queen Elizabeth never saw herself, after she became old, in a true glass; they painted her, and sometimes would vermilion her nose. She had always about Christmas evens-set dice, that threw sixes or five, and she knew not they were other, to make her win and esteem herself fortunate. That she had a membrana on her which made her incapable of man, though for her delight she tried many. At the coming of 'Monsieur' [Duke of Anjou], there was a French surgeon who took in hand to cut it, yet fear stayed her, and his death.

Ben Jonson, Conversations with William Drummond (1619; pub. 1711)

THE COURT

QUEEN ELIZABETH ON PROGRESS: A BIT OF A DO

THE HONOURABLE ENTERTAINMENT GIVEN TO THE QUEEN'S MAJESTY IN PROGRESS AT ELVETHAM IN HAMPSHIRE, BY THE RIGHT HONOURABLE THE EARL OF HERTFORD.

Elvetham House being situate in a park but of two miles in compass or thereabouts, and of no great receipt [not able to receive many], as being none of the Earl's chief mansion houses, yet for the desire he had to show his unfeigned love and loyal duty to Her Most Gracious Highness purposing to visit him in this her late progress, whereof he had to understand by the ordinary guess, as also by his honourable good friends in Court near to Her Majesty, his Honour with all expedition set artificers a-work, to the number of three hundred, many days before Her Majesty's arrival, to enlarge his house with new rooms and offices. Whereof I omit to speak how many were destined to the offices of the Queen's household, and will only make mention of other such buildings as were raised on the sudden, fourteen score off from the house on a hillside, within the said park, for entertainment of nobles, gentlemen and others whatsoever.

First there was made a room of estate for the nobles, and at the end thereof a withdrawing place for Her Majesty. The outsides of the walls were all covered with boughs and clusters of ripe hazelnuts, the insides with arras, the roof of the place with work of ivy leaves, the floor with sweet herbs and green rushes.

Near adjoining unto this were many offices newly builded, as namely, spicery, lardery, chaundery [candle-store], wine-cellar, ewery [plate store] and pantry; all which were tiled. Not far off was erected a large hall for entertainment of knights, ladies and gentlemen of chief account.

There was also a several place for Her Majesty's footmen and their friends.

Then there was a long bower for Her Majesty's Guard.

Another for other offices of Her Majesty's house.

Another to entertain all comers, suitors and suchlike.

Another for my Lord's steward, to keep his table in.

Most of these aforesaid rooms were furnished with tables, and the tables carried 23 yards in length.

Moreover on the same hill there was raised a great common buttery [store-room for drink and provisions].

A pitcher house [store-room for ale and wine].

A large pastery [pastry-kitchen], with five new ovens built, some of them 14 foot deep.

A great kitchen, with four ranges and a boiling place for small boiled meats.

Another kitchen with a very long range, for the waste, to serve all commoners.

A boiling house for the great boiler.

A room for the scullery.

Another room for the cooks' lodgings.

Some of these were covered with canvas, and other some with boards.

Between my Lord's house and the aforesaid hill where these rooms were raised, there had been made in the bottom, by handy labour, a goodly pond, cut to the perfect figure of a half-moon. In this pond were three notable grounds, where hence to prevent [provide] Her Majesty with sports and pastimes. The first was a Ship Isle of 100 foot in length and 40 foot broad, bearing three trees orderly set for three masts. The second was a Fort 20 foot square every way, and overgrown with willows. The third and last was a Snail Mount, rising to four circles of green privet hedges, the whole in height 20 foot, and forty foot at the bottom. These three places were equally distant from the sides of the pond, and every one by a just measured proportion distant from other. In the said water were divers boats prepared for music, but especially there was a pinnace, full furnished with masts, yards, sails, anchors, cables and all other ordinary tackling, and with iron pieces [cannon], and lastly with flags, streamers and pendants, to the number of twelve, all painted with divers colours and sundry devices. To what use these particulars served, it shall evidently appear by that which followeth . . .

On Wednesday morning, about nine of the clock, as Her Majesty opened a casement of her gallery window, there were three excellent musicians, who, being disguised in ancient country attire, did greet her with a pleasant song of Corydon and Phyllida, made in three parts of purpose. The song, as well for the worth of the ditty as for the aptness of the note thereto applied, it pleased Her Majesty, after it had been once sung, to command it again, and highly to grace it with her cheerful acceptance and commendation. . . .

The same day after dinner, about three of the clock, ten of my Lord of Hertford's servants, all Somersetshire men, in a square green court before Her Majesty's window, did hang up lines, squaring out the form of a tennis court, and making a cross line in the middle. In this square they (being stripped out of their doublets) played five to five with the hand ball at board and cord (as they term it) to so great liking of Her Highness that she graciously deigned to behold their pastime more than an hour and a half.

After supper there were two delights presented unto Her Majesty: curious fireworks, and a sumptuous banquet, the first from the three islands in the pond, the second in a low gallery in Her Majesty's privy garden. But I first will briefly speak of the fireworks.

First there was a peal of a hundred chambers [small cannon] discharged from the Snail Mount, in counter whereof a like peal was discharged from the Ship Isle, and some great ordnance withal. Then was there a castle of fireworks of all sorts, which played in the Fort. Answerable to that there was in the Snail Mount a globe of all manner of fireworks, as big as a barrel. When these were spent on either side, there were many running rockets upon lines, which passed between the Snail Mount and the Castle in the Fort. On either side were many fireworks, pikes of pleasure and balls of wildfire which burned in the water.

During the time of these fireworks in the water, there was a banquet served all in glass and silver into the low gallery in the garden, from a hillside fourteen score off, by two hundred of my Lord of Hertford's gentlemen, every one carrying so many dishes that the whole number amounted to a thousand, and there were to light them in their way a hundred torchbearers. To satisfy the curious, I will here set down some particulars in the banquet.

Her Majesty's Arms in sugar-work.

The several Arms of all our nobility in sugar-work.

Many men and women in sugar-work, and some enforced by hand [shaped by hand, not moulded].

Castles, forts, ordnance, drummers, trumpeters and soldiers of all sorts, in sugar-work.

Lions, unicorns, bears, horses, camels, bulls, rams, dogs, tigers, elephants, antelopes, dromedaries, apes and all other beasts in sugar-work.

Eagles, falcons, cranes, bustards, heronshaws [herons], bitterns, pheasants, partridges, quails, sparrows, pigeons, cocks, owls and all that fly, in sugar-work.

Snakes, adders, vipers, frogs, toads, and all kinds of worms, in sugar-work.

Mermaids, whales, dolphins, congers [eels], sturgeons, pikes, carps, breams, and all sorts of fishes, in sugar-work.

All these were standing dishes of sugar-work. The selfsame devices were also there all in flat work. Moreover, these particulars following, and many suchlike, were in flat sugar-work and cinnamon:

Marchpanes [marzipan cakes], grapes, oysters, mussels, cockles, periwinkles, crabs, lobsters.

Apples, pears, plums of all sorts.

Preserves, succades [preserved fruit], jellies, leaches [meat or eggs or fruit in aspic or jelly], marmalades, pastes, comfits, [sweets] of all sorts.

William Lyly, 1591 (J. Nichols, *Progresses . . . of Queen Elizabeth*, 1823)

A COURTIER'S BUSY DAY

[FROM A LETTER REPORTING THE QUEEN'S VISIT TO KENILWORTH IN 1575]

A-mornings, I rise ordinarily at seven o'clock. Then ready, I go into the Chapel; soon after eight, I get me commonly into my Lord's chamber, or into my Lord President's. There, at the cupboard, after I have eaten the manchet [white bread] served overnight for livery [provisions] (for I dare be as bold, I promise you, as any of my friends the servants there; and indeed, could I have fresh, if I would tarry, but I am of wont jolly and dry, a-mornings), I drink me up a good bowl of ale. When in a sweet pot it is defecated [cleared] by all night's standing, drink is the better: take that of me; and a morsel in a morning, with a sound draught, is very wholesome and good for the eyesight. Then I am as fresh all the forenoon after, as I had eaten a whole piece of beef.

Now, sir, if the Council sit, I am at hand – wait at an inch, I warrant you. If any make babbling, 'Peace!' say I, 'wot ye where ye are?' If I take a listener, or a pryer-in at the chinks or at the look-hole, I am by and by in the bones of him. But now they keep good order; they know me well enough. If 'a be a friend, or such one as I like, I make him sit down by me on a form, or chest; let the rest walk, 'a God's name!

And here doth my languages now and then stand me in good stead, my French, my Spanish, my Dutch and my Latin: sometime among ambassadors' men, if their masters be within with the Council, sometime with the ambassador himself; if he bid call his lackey, or ask me, what's o'clock; and I warrant you, I answer him roundly, that they marvel to see such a fellow there; then laugh I, and say nothing.

Dinner and supper, I have twenty places to go to, and heartily prayed to; and sometime get I to Master Pinner, by my faith a worshipful gentleman, and as careful for his charge as any Her Highness hath. There find I alway good store of very good viands: we eat and be merry, thank God and the Queen! Himself in feeding, very temperate and moderate as ye shall see any; and yet, by your leave, of a dish – as a cold pigeon or so, that hath come to him at meat, more than he looked for – I have seen him e'en so by and by surfeit, as he hath plucked off his napkin, wiped his knife, and eat not a morsel more: like enough to stick in his stomach a two days after (some hard message from the higher officers, perceive ye me?). Upon search, his faithful dealing and diligence hath found him faultless.

In afternoons and a-nights, sometimes am I with the right worshipful Sir George Howard, as good a gentleman as any lives; and sometimes at my good Lady Sidney's chamber, a noblewoman that I am as much bound unto as any poor man may be unto so gracious a lady; and sometimes in another place. But always among the gentlewomen, by my good will (O, ye know that come always of a gentle spirit); and when I see company according, then can I be as lively, too. Sometimes I foot it with dancing; now with my gittern, and else with my cittern [both like guitars], then at the virginals [a small spinet] ye know nothing comes amiss to me. Then carol I up a song withal, that by and by they come flocking about me like bees to honey; and ever they cry, 'Another, good Langham, another!' Shall I tell you? When I see Mistress —— (A! see a mad knave! I had almost told all!), that she gives once but an eye or an ear, why, then, man, am I blest! My grace, my courage, my cunning is doubled. She says sometimes she likes it, and then I like it much the better; it doth me good to hear how well I can do. And, to say truth, what with mine eyes, as I amorously gloit it [glance amorously], with my Spanish sospires [sighs], my French heys [cries], mine Italian dulcets [sweet notes], my Dutch hoves [pauses], my double release, my high reaches, my fine feigning, my deep diapason, my wanton warbles, my running, my timing, my tuning and my twinkling. I can gracify the matters as well as the proudest of them; and was yet never stained, I thank God. By my troth, countryman, it is sometimes by midnight ere I can get from them. And thus have I told

ye most of my trade all the livelong day. What will ye more? God save
the Queen, and my Lord! I am well, I thank you.

Robert Langham, *A Letter* (1575)

COURT CHATTER

. . . More than ten Holinsheds, or Halls or Stows,   [famous chroniclers]
Of trivial household trash he knows; he knows
When the Queen frowned, or smiled, and he knows what
A subtle statesman may gather of that;
He knows who loves; whom; and who by poison
Hastes to an office's reversion;   [inheritance]
He knows who hath sold his land, and now doth beg
A licence, old iron, boots, shoes, and egg-
shells to transport; shortly boys shall not play
At span-counter or blow-point, but they pay [games: like marbles; and
Toll to some courtier, and, wiser than all us,   with laces]
He knows what lady is not painted . . .
. . . He, like a privileged spy, whom nothing can
Discredit, libels now 'gainst each great man.
He names a price for every office paid;
He saith, our wars thrive ill, because delayed;
That offices are entailed, and that there are
Perpetuities of them, lasting as far
As the last day; and that great officers
Do with the pirates share, and Dunkirkers.   [privateers]
Who wastes in meat, in clothes, in horse, he notes;
Who loves whores, who boys, and who goats. . . .
  'Tis ten a-clock and past; all whom the mews   [stables]
 Balloon, tennis, diet, or the stews,   [game like volleyball; brothels]
Had all the morning held, now the second
Time made ready, that day, in flocks, are found
In the Presence, and I (God pardon me).
As fresh and sweet their apparels be, as be
The fields they sold to buy them; 'For a King
Those hose are,' cry the flatterers; and bring
Them next week to the theatre to sell;

THE COURT

Wants reach all states; me seems they do as well
At stage, as Court; all are players; whoe'er looks
(For themselves dare not go) o'er Cheapside books   [tailors'
Shall find their wardrobes' inventory. Now,   account-books]
The ladies come; as pirates, which do know
That there came weak ships fraught with cochineal, [expensive scarlet
The men board them; and praise, as they think, well   dye]
Their beauties; they, the men's wits; both are bought. . . .

John Donne, *Fourth Satire* (c. 1597)

A COURTIER

To all men's thinking is a man, and to most men the finest; all things else are defined by the understanding, but this by the senses; but his surest mark is, that he is to be found only about princes. He smells; and putteth away much of his judgement about the situation of his clothes. He knows no man that is not generally known. His wit, like the marigold, openeth with the sun, and therefore he riseth not before ten of the clock. He puts more confidence in his words than meaning, and more in his pronunciation than his words. Occasion is his Cupid, and he hath but one receipt of making love. He follows nothing but inconstancy, admires nothing but beauty, honours nothing but fortune, loves nothing. The sustenance of his discourse is news, and his censure like a shot depends upon the charging. He is not, if he be out of court, but fish-like breathes destruction if out of his own element. Neither his motion or aspect are regular, but he moves by the upper spheres, and is the reflection of higher substances.

If you find him not here, you shall in Paul's, with a pick-tooth in his hat, a cape-cloak, and a long stocking.

Sir Thomas Overbury, *Characters* (1614–16)

COURT LADIES

Just to dinner they will arise, and after dinner go to bed again, and lie until supper. Yea, sometimes, by no sickness occasioned, they will be in bed three days together, provided every morning before four o'clock

151

they have their broths and their cullises [strong broths] with pearl and gold sodden in them. If haply they break their hours and rise more early to go a-banqueting, they stand practising half a day with their looking-glass how to pierce and to glance and to look alluringly amiable. Their feet are not so well framed to the measures as are their eyes to move and bewitch. Even as angels are painted in church windows with glorious golden fronts beset with sunbeams, so beset they their foreheads on either side with glorious borrowed gleamy bushes; which, rightly interpreted, should signify beauty to sell, since a bush is not else hanged forth but to invite men to buy [an ivy-bush was a vintner's sign]. . . .

Their heads, with their top and top-gallant [ships' upper sails] lawn baby-caps and snow-resembled silver curlings, they make a plain puppet stage of. Their breasts they embusk up on high, and their round roseate buds immodestly lay forth, to show at their hands there is fruit to be hoped. In their curious antic [strangely]-woven garments they imitate and mock the worms and adders that must eat them. They show the swellings of their minds in the swellings and plumpings-out of their apparel. Gorgeous ladies of the Court, never was I admitted so near any of you to see how you torture poor old Time with sponging, pinning and pouncing [ornamental trimming]; but they say his sickle you have burst in twain to make your periwigs more elevated arches of. . . .

It is not your pinches [pleats], your purls [frills], your flowery jaggings [cut edges, fringes], superfluous interlacings and puffings up that can any way offend God, but the puffings up of your souls which therein you express. For as the biting of a bullet is not that which poisons a bullet, but the lying of the gunpowder in the dint of the biting, so it is not the wearing of costly burnished apparel that shall be objected unto you for sin, but the pride of your hearts, which, like the moth, lies closely shrouded amongst the threads of that apparel. Nothing else is garish apparel but Pride's ulcer broken forth. How will you attire yourselves, what gown, what head-tire will you put on, when you shall live in hell amongst hags and devils?

As many jags, blisters and scars shall toads, cankers and serpents make on your pure skins in the grave, as now you have cuts, jags or raisings upon your garments. Your morn-like crystal countenances shall be netted over and, masker-like, caul-vizarded [masked with a close web] with crawling venomous worms. Your orient [shining] teeth, toads shall steal into their heads for pearl; of the jelly of your decayed eyes shall they engender the[ir] young. In their hollow caves (their transplendent juice so pollutionately employed) shelly snails shall keep house.

Thomas Nashe, *Christ's Tears over Jerusalem* (1593)

THE DREAM OF SIMON FORMAN (THE ASTROLOGER)

I dreamt [January 1597] that I was with the Queen, and that she was a little elderly woman in a coarse white petticoat all unready. She and I walked up and down through lanes and closes, talking and reasoning. At last we came over a great close where were many people, and there were two men at hard words. One of them was a weaver, a tall man with a reddish beard, distract of his wits. She talked to him and he spoke very merrily unto her, and at last did take her and kiss her. So I took her by the arm and did put her away; and told her the fellow was frantic. So we went from him and I led her by the arm still, and then we went through a dirty lane. She had a long white smock very clean and fair, and it trailed in the dirt and her coat behind. I took her coat and did carry it up a good way, and then it hung too low before. I told her she should do me a favour to let me wait on her, and she said I should. Then said I, 'I mean to wait *upon* you and not under you, that I might make this belly a little bigger to carry up this smock and coat out of the dirt.' And so we talked merrily; then she began to lean upon me, when we were past the dirt and to be very familiar with me, and methought she began to love me. When we were alone, out of sight, methought she would have kissed me.

Simon Forman, *Diary*

[By permission, Bodleian Library, Oxford: MS Ashmole 226, fol. 44r.]

THE DEATH OF THE QUEEN

Imprimis. Her Majesty being in very good health, one day Sir John Stanhope, being the vice-chamberlain, and Secretary Cecil's [Lord Burghley] dependant and familiar, came and presented Her Majesty with a piece of gold of the bigness of an angel [coin], full of characters, which, he said, an old woman in Wales bequeathed her on her deathbed; and thereupon he discoursed how the said old woman, by virtue of the same, lived to the age of one hundred and twenty years; and in that age, having all her body withered and consumed, and wanting nature to nourish, she died, commanding the said piece of gold to be carefully sent to Her Majesty; alleging further that, as long as the said old woman wore it upon her body, she could not die.

The Queen, upon the confidence she had hereof, took the said gold, and wore it about her neck. Now, though she fell not suddenly sick, yet daily decreased of her rest and feeding; and, within fifteen days, fell downright sick; and the cause being wondered at by my Lady Scrope, with whom she was very private and confidant, being her near kinswoman, Her Majesty told her (commanding her to conceal the same) that she saw, one night, in her bed, her body exceeding lean and fearful, in the light of fire. This sight was at Whitehall, a little before she departed thence to Richmond, and may be testified by another lady, who was one of the nearest about her person, of whom the Queen demanded, whether she was not wont to see sights in the night, telling her of the bright flame she had seen. Afterward, in the melancholy of her sickness, she desired to see a true looking-glass, which, in twenty years before, she had not seen, but only such a one which of purpose was made to deceive her sight; which glass being brought her, she fell presently exclaiming at all those which had so much commended her, and took it so offensively, that all those which had before flattered her durst not come in her sight.

Now falling into extremity, she sat two days and three nights upon her stool, ready dressed and could never be brought by any of her Council to go to bed, or eat, or drink; only my Lord Admiral one time persuaded her to drink some broth. For any of the rest, she would not answer them to any question; but said softly to my Lord Admiral's earnest persuasions that, if he knew what she had seen in her bed, he would not persuade her as he did. And Secretary Cecil, overhearing her, asked if Her Majesty had seen any spirits, to which she said she scorned to answer him to so idle a question. Then he told her how, to content the people, Her Majesty must go to bed; to which she smiled, wonderfully contemning him, saying that the word *must* was not to be used to princes; and thereupon said, 'Little man, little man, if your father had lived, ye durst not have said so much: but thou knowest I must die, and that maketh thee so presumptuous.' And presently, commanding him and the rest to depart from her chamber, she willed my Lord Admiral to stay; to whom she shook her head, and, with a pitiful voice said, 'My lord, I am tied with a chain of iron about my neck.' He alleging her wonted courage to her, she replied, 'I am tied, and the case is altered with me.'

Then two ladies, waiting on her in her chamber, discovered in the bottom of her chair the Queen of Hearts, with a nail of iron knocked through the forehead of it; the which the ladies durst not pull out, remembering that the like thing was used to the old lady of Sussex, and proved afterwards for a witchcraft, for the which certain were hanged, as instruments of the same. The Lady Elizabeth Guildford, then waiting on the Queen, and leaving her asleep in her privy chamber, met her, as she thought, three or four chambers off and, fearing she would have been displeased that she left her alone, came towards her to excuse herself; and she vanished away; and when she returned into the same chamber where she had left her, found her asleep as before. So growing past recovery (having kept her bed fifteen days, besides three days she sat upon her stool), one day, when being pulled up by force, she stood on her feet fifteen hours; the Council sent to her the Bishop of Canterbury and other of the prelates, upon sight of whom she was much offended, cholericly rating them, bidding them be packing, saying she was no atheist, but knew full well that they were hedge priests, and took it for an indignity that they should speak to her.

Now being given over by all, and at the last gasp, keeping still her sense in everything, and giving, ever, when she spake, apt answers, though she spake very seldom, having then a sore throat, she desired to wash it, that she might answer more freely to what the Council demanded; which was, to know whom she would have King. But they, seeing her throat troubled her so much, desired her to hold up her finger, when they named whom liked her. Whereupon they named the King of France, the King of Scotland, at which she never stirred. They named my Lord Beauchamp, whereto she said, 'I will have no rascal's son in my seat, but one worthy to be a king.' Hereupon, instantly she died.

Then the council went forth and reported she meant the K. of Scots, whereupon they went to London to proclaim him, leaving her body with charge not to be opened, such being her desire; but Cecil having a secret warrant to the surgeons, they opened her, which the rest of the Council afterwards passed it over, though they meant it not so. Now her body, being cered [wrapped] up, was brought to Whitehall, where, being watched every night by 6 several ladies, my self that night there watching as one of them, being all about the body, which was fast nailed up in a board coffin with leaves of lead covered with velvet, her body and head broke with such a crack that splitted the wood, lead and cerecloth [waxed winding-sheet]. Whereupon the next day, she was fain to be new trimmed up; whereupon they gave their verdicts that if she had not been opened the breath of her body would have been much worse; but no man durst speak it publicly for displeasing Secretary Cecil. [Lady Elizabeth Southwell was Maid of Honour to the Queen; she later ran away with Robert Dudley; they converted to Roman Catholicism and married, 1605.]

> Lady Elizabeth Southwell, *A true relation of what*
> *succeeded in the sickness and death of queen Elizabeth* (c. 1607)
> [By permission, Stonyhurst College: Stonyhurst MSS, *Anglia*, iii, 77.]

THE REPORT OF HER DEATH

Death made him [Sickness] his herald, attired him like a courtier, and in his name charged him to go into the Privy Chamber of the English Queen, to summon her to appear in the Star Chamber [high court] of Heaven.

The summons made her start, but, having an invincible spirit, did not amaze her; yet whom would not the certain news of parting from a kingdom amaze! But she knew where to find a richer, and therefore lightly regarded the loss of this, and thereupon made ready for that heavenly Coronation, being (which was most strange) most dutiful to obey, that had so many years so powerfully commanded. She died, resigning her sceptre to posterity and her soul to immortality.

The report of her death, like a thunderclap, was able to kill thousands, it took away hearts from millions: for having brought up (even under her wing) a nation that was almost begotten and born under her, that never shouted any other *Ave* than for her name, never saw the face of any other prince but herself, never understood what that strange outlandish word *Change* signified, how was it possible but that her sickness should throw abroad an universal fear, and her death an astonishment? She was the courtier's treasure, therefore he had cause to mourn; the lawyer's sword of justice, he might well faint; the merchant's patroness, he had reason to look pale; the citizen's mother, he might best lament; the shepherd's goddess, and should not he droop? Only the soldier, who had walked a long time upon wooden legs and was not able to give up arms, though he were a gentleman, had bristled up the quills of his stiff porcupine moustachio, and swore by no beggars that now was the hour come for him to bestir his stumps. Usurers and brokers (that are the Devil's ingles [pets], and dwell in the long-lane of hell [Long Lane, Aldersgate had tenements for brokers]) quaked like aspen leaves at his oaths; those that before were the only cut-throats in London, now stood in fear of no other death; but my Signior Soldado was deceived, the tragedy went not forward . . .

She came in with the fall of the leaf, and went away in the spring; her life, which was dedicated to virginity, both beginning and closing up a miraculous maiden circle: for she was born upon a Lady Eve [7.9.33, eve of the nativity of the Virgin Mary], and died upon a Lady Eve [24.3.03, eve of the Annunciation], her nativity and death being memorable by this wonder; the first and last years of her reign by this, that a Leigh was Lord Mayor when she came to the throne, and a Lee Lord Mayor when she departed from it.

Thomas Dekker, The Wonderful Year (1603)

OLD QUEEN, NEW COURT

LETTER TO LORD THOMAS HOWARD, 1603:
Many have been the madcaps rejoicing at our new King's coming, and who in good troth dared not have set forth their good affection to him a month or two ago; but, alas, what availeth truth when profit is in quest? You were true and liege bondman to her late Highness, and felt her sweet bounties in full force and good favour. Nor did I my poor self unexperience her love and kindness on many occasions; but I cannot forbear remembering my dread at her frowns in the Irish affair, when I followed my General (and what should a captain do better?) to England a little before his time. If Essex had met his *appointed time*, as David saith, to die, it had fared better than to meet his folly and his fate too. But enough of old tales; a new King will have new soldiers, and God knoweth what men they will be. One saith he will serve him by day, another by night; the women who love to talk as they like are for serving him both day and night. It pleaseth me to think I am not under their command who offer so bountifully what perchance they would be glad to receive at others' hands. But I am a cripple, and not made for sports in new Courts. . . .

Sir John Harington, Nugae Antiquae (1769)

How to Succeed at Court

FROM LORD THOMAS HOWARD, LORD CHAMBERLAIN, TO SIR
JOHN HARINGTON:

If you have good will and good health to perform what I shall
commend, you may set forward for Court whenever it suiteth your own
conveniency: the King hath often inquired after you, and would readily
see and converse again with the 'merry blade', as he hath oft called you
since you was here. I will now premise certain things to be observed by
you, toward well gaining our prince's good affection.

He doth wondrously covet learned discourse, of which you can
furnish out ample means; he doth admire good fashion in clothes,
I pray you give good heed hereunto. Strange devices oft come into
man's conceit: some one regardeth the endowments of the inward
sort, wit, valour or virtue; another hath, perchance, special affection
towards outward things, clothes, deportment and good countenance. I
would wish you to be well trimmed; get a new jerkin, well bordered,
and not too short: the King saith he liketh a flowing garment. Be sure it
be not all of one sort, but diversely coloured . . .

Robert Carr is now most likely to win the Prince's affection, and
doth it wondrously in a little time [1603, Groom of the Bedchamber;
1607, Gentleman of the Bedchamber; 1611, Viscount Rochester; 1613,
Earl of Somerset]. The Prince leaneth on his arm, pinches his cheek,
smoothes his ruffled garment and, when he looketh at Carr, directeth
discourse to divers others. This young man doth much study all art
and device; he hath changed his tailors and tiremen many times, and
all to please the Prince, who laugheth at the long grown fashion of our
young courtiers, and wisheth for change every day. You must see Carr
before you go to the King, as he was with him a boy in Scotland, and
knoweth his taste and what pleaseth.

In your discourse you must not dwell too long on any one subject,
and touch but lightly on religion. Do not of yourself say, 'This is good
or bad', but, 'If it were your Majesty's good opinion, I myself should
think so and so.' Ask no more questions than what may serve to know
the Prince's thought. In private discourse, the King seldom speaketh
of any man's temper, discretion or good virtues: so, meddle not at
all, but find out a clue to guide you to the heart and most delightful
subject of his mind. I will advise one thing – the roan jennet, whereon

the King rideth every day, must not be forgotten to be praised; and the good furniture [harness] above all, what lost a great man much notice the other day. A noble did come in suit of a place, and saw the King mounting the roan; delivered his petition, which was heeded and read, but no answer was given. The noble departed, and came to Court the next day, and got no answer again. The Lord Treasurer was then pressed to move the King's pleasure touching the petition. When the King was asked for answer thereto, he said, in some wrath, 'Shall a King give heed to a dirty pauper, when a beggar noteth not his gilt stirrups?' Now it fell out that the King had new furniture when the noble saw him in the courtyard, but he was overcharged with confusion, and passed by admiring the dressing of the horse. Thus, good knight, our noble failed in his suit. . . .

You are not young, you are not handsome, you are not finely, and yet will you come to Court and think to be well favoured? Why, I say again, good knight, that your learning may somewhat prove worthy hereunto; your Latin and your Greek, your Italian, your Spanish tongues, your wit and discretion may be well looked unto for a while, as strangers at such a place; but these are not the things men live by nowadays.

Sir John Harington, *Nugae Antiquae* (1769)

THE FEAST OF REASON

The King's table was a trial of wits. The reading of some books before him was very frequent, while he was at his repast. Otherwise he collected knowledge by variety of questions, which he carved out to the capacity of his understanding writers. Methought his hunting humour was not off so long as his courtiers, I mean the learned, stood about him at his board. He was ever in chase after some disputable doubts, which he would wind and turn about with the most stabbing objections that ever I heard. And was as pleasant and fellow-like in all those discourses as with his huntsmen in the field. They that in many such genial and convivial conferences were ripe and weighty in their answers were indubiously designed to some place of credit and profit.

John Hacket, *Scrinia Reserata: A Memorial* (1692)

SHAKESPEARE'S ENGLAND

COURT FESTIVITIES

TO MR SECRETARY BARLOW [1606]:

I came here a day or two before the Danish King came, and from the day he did come until this hour, I have been well nigh overwhelmed with carousal and sports of all kinds. The sports began each day in such manner and such sort as well nigh persuaded me of Mahomet's paradise. We had women, and indeed wine too, of such plenty, as would have astonished each sober beholder. Our feasts were magnificent, and the two royal guests did most lovingly embrace each other at table. I think the Dane hath strangely wrought on our good English nobles; for those whom I could never get to taste good liquor now follow the fashion, and wallow in beastly delights. The ladies abandon their sobriety, and are seen to roll about in intoxication. In good sooth, the Parliament did kindly provide His Majesty so seasonably with money, for there hath been no lack of good living: shows, sights and banqueting from morn to eve.

One day, a great feast was held, and, after dinner, the representation of Solomon his Temple, and the coming of the Queen of Sheba was made, or (as I may better say) was meant to have been made, before their Majesties, by device of the Earl of Salisbury and others. But, alas! As all earthly things do fail to poor mortals in enjoyment, so did prove our presentment hereof. The Lady who did play the Queen's part did carry most precious gifts to both their Majesties; but, forgetting the steps arising to the canopy, overset her caskets into his Danish Majesty's lap, and fell at his feet, though I rather think it was in his face. Much was the hurry and confusion; cloths and napkins were at hand, to make all clean. His Majesty then got up and would dance with the Queen of Sheba; but he fell down and humbled himself before her, and was carried to an inner chamber and laid on a bed of state, which was not a little defiled with the presents of the Queen which had been bestowed on his garments, such as wine, cream, jelly, beverage, cakes, spices and other good matters. The entertainment and show went forward, and most of the presenters went backward, or fell down, wine did so occupy their upper chambers.

Now did appear, in rich dress, Hope, Faith and Charity. Hope did essay to speak, but wine rendered her endeavours so feeble that she withdrew, and hoped the King would excuse her brevity. Faith was then all alone, for I am certain she was not joined with good works; and left the Court in a staggering condition. Charity came to the King's feet, and seemed to cover the multitude of sins her sisters had committed; in some sort she made obeisance and brought gifts, but said she would return home again, as there was no gift which Heaven had not already given His Majesty; she then returned to Hope and Faith, who were both sick and spewing in the lower hall.

Next came Victory, in bright armour, and presented a rich sword to the King (who did not accept it, but put it by with his hand) and, by a strange medley of versification, did endeavour to make suit to the King; but Victory did not triumph long, for, after much lamentable utterance, she was led away like a silly captive and laid to sleep in the outer steps of the ante-chamber. Now did Peace make entry, and strive to get foremost to the King; but I grieve to tell you how great wrath she did discover unto those of her attendants, and, much contrary to her own semblance, most rudely made war with her olive branch, and laid on the pates of those who did oppose her coming.

I have much marvelled at these strange pageantries, and they do bring to my remembrance what passed of this sort in our Queen's days, of which I was sometime an humble presenter and assistant; but I never did see such lack of good order, discretion and sobriety, as I have now done. I have passed much time in seeing the royal sports of hunting and hawking, where the manners were such as made me devise the beasts were pursuing the sober creation, and not man in quest of exercise or food. I will now, in good sooth, declare to you who will not blab, that the Gunpowder fright is got out of all our heads, and we are going on hereabouts as if the Devil was contriving every man should blow up himself by wild riot, excess and devastation of time and temperance. The great ladies do go well masked, and indeed it be the only show of their modesty, to conceal their countenance; but alack, they meet with such countenance to uphold their strange doings, that I marvel not at aught that happens.

Sir John Harington, *Nugae Antiquae* (1769)

Touching for the King's Evil (scrofula)

As it was now the time for divine service, the King made his appearance in company with the young Prince Charles. He was dressed in a satin robe of an ash colour, thickly covered with gold lace chevron-wise, and a rather long cloak of black cloth, lined with velvet. In his hat was a magnificent jewel, with three large precious stones one above the other, set in gold. . . .

The service lasted about an hour and a half. When it was concluded, His Majesty stood up, his chair was removed to the table, and he seated himself in it. Then immediately the Royal Physician brought a little girl, two boys, and a tall strapping youth, who were afflicted with incurable diseases, and bade them kneel down before His Majesty; and as the Physician had already examined the disease (which he is always obliged to do, in order that no deception may be practised), he then pointed out the affected part in the neck of the first child to His Majesty, who thereupon touched it, pronouncing these words, 'Le Roy vous touche, Dieu vous guery' ('The King touches, may God heal thee') and then hung a rose-noble round the neck of the little girl with a white silk ribbon. He did likewise with the other three. During the performance of this ceremony, the above-mentioned Bishop, who stood close to the King, read from the Gospel of St John, and lastly a prayer, whilst another clergyman knelt before him and made occasional responses during the prayer. Now when this was concluded, three lords – among whom were the Earl of Montgomery and his brother – came forward at the same time, one bearing a golden ewer, another a basin, and the third a towel. They fell on their knees thrice before the King, who washed himself, and then went with the young Prince (who, with His Highness [the Duke of Saxe-Weimar] walked before His Majesty) though the ante-room again into his apartment. . . . This ceremony of healing is understood to be very distasteful to the King, and it is said he would willingly abolish it; but he cannot do so, because he assumes the title of King of France as well; for he does not cure as King of England, but as a King of France, who ever had such a gift from God.

J.W. Neumayr von Ramssla, *The Visit of the Duke of
Saxe-Weimar* (1620),
in W.B. Rye, *England as Seen by Foreigners* (1865)

8

LONDON

At length they all to merry London came . . .
Edmund Spenser, *Prothalamion* (1596)

An unnerving as well as exciting experience it must have been, for
the many hundreds who came to London every year: the largest
city in England by far (expanding from about 12,000 in 1550 to
200,000 in 1600, with the unregulated suburbs growing even
faster), the centre of government and law, the chief continental
port, it seemed to many, as to William Camden, 'the epitome and
breviary of all Britain'.

At its heart was the City, still with its medieval walls, containing
the commercial centre, dominated by the trade guilds. The Lord
Mayor, Aldermen and the Common Council ran the City, issuing
licences, controlling markets, courts, jails, ward and parish
constables, overseeing supplies of water (from various street
conduits, delivered by water-carriers) and grain (from municipal
granaries, in time of dearth), and working for social stability in
a time of unprecedented social and economic instability. The
guilds in particular oversaw standards of trading and apprentice
training, sought to control imports and provided some charitable
relief (10 to 15 per cent of London's population needed regular or
occasional poor relief).

Trade tended to be localized, fishmongers, goldsmiths or
shoemakers congregating in their own areas. A few streets, such
as Cheapside, were broad, business thoroughfares, but most were
narrow and crowded, noisy with traders' cries, the passage of
wagons and animals, darkened by jettied, overhanging buildings,
nasty underfoot from midstreet gutters and open drains. The great

open drains of Fleet Ditch and Moorditch were often clogged and stinking. Foul water caused outbreaks of typhoid (which killed the Prince of Wales), while marshy areas (as on the south bank) produced malaria. Plague killed over 10,000 in 1593, over 25,000 in 1603 and over 26,000 in 1625. Syphilis ('the old bone-ache') kept hospitals, 'hot-houses' and moralists busy. Yet immigrants kept on coming – country people driven out by enclosures and dearth, unpaid soldiers, foreign refugees with new and useful skills (not always welcome to resident workers); every year came 750 upper-class young men to the Inns of Court, and 4,000 others (including some younger sons of gentry) as apprentices: it was a relatively youthful population. Overcrowding was a constant problem, especially for the very poor, crammed into the insanitary alleys.

In the western part of the City, by Ludgate and Newgate (with its prison) was the medieval St Paul's Cathedral, not only a religious centre but a business centre, and major venue for booksellers, barbers, beggars and cutpurses. To the west were the lawyers' Inns of Court, in practice the country's third university – or finishing-school; outside, along the Strand, was the way to Westminster, to Court and Parliament. Not surprisingly, the route there was soon developed, with the great houses of the wealthy stretching down to the river. To the north were the weavers and brewers of Cripplegate, the open fields of Finsbury and Moorfields, used for grazing, archery-practice and laundry-drying, with the Bedlam asylum and workhouse and first theatres nearby (The Red Bull at Clerkenwell, The Theatre and The Curtain near Shoreditch). Also at Shoreditch, Highgate and Whitechapel were the great 'laystalls' or dunghills (still in use until the 1850s). To the east was the great Tower of London with its lions and political prisoners, and, down-river, the shipfitters, wharves and whores of Shadwell, Wapping and Limehouse, servicing the cargo vessels unable to pass London Bridge.

Boatmen ferried one up and down the Thames, with its swans, salmon and sewage, or across it, if one were not using London Bridge, itself a shopping street and display centre for traitors' severed heads. South of the river were the notorious suburbs of Southwark and Bankside, known as 'the liberties' (originally monastic land, they remained beyond the City's jurisdiction until 1608). Here were the Marshalsea, Queen's Bench and Clink prisons, ale-houses, brothels, animal-baiting arenas (Paris Gardens) and some theatres (notably The Swan, The Rose and The Globe). Here too was much smelly industry: felt-making, tanning, brewing, soap- and sugar-boiling; and hospitals and poor-houses.

Described as the engine of industry and an eater of people, London was a city of contrasts, notably between the great wealth and conspicuous consumption of the few, the sober industry of the Protestant bourgeoisie, and the poverty of many. The common theme of plays, satires and pamphlets is social change and conflict, prodigal gentry versus upstart merchant and the potentially threatening 'many-headed multitude', in a stressful but dynamic economy.

The world is a Royal Exchange, where all sorts of men are merchants . . . [and] have their trading in particular merchandises. . . . They talk in several tongues, and like the murmuring fall of waters is the hum of their several businesses: insomuch that the place seems a babel, a confusion of tongues. The best, yet most incertain, commodity which all those merchants strive for, is Life.

Thomas Dekker, *The Blacke and White Rod* (1630)

LONDON BRIDGE

The bridge at London is worthily to be numbered among the miracles of the world, if men respect the building and foundation laid artificially and stately over an ebbing and flowing water upon 21 piles of stone, with 20 arches, under which barks may pass, the lowest foundation being (as they say) packs of wool, most durable against the force of water, and not to be repaired but upon great fall of the waters and by artificial turning or stopping the course of them; or if men respect the houses built upon the bridge, as great and high as those of the firm land, so as a man cannot know that he passeth a bridge, but would judge himself to be in the street, save that the houses on both sides are combined in the top, making the passage somewhat dark, and that in some few open places the river of Thames may be seen on both sides.

Fynes Moryson, An Itinerary (1617)

THE THAMES

What should I speak of the fat and sweet salmons daily taken in this stream, and that in such plenty (after the time of the smolt [migratory stage of the salmon] be past) as no river in Europe is able to exceed it. What store also of barbels, trouts, chevins [chub], perches, smelts, bream, roach, dace, gudgeon, flounders, shrimps, etc., are commonly to be had therein, I refer me to them that know by experience better than I, by reason of their daily trade of fishing in the same. . . .

In like manner I could entreat of the infinite number of swans daily to be seen upon this river, the two thousand wherries and small boats, whereby three thousand poor watermen are maintained through the carriage and recarriage of such persons as pass or repass from time to time upon the same; beside those huge tide-boats, tiltboats [large covered passenger-boats] and barges, which either carry passengers or bring necessary provision . . . into the city of London.

1573. A monstrous fish is taken in Thanet upon the xi th [11] of July, of 66 foot in length; one of whose eyes was a full cart load, and the diameter or thickness thereof, full two yards, or 6 of our English feet . . .

1576. The tower on the drawbridge upon London Bridge is taken down in April, being in great decay, and soon after made a pleasant and beautiful dwelling house; and whereas the heads of such as were executed for treason were wont to be placed upon this tower, they were now removed, and fixed over the gate which leadeth from Southwark into the City by that bridge.

William Harrison, A Description of England (1587)

LONDON

THE STREETS OF LONDON

(I)

In every street, carts and coaches make such a thundering as if the world ran upon wheels; at every corner, men, women and children meet in such shoals, that posts are set up of purpose to strengthen the houses, lest with jostling one another they should shoulder them down. Besides, hammers are beating in one place, tubs hooping in another, pots clinking in a third, water-tankards [water-carts] running at tilt in a fourth. Here are porters sweating under burdens, there merchants' men bearing bags of money. Chapmen (as if they were at leap-frog) skip out of one shop into another. Tradesmen (as if they were dancing galliards) are lusty at legs and never stand still. All are as busy as country attorneys at assizes.

Thomas Dekker, *The Seven Deadly Sinnes of London* (1606)

(II)

'Tis thought the way through this street [Cheapside] is not good, because so broad and so many go in it; yet though it be broad, it's very straight, because without any turnings. It is suspected here are not many sufficient able men, because they would sell all; and but little honesty, for they show all, and, some think, more sometimes than their own; they are very affable, for they'll speak to most that pass by; they care not how few be in the streets, so their shops be full; they that bring them money seem to be used worst, for they are sure to be paid soundly; their books of accounts are not like to their estates, for the latter are best without, but the other with, long crosses. There are a great company of honest men in this place, if all be gold that glisters: their parcel-gilt [partly gilded] plate is thought to resemble themselves, most of them have better faces than heart; their moneys and coins are used as prisoners at sea, kept under hatches. One would think them to be good men, for they deal with the purest and best metals, and every one strives to work best, and stout too, for they get much by knocking and especially by leaning on their elbows. Puritans do hold it for a fine street but something addicted to popery, for adoring the cross [on coins] too much. The inhabitants seem not to affect the standard: the kings and queens would be offended with and punish them, knew they how these batter their faces on their coins. Some of their wives

167

would be ill prisoners, for they cannot endure to be shut up; and as bad nuns, the life is so solitary. There are many virtuous and honest women, some truly so, others are so for want of opportunity. They hold that a harsh piece of Scripture, that women must be no goers or gadders abroad. In going to a lecture [sermon by an itinerant preacher] many use to visit a tavern: the young attendant must want his eyes [see or not see] and change his tongue according as his mistress shall direct; though many times they do mistake the place, yet they will remember the time an hour and half, to avoid suspicion. Some of the men are cunning launders of plate, and get much by washing that plate they handle [rinsing off gold with acid], and it hath come from some of them like a man from the [pawn]broker's that hath cashiered his cloak, a great deal the lighter. Well, if all the men be rich and true, and all the women fair and honest, then Cheapside shall stand beside Charing Cross for a wonder, and I will make no more characters. But I proceed.

Donald Lupton, *London and the Countrey carbonadoed* (1632)

WILL AND TESTAMENT: A FAREWELL TO LONDON

The time is come I must depart
From thee, O famous City:
I never yet, to rue my smart,
Did find that thou hadst pity . . .
I whole in body, and in mind,
But very weak in purse,
Do make and write my testament,
For fear it will be worse . . .
I first of all to London leave,
Because I there was bred,
Brave buildings rare, of churches store,
And Paul's unto the head. . . .
First for their food, I butchers leave,
That every day shall kill;
By Thames you shall have brewers' store,
And bakers at your will;

And such as others do observe
  And eat fish thrice a week,
I leave two streets full fraught therewith,
  They need not far to seek.
Watling Street and Canwick Street   [Candlewick]
  I full of woollen leave,
And linen store in Friday Street,
  If they me not deceive.
And those which are of calling such
  That costlier they require,
I mercers leave, with silks so rich
  As any would desire.
In Cheap, of them they store shall find,
  And likewise in that street
I goldsmiths leave, with jewels such
  As are for ladies meet.
And plate to finish cupboards with
  Full brave there shall you find,
With purl of silver and of gold   [thread]
  To satisfy your mind;
With hoods, bongraces, hats or caps,   [cloth sunshades on
  Such store are in that street,   hats]
As, if on t'one side you should miss,
  The t'other serves you feat.   [well]
For nets of every kind of sort
  I leave within the Pawn   [upper arcade in the Royal Exchange]
French ruffs, high purls,* gorgets and sleeves [ruff-pleats;* wimples]
  Of any kind of lawn.   [fine linen]
For purse or knives, for combs or glass,
  Or any needful knack,
I by the Stocks have left a boy   [market in Walbrook]
  Will ask you what you lack.
I hose do leave in Birchin Lane,
  Of any kind of size,
For women stitched, for men both trunks
  And those of Gascoyne guise.   [gaskins, wide breeches]
Boots, shoes, or pantables good store   [over-slippers]
  St Martin's hath for you;

In Cornwall, there I leave you beds   [in Vintry ward]
　　And all that 'longs thereto.
For women shall you tailors have,
　　By Bow the chiefest dwell: [St Mary Bow]
In every lane you some shall find
　　Can do indifferent well.
And for the men, few streets or lanes
　　But body-makers be,   [tailors]
And such as make the sweeping cloaks
　　With guards beneath the knee.   [ornamental trimming]
Artillery at Temple Bar   [weaponry]
　　And dags at Tower Hill;   [pistols]
Swords and bucklers of the best
　　Are nigh the Fleet until.
Now when thy folk are fed and clad
　　With such as I have named,
For dainty mouths and stomachs weak,
　　Some junkets must be framed.
Wherefore I 'potecaries leave,   [sellers of spices, drugs, sweets]
　　With banquets in their shop;   [fancy dishes]
Physicians also for the sick,
　　Diseases for to stop.
Some roisters still must bide in thee,   [riotous swaggerers]
　　And such as cut it out,
That with the guiltless quarrel will,
　　To let their blood about.
For them I cunning surgeons leave,
　　Some plasters to apply,
That ruffians may not still be hanged
　　Nor quiet persons die.
For salt, oatmeal, candles, soap,
　　Or what you else do want,
In many places shops are full,
　　I left you nothing scant.
If they that keep what I you leave
　　Ask money when they sell it,
At Mint there is such store, it is
　　Unpossible to tell it.

LONDON

At Steelyard, store of wines there be,   [Hanseatic merchants' store]
   Your dullèd minds to glad,
And handsome men, that must not wed,
   Except they leave their trade.   [apprentices]
They oft shall seek for proper girls,
   And some perhaps shall find,
That need compels or lucre lures,
   To satisfy their mind.
And near the same I houses leave
   For people to repair
To bathe themselves, so to prevent
   Infection of the air.
On Saturdays I wish that those
   Which all the week do drudge,
Shall thither trudge to trim them up
   On Sundays to look smug. . . .   [smart]
And that the poor, when I am gone,
   Have cause for me to pray,
I will to prisons portions leave,   [to supply poor prisoners]
   What though but very small . . .
The Newgate once a month shall have
   A Sessions for his share,   [a Court Sessions]
Lest, being heaped, infection might
   Procure a further care.
And at those Sessions some shall 'scape
   With burning near the thumb,   [and not hanging]
And afterward to beg their fees,   [prison charges]
   Till they have got the sum. . . .
To all the bookbinders by Paul's,
   Because I like their art,
They every week shall money have,
   When they from books depart. . . .
For maidens poor, I widowers rich
   Do leave, that oft shall dote,
And by that means shall marry them,
   To set the girls afloat.
And wealthy widows will I leave,
   To help young gentlemen,

Which when you have, in any case
  Be courteous to them then . . .
To Smithfield I must something leave,
  My parents there did dwell:
So careless for to be of it,
  None would account it well.
Therefore it thrice a week shall have   [for the market]
  Of horse and neat good store,   [oxen]
And in his Spital, blind and lame   [hospital]
  To dwell for evermore.
And Bedlam must not be forgot,   [lunatic asylum]
  For that was oft my walk:
I people there too many leave,
  That out of tune do talk.
At Bridewell there shall be beadles be,   [house of correction]
  And Matrons that shall still
See chalk well chopped, and spinning plied,
  And turning of the mill. . . .
And also leave I at each Inn
  Of Court or Chancery,
Of gentlemen, a youthful rout,
  Full of activity,
For whom I store of books have left
  At each bookbinder's stall,
And part of all that London hath,
  To furnish them withal.
And when they are with study cloyed,
  To recreate their mind,
Of tennis courts, of dancing-schools,
  And fence, they store shall find.
And every Sunday at the least,
  I leave, to make them sport,
In divers places, players, that
  Of wonders shall report.
Now London have I, for thy sake,
  Within thee, and without,
As come into my memory
  Dispersèd round about

Such needful things, as they should have
   Here left now unto thee:
When I am gone, with conscience
   Let them dispersèd be. . . .

Isabella Whitney, Wyll and Testament (1573)

PAUL'S WALK

THE TOWER OF ST PAUL'S SPEAKS:

For whereas I was at first consecrated to a mystical and religious purpose (the ceremonies of which are daily observed in the better part of me, for my heart is even to this hour an altar upon which are offered the sacrifices of holy prayers for men's sins) yet are some limbs of my venerable body abused and put to profane, horrid and servile customs, No marvel though my head rots [the steeple collapsed in 1561 and was not rebuilt], when the body is full of diseases; no marvel if the Divine Executioner cut me off by the shoulders, when in my bosom is so much horrible and close treason practiced against the King of the whole world.

For albeit I never yet came down all my stairs to be an ocular witness-bearer of what I speak, and what is (sometimes spoke openly and sometimes spoke in private) committed in my walks, yet doth the daily sound and echo of much knavish villainy strike up into mine ear. What whispering is there in Term times, how by some sleight to cheat the poor country client of his full purse that is stuck under his girdle? What plots are laid to furnish young gallants with ready money (which is shared afterwards at a tavern) thereby to disfurnish him of his patrimony? What buying up of oaths out of the hands of Knights of the Post [professional court 'witnesses'], who for a few shillings do daily sell their souls? What laying of heads is there together and sifting of the brain, still and anon, as it grows toward eleven of the clock (even amongst those that wear gilt [expensive scabbards] by their sides) where for that noon they may shift from Duke Humphrey [Sir John Beauchamp's tomb, thought to be that of Humphrey, Duke of Gloucester, in the south side of the nave, where the penniless dinnerless loitered] and be furnished with a dinner at some meaner man's table? What damnable bargains of unmerciful brokery and of unmeasurable usury are there clapped up? What swearing is there, yea, what swaggering, what facing and outfacing? What shuffling, what shouldering, what jostling, what jeering, what biting of thumbs to beget quarrels [see *Romeo and Juliet*], what holding up of fingers to remember drunken meetings, what braving [swaggering] with feathers [in hats], what bearding with moustaches, what casting open of cloaks to publish new clothes, what muffling in cloaks to hide broken elbows, so that when I hear such trampling up and down, such spitting, such hawking and such humming (every man's lips making a noise, yet not a word to be understood), I verily believe that I am the Tower of Babel newly to be builded up, but presently despair of ever being finished, because there is in me such confusion of languages.

For at one time, in one and the same rank, yea, foot by foot and elbow by elbow, shall you see walking, the knight, the gull, the gallant, the upstart, the gentleman, the clown [rustic], the captain [soldier], the apple-squire [pimp], the lawyer, the usurer, the citizen, the bankrupt, the scholar, the beggar, the doctor, the idiot, the ruffian, the cheater, the puritan, the cut-throat, the high man, the low man, the true man, and the thief; of all trades and professions some, of all countries some; and thus doth my middle aisle show like the Mediterranean Sea, in which as well the merchant hoists up sails to purchase wealth honestly, as the rover to light upon prize unjustly. Thus am I like a common mart where all commodities (both the good and the bad) are to be bought and sold. Thus whilst devotion kneels at her prayers, doth profanation walk under her nose in contempt of religion.

Thomas Dekker, *The Dead Term* (1608)

STREET CRIES

My masters, all attend you,
  If mirth you love to hear,
And I will tell you what they cry
  In London all the year.
I'll please you if I can,
  I will not be too long,
I pray you all attend a while,
  And listen to my song.

The fishwife first begins,
  ' 'ny mussels lily-white?   [any]
Herrings, sprats, or plaice,
  Or cockles for delight?
'ny Wallfleet oysters?'   [from Essex]
  Then she doth change her note,
She had need to hane her tongue by grease,   [?oil]
  For she rattles in the throat.

For why, they are but Kentish,
  To tell you out of doubt,
Her measure is too little –
  Go beat the bottom out.
Half a peck for two pence,   [dry goods measure of
  I doubt it is a bodge,   one gallon]
Thus all the city over,
  The people they do dodge. . . .

The weaver and the tailor,
  Cozens they be sure: [cousins, cheats]
They cannot work but they must steal,
  To keep their hands in ure,   [practice]
For it is a common proverb,
  Throughout all the town:
The tailor he must cut three sleeves
  For every woman's gown.

Mark but the water man
  Attending for his fare:
Of hot and cold, of wet and dry,
  He always takes a share.
He carrieth bonny lasses
  Over to the plays,
And here and there he gets a bit,
  And that his stomach stays. . . .

'Old shoes for new brooms!'

The broom man he doth sing,
'For hats or caps or buskins,   [ankle boots]
  Or any old pouch rings.   [rings to close purses]
Buy a mat, a bed-mat,
  A padlock or a pess,   [hassock, cushion]
A cover for a close-stool,   [chamber-pot]
  A bigger or a less.'

'Ripe cherry, ripe!'
  The costermonger cries,
'Pippins fine, or pears!'
  Another after hies,
With basket on his head,
  His living to advance,
And in his purse a pair of dice,
  For to play at mumchance. . . .   [gambling game]

'Buy black,' saith the blacking man,
  'The best that e'er was seen!'
'Tis good for poor men citizens,
  To make their shoes to shine;
Oh, 'tis a rare commodity,
  It must not be forgot:
It will make them glister gallantly,
  And quickly make them rot. . . .

W. Turner, *Turners Dish of Lenten Stuff* (1612)

LONDON SPORTS AND PASTIMES

Of late time . . . hath been used comedies, tragedies, interludes and histories, both true and feigned: for the acting whereof certain public places have been erected. Also cocks of the game are yet cherished by divers men for their pleasures, much money being laid on their heads, when they fight in pits, whereof some be costly made for that purpose. The ball is used by noble men and gentlemen in tennis courts, and by people of meaner sort in the open fields and streets.

LONDON

The marching forth of citizens' sons, and other young men on horseback, with disarmed lances and shields, there to practise feats of war, man against man, hath long since been left off, but in their City, they have used on horseback to run at a dead mark called a quintain . . . in the feast of Christmas, I have seen a quintain set upon Cornhill by the Leadenhall, where the attendants on the Lords of Merry Disports have run and made great pastime, for he that hit not the broad end of the quintain was of all men laughed to scorn, and he that hit it full, if he rode not the faster, had a sound blow on the back of the neck with a bag full of sand hanged on the other end. I have also in the summer season seen some upon the river of Thames rowed in wherries, with staves in their hands, flat at the fore end, running one against another, and, for the most part, one or both overthrown and well ducked.

On the holydays in summer the youths of this City have in the field exercised themselves, in leaping, dancing, shooting, wrestling, casting of the stone or ball, etc. . . .

The youths of this City also have used on holy days after evening prayer, at their masters' doors, to exercise their wasters [fencing cudgels] and bucklers; and the maidens, one of them playing on a timbrel, in sight of their masters and dames, to dance for garlands hanged thwart the streets, which open pastimes in my youth, being now suppressed, worser practices within doors are to be feared; as for the baiting of bulls and bears, they are till this day much frequented, namely in beargardens on the Bankside, wherein be prepared scaffolds for beholders to stand upon. Sliding upon the ice is now but children's play; but in hawking and hunting many grave citizens at this present have great delight, and do rather want leisure than good will to follow it.

John Stow, *The Survay of London* (1598, 1603)

LONDON BY CANDLE-LIGHT

Let the world therefore understand, that this tallow-faced gentleman called Candlelight, so soon as ever the sun was gone out of sight, and that darkness like a thief out of a hedge crept upon the earth, sweat till he dropped again with bustling to come into the city. For having no more but one only eye, and that fiery red with drinking and sitting up late, he was ashamed to be seen by day, knowing he should be laughed to scorn and hooted at. He makes his entrance therefore at Aldersgate of set purpose, for though the street be fair and spacious, yet, few lights in misty evenings using there to thrust out their golden heads, he thought that the aptest circle for him to be raised in, because there his glittering would make greatest show.

What expectation was there of his coming? Setting aside the bonfires, there is not more triumphing on midsummer night. No sooner was he advanced up into the most famous streets, but a number of shops for joy began to shut in: mercers rolled up their silks and velvet; the goldsmiths drew back their plate, and all the City looked like a private playhouse [e.g. Blackfriars], when the windows are clapped down, as if some nocturnal or dismal tragedy were presently to be acted before all the tradesmen. But Cavaleiro Candlelight came for no such solemnity; no, he had other crackers in hand to which he watched but his hour to give fire. Scarce was his entrance blown abroad, but the bankrupt, the felon and all that owed any money and for fear of arrests or justices' warrants had, like so many snails, kept their houses over their heads all the day before, began now to creep out of their shells and to stalk up and down the streets as uprightly and with as proud a gait as if they meant to knock against the stars with the crowns of their heads.

The damask-coated citizen, that sat in his shop both forenoon and afternoon, and looked more sourly on his poor neighbours than if he had drunk a quart of vinegar at a draught, sneaks out of his own doors and slips into a tavern where, either alone or with some other that battels their money together [pool funds], they so ply themselves with penny pots, which, like small-shot, go off, pouring into their fat paunches, that at length they have not an eye to see withal, nor a good leg to stand upon. In which pickle, if any of them happen to be jostled down by a post, that in spite of them will take the wall, and so reels them into the kennel [gutter], who takes them up or leads them home? Who has them to bed, and with a pillow smoothes this stealing so of good liquour, but that brazen-face Candlelight? Nay more, he entices their very prentices to make their desperate sallies out and quick retires in (contrary to the oath of their indentures which are seven years a-swearing) only for their pints, and away.

Tush, this is nothing! Young shopkeepers that have but newly ventured upon the pikes of marriage, who are every hour showing their wares to their customers, plying their business all day harder than Vulcan does his anvil, and seem better husbands than fiddlers that scrape for a poor living both day and night, yet even if they can but get Candlelight to sit up all night with them in any house of reckoning (that's to say in a tavern) they fall roundly to play the London prize, and that's at three several weapons, drinking, dancing and dicing; their wives lying all that time in their beds sighing like widows, which is lamentable; the giddy-brained husbands wasting the portion they had with them, which lost once, they are (like maidenheads) never recoverable. Or worse, this going a-bat-fowling a-nights being noted by some wise young man or other that knows how to handle such cases, the bush is beaten for them at home, whilst they catch the bird abroad. But what bird is it? The woodcock [dupe, cuckold].

Never did any city pocket up such wrongs at the hands of one over whom she is so jealous and so tender, that in winter nights if he be but missing and hide himself in the dark, I know not how many beadles are sent up and down the streets to cry him; yet, you see, there is more cause she should send out to curse him. For what villainies are not abroad so long as Candlelight is stirring? The serving-man then dare walk with his wench; the private punk [whore] (otherwise called one that boards [bawds] in London) who like a pigeon sits billing all day within doors and fears to step over the threshold, does then walk the round till midnight, after she hath been swaggering amongst pottlepots [two-quart tankards, drunks] and vintners' boys. Nay, the sober perpetuana [long-lasting wool]-suited puritan that dares not (so much as by moonlight) come near the suburb-shadow of a house where they set stewed prunes [brothel whores] before you, raps as boldly at the hatch, when he knows Candlelight is within, as if he were a new-chosen constable. When all doors are locked up, when no eyes are open, when birds sit silent in bushes, and beasts lie sleeping under hedges, when no creature can be smelt to be up but they that may be smelt every night a street's length ere you come at them [the dung-carts], even then doth this *ignis fatuus* Candlelight walk like a fire-drake [dragon] into sundry corners. If you will not believe this, shoot but your eye through the iron grates into the cellars of vintners: there you shall see him hold his neck in a gin made of a cleft hoopstick, to throttle him from telling tales, whilst they most abominably jumble together all the papistical drinks that are brought from beyond sea. The poor wines are racked [strained, tortured] and made to confess anything; the Spanish and the French, meeting both in the bottom of the cellar, conspire together in their cups to lay the Englishman (if he ever come into their company) under the board. To be short, such strange mad music do they play upon their sack-butts [wine-barrels, bass trumpets], that if Candlelight, being overcome with the steam of new sweet wines when they are at work, should not tell them 'tis time to go to bed, they would make all the hogsheads that use to come to the house to dance the canaries [Spanish dance, wine] till they reel again.

When the grape-mongers and he are parted, he walks up and down the streets squiring old midwives to any house (very secretly) where any bastards are to be brought into the world. From then, about the hour when spirits walk and cats go a-gossiping, he visits the watch, where, creeping into the beadle's cot-house [shelter] (which stands between his legs, that are lapped about with pieces of rug, as if he had new struck off shackles) and seeing the watchmen to nod at him, he hides himself presently (knowing the token) under the flap of a gown, and teaches them by instinct how to steal naps into their heads, because he sees all their cloaks have not one good nap upon them; and upon his warrant, snort [snore] they so loud, that to those night-walkers (whose wits are up so late) it serves as a watchword to keep out of the reach of their brown bills [halberds], by which means they never come to answer the matter before master constable, and the bench upon which his men, that should watch, do sit: so that the Counters [jails] are cheated of prisoners, to the great damage of those that should have their morning's draught out of the garnish [bribe paid to the jailers].

O Candlelight, Candlelight! To how many costly sack-possets and rear-banquets [after-dinner snacks] hast thou been invited by prentices and kitchen maidens? When the bellman for anger to spite such a purloiner of so many citizens' goods hath bounced at the door like a madman, at which (as if Robin Goodfellow had been conjured up amongst them) the wenches have fallen into the hands of the green-sickness [fainting, chlorosis], and the young fellows into cold agues, with very fear lest their master (like old Jeronimo and Isabella his wife after him [in Kyd's *The Spanish Tragedy*] starting out of his naked bed should come down with a weapon in his hand and this in his mouth: 'What outcries pull us from our naked bed? Who calls, etc.' as the players can tell you. O Candlelight, how hast thou stunk then, when they have popped thee out of their company; how hast thou taken it in snuff [been extinguished, resented it] when thou hast been smelt out, especially the master of the house exclaiming, that by day that deed of darkness had not been. One veney [bout] more with thee, and then I have done.

How many lips have been worn out with kissing at the street door or in the entry, in a winking blind evening? How many odd matches and uneven marriages have been made there between young prentices and their masters' daughters, whilst thou, O Candlelight, hast stood watching at the stair's head, that none could come stealing down by thee, but they must be seen?

It appears by these articles put in against thee, that thou art partly a bawd to divers loose sins, and partly a cozener.

Thomas Dekker, *The Seven Deadly Sins of London* (1606)

WALKING HOME LATE: ADVICE

After the sound of pottle-pots is out of your ears and that the spirit of wine and tobacco walks in your brain, the tavern-door being shut upon your back, cast about to pass through the widest and goodliest streets in the city. And if your means cannot reach to the keeping of a boy, hire one of the drawers to be as a lantern unto your feet and to light you home. And still as you approach near any night-walker that is up as late as yourself, curse and swear, like one that speaks High Dutch, in a lofty voice, because your men have used you so like a rascal in not waiting upon you, and vow the next morning to pull their blue cases [livery] over their ears; though if your chamber were well searched, you give only sixpence a week to some old woman to make your bed, and that she is all the serving creatures you give wages to.

If you smell a watch (and that you may easily do, for commonly they eat onions to keep them in sleeping, which they account a medicine against cold), but if you come within danger of their brown bills, let him that is your candlestick and holds up your torch from dropping (for to march after a link [torch] is shoemaker-like), let *ignis fatuus*, I say, being within reach of the constable's staff, ask aloud, 'Sir Giles,' or 'Sir Abr'am, will you turn this way,' or 'down that street?'. It skills not that there be none dubbed in your bunch, the watch will wink at you only for the love they bear to arms and knighthood. Marry, if the sentinel and his court of guard stand strictly upon his martial law, and cry 'Stand!', commanding you to give the word and to show reason why your ghost walks so late, do it in some jest, for that will show you have a desperate wit and perhaps make him and his halberdiers afraid to lay foul hands upon you; or if you read a *mittimus* [jail-warrant] in the constable's look, counterfeit to be a Frenchman, a Dutchman or any other nation whose country is in peace with your own, and you may pass the pikes; for being not able to understand you, they cannot by the customs of the City take your examination, and so by consequence they have nothing to say to you. . . .

All the way as you pass, especially being approached near some of the gates, talk of none but lords, and such ladies with whom you have played at primero [a card game] or danced in the Presence [-chamber at Court] the very same day. And being arrived at your lodging door, which I would counsel you to choose in some rich citizen's house, salute at parting no man but by the name of 'Sir', as though you had supped with knights, albeit you had none in your company but your perinado [catamite, rent-boy] or your ingle [male lover].

Thomas Dekker, *The Gull's Hornbook* (1609)

STEWS AND STRUMPETS

London, what are thy suburbs but licensed stews? Can it be so many brothel-houses of salary sensuality and sixpenny whoredom (the next door to the magistrate's) should be set up and maintained, if bribes did not bestir them? I accuse none, but certainly justice somewhere is corrupted. Whole hospitals of ten-times-a-day dishonested strumpets have we cloistered together. Night and day the entrance unto them is as free as to a tavern. Not one of them but hath a hundred retainers. Prentices and poor servants they encourage to rob their masters. Gentlemen's purses and pockets they will dive into and pick, even whiles they are dallying with them.

No Smithfield ruffianly swashbuckler will come off with such harsh hell-raking oaths as they. Every one of them is a gentlewoman, and either the wife of two husbands or a bed-wedded bride before she was ten years old. The speech-shunning sores and sight-irking botches of their unsatiate intemperance they will unblushingly lay forth and jestingly brag of, wherever they haunt. To church they never repair. Not in all their whole life would they hear of GOD, if it were not for their huge swearing and forswearing by Him.

Great cunning do they ascribe to their art, as, the discerning by the very countenance a man that hath crowns in his purse; the fine closing in with the next Justice, or Alderman's deputy of the ward; the winning love of neighbours round about to repel violence if haply their houses should be environed [beset], or any in them prove unruly, being pilled and polled [stripped and shaven, robbed] too unconscionably. They forecast [look out] for backdoors to come in and out by undiscovered. Sliding windows also and trapdoors in floors to hide whores behind and under, with false counterfeit pane[l]s in walls, to be opened and shut like a wicket[-gate]. Some one gentleman generally acquainted they give his admission to sans fee, and free privilege thenceforward in their nunnery, to procure them frequentance.

Awake your wits, grave authorised law-distributors, and show yourselves as insinuative-subtle in smoking this city-sodoming trade out of his starting-hole as the professors of it are in underpropping it.

Thomas Nashe, *Christ's Tears over Jerusalem* (1593)

Voyage to the Underworld, with a Paddle

[A mock-epic account of a midnight journey down the Fleet Ditch main sewer]

> . . . In the first jaws appeared that ugly monster,
> Ycleped Mud, which, when their oars did once stir,
> Belched forth an air as hot as at the muster
> Of all your night-tubs, when the carts do cluster,   [dung-carts]
> Who shall discharge first his merd-urinous load:
> Through her womb they make their famous road
> Between two walls, where, on one side, to scare men,
> Were seen your ugly Centaurs ye call car-men, [dungcart drivers]
> Gorgonian scolds and harpies; on the other
> Hung stench, diseases, and old filth, their mother,
> With famine, wants and sorrows many a dozen,
> The least of which was to the plague a cousin. . . .
> All was to them the same, they were to pass;

And so they did, from Styx to Acheron,   [river in Hades]
The ever-boiling flood, whose banks upon
Your Fleet-lane furies and hot cooks do dwell,
That, with still-scalding steams, make the place hell.
The sinks ran grease and hair of measled hogs,
 The heads, houghs, entrails and the hides of dogs;   [leg-joints]
For to say truth, what scullion is so nasty
To put the skins and offal in a pasty?
Cats there lay, divers had been flayed and roasted,
And, after mouldy grown, again were toasted;
Then, selling not, a dish was ta'en to mince 'em,
But still, it seemed, the rankness did convince 'em.   [expose
                                                          or condemn]

. . . And now, above the pool, a face right fat
With great gray eyes, is lifted up, and mewed;
Thrice did it spit, thrice dived. At last, it viewed
Our brave heroes with a milder glare,
And, in a piteous tune, began: 'How dare
Your dainty nostrils (in so hot a season,
When every clerk eats artichokes and peason,   [peas]
Laxative lettuce, and such windy meat)
Tempt such a passage? When each privy's seat
Is filled with buttock? and the walls do sweat
Urine and plasters? when the noise doth beat
Upon your ears of discords so unsweet?
And outcries of the damnèd in the Fleet?   [prison]
Cannot the plague-bill keep you back? nor bells
Of loud Sepulchre's, with their hourly knells,   [St Sepulchre's
                                                          Church]

But you will visit grisly Pluto's hall?' . . .
  In memory of [this] most liquid deed,
The city since hath raised a pyramid.   [memorial; dungheap]
And I could wish, for their eternised sakes,
My Muse had ploughed with his, that sung A-jax.

[Sir John Harington celebrated his invention of the water-closet (a jakes)
with a poem, *The Metamorphosis of Ajax* (1596)]
                                Ben Jonson, *On the Famous Voyage* (pub. 1616)

LONDON

THE PLAGUE OF 1603

Apollo . . . and you bewitching silver-tongued Muses, get you gone, I invocate none of your names; Sorrow and Truth, sit you on each side of me whilst I am delivered of this deadly burden; prompt me that I may utter ruthful and passionate condolement; arm my trembling hand, that it may boldly rip up and anatomise the ulcerous body of this anthropophagised [man-eating] plague; lend me art (without any counterfeit shadowing) to paint and delineate to the life the whole story of this mortal and pestiferous battle, and you, the ghosts of those more (by many) than 40,000, that with the virulent poison of infection have been driven out of your earthly dwellings . . .

What an unmatchable torment were it for a man to be barred up every night in a vast, silent charnelhouse? Hung, to make it more hideous, with lamps dimly and slowly burning, in hollow and glimmering corners, where all the pavement should, instead of green rushes, be strewed with blasted rosemary, withered hyacinths, fatal cypress and yew, thickly mingled with heaps of dead men's bones. The bare ribs of a father that begat him, lying there; here the chapless [jawless] hollow skull of a mother that bore him; round about him a thousand corpses, some standing bolt upright in their knotted winding-sheets; others half mouldered in rotten coffins, that should suddenly yawn wide open, filling his nostrils with noisome stench, and his eyes with the sight of nothing but crawling worms. And to keep such a poor wretch waking, he should hear no noise but of toads croaking, screech-owls howling, mandrakes shrieking. Were not this an infernal prison? Would not the strongest-hearted man, beset with such a ghastly horror, look wild, and run mad, and die? And even such a formidable shape did the diseased City appear in: for he that durst, in the dead hour of gloomy midnight, have been so valiant as to have walked through the still and melancholy streets, what think you should have been his music? Surely the loud groans of raving, sick men; the struggling pangs of souls departing; in every house grief striking up an alarum; servants crying out for masters, wives for husbands, parents for children, children for their mother. Here he should have met some frantically running to knock up sextons; there, others fearfully sweating with coffins, to steal forth dead bodies, lest the fatal handwriting of death should seal up their doors [a large red cross and the words 'Lord have mercy upon us' were painted on the doors of infected houses, which were shut up for twenty-eight days]. And to make this dismal concert more full, round about him bells heavily tolling in one place, and ringing out in another. The dreadfulness of such an hour, is unutterable: let us go no further. . . .

It is now day, let us look forth and try what consolation rises with the sun: not any, not any. For before the jewel of the morning be fully set in silver, an hundred hungry graves stand gaping, and every one of them, as at a breakfast, hath swallowed down ten or eleven lifeless carcasses; before dinner, in the same gulf are twice so many more devoured; and before the sun takes his rest, those numbers are doubled. Threescore that not many hours before had every one several lodgings very delicately furnished, are now thrust altogether into one close room; a little, little noisome room; not fully ten foot square. . . .

Imagine then that all this while, Death (like a Spanish leaguer [siege soldier], or rather like stalking Tamburlaine [in Marlowe's play]) hath pitched his tents (being nothing but a heap of winding-sheets tacked together) in the sinfully-polluted suburbs. The Plague is muster-master and marshal of the field; burning fevers, boils, blains and carbuncles, the leaders, lieutenants, sergeants and corporals, the main army consisting (like Dunkirk [pirate haven]) of a mingle-mangle, viz. dumpish mourners, merry sextons, hungry coffin-sellers, scrubbing bearers and nasty grave-makers; but indeed, they are the pioneers of the camp, that are employed only (like moles) in casting up of earth and digging of trenches. Fear and Trembling, the two catchpoles [arresting officers] arrest everyone: no parley will be granted, no composition [scruples] stood upon, but the alarum is struck up, the tocsin rings out for life, and no voice heard but, '*Tue, tue*: kill, kill.' The little bells only (like small shot) do yet go off, and make no great work for worms, a hundred or two lost in every skirmish, or so; but alas, that's nothing. Yet by these desperate sallies, what by open setting upon them by day, and secret ambuscadoes by night, the skirts of London were pitifully pared off, by little and little; which they within the gates perceiving, it was no boot [use] to bid them take their heels, for away they trudge thick and threefold, some riding, some on foot, some without boots, some in their slippers, by water, by land. In shoals swam they westward, marry, to Gravesend none went unless they were driven, for whosoever landed there never came back again. Hackneys, watermen and wagons were not so terribly employed many a year: so that within a short time, there was not a good horse in Smithfield, nor a coach to be set eye on, for after the world had once run upon the wheels of the Pest-cart, neither coach nor caroche durst appear in his likeness. . . .

I am amazed to remember what dead marches are made of three thousand trooping together [in several weeks the weekly mortality bills exceeded 3,000]; husbands, wives and children being led as ordinarily to one grave as if they had gone to one bed. And those that could shift for a time, and shrink their heads out of the collar (as many did) yet went they (most bitterly) miching [skulking] and muffled up and down with rue and wormwood stuffed into their ears and nostrils, looking like so many boars' heads stuck with branches of rosemary, to be served in for brawn at Christmas.

Thomas Dekker, *The Wonderful Year* (1603)

THE PLAGUE FULL SWIFT GOES BY

Song

Adieu, farewell, earth's bliss,
This world uncertain is;
Fond are life's lustful joys,
Death proves them all but toys,
None from his darts can fly.
I am sick, I must die.
    Lord have mercy on us.

Rich men, trust not in wealth,
Gold cannot buy you health;
Physic himself must fade,
All things to end are made.
The plague full swift goes by;
I am sick, I must die.
    Lord have mercy on us.

Beauty is but a flower
Which wrinkles will devour,
Brightness falls from the air,
Queens have died young and fair,

Dust hath closed Helen's eye.
I am sick, I must die.
   Lord have mercy on us.

Strength stoops unto the grave,
Worms feed on Hector brave,
Swords may not fight with fate.
Earth still holds ope her gate;
Come, come, the bells do cry.
I am sick, I must die.
   Lord have mercy on us.

Wit with his wantonness
Tasteth death's bitterness;
Hell's executioner
Hath no ears for to hear
What vain art can reply.
I am sick, I must die.
   Lord have mercy on us.

Haste, therefore, each degree,
To welcome destiny.
Heaven is our heritage,
Earth but a player's stage;
Mount we unto the sky.
I am sick, I must die.
   Lord have mercy on us.

Thomas Nashe, *Summer's Last Will and Testament*
(1592; pub. 1600)

9

ARTS AND PLEASURES

The courts of kings for stately measures; the City for light heels and nimble footing; the country for shuffling dances; western men for gambols; Middlesex men for tricks above ground; Essex men for the hey [dance]; Lancashire for hornpipes; Worcestershire for bagpipes; but Herefordshire for a morris dance.

Anon., *Old Meg of Herefordshire* (1609)

The Renaissance came late to England; but after a hiccup in the mid-sixteenth century, its shaping force was apparent from the early 1580s, Virgil, Ovid, Seneca, Petrarch all speaking in English accents. 'High' art worked down into a still vigorous popular culture.

Shakespeare and his fellow playwrights provided drama for the City; Byrd, Campion and Morley provided music for the Court and gentry; Greene and Lodge wrote romances for readers anywhere; but there were many other entertainments for the people at large. Although working long hours, they also displayed what modern social historians coolly call 'the high leisure preference common to underdeveloped agrarian economies'; most people, in country and town, still had their work, leisure and imaginations moulded in varying degree by the old religious (even pre-Christian) calendar and its values, providing release and pleasures beyond that of commercial entertainment.

Thus, Shrove Tuesday was an occasion for carnival, associated with wild football games, food, drink and riot (especially by apprentices); St Valentine's Day celebrated sexuality; if Lent meant fasting and fish, Easter was a time of rejoicing, with mummers' plays, when mean Jack-a-Lent was driven out and replaced by virile Jack-in-the-Green. St George's Day still had mummers' plays with dragons and processions, but May Day was more popular, with phallic maypoles, sexual frolics, morris dances and Robin Hood (and unmaidenly Maid Marian) plays. Whitsuntide was linked with new growth, new clothes and festivities (the 'Whitsun pastorals' of *The Winter's Tale*). Midsummer, 24 June, was marked by bonfires and pageants, especially in London, which also had, a month later, the great carnivalesque Bartholomew's Fair (see Jonson's play). On 15 August there were horn-dances (*As You Like It*). The twelve days of Christmas had masques, plays and dancing, holly and ivy, the burning of the Yule log. Plough Monday, 11 January, again had plays and dances to mark the return to work; on Lady Day, 25 March, the year began.

Until they were officially suppressed in 1547 there were the great Christian Mystery plays, performed by guilds, on pageants, in Coventry, York, Wakefield, Chester and elsewhere (some survived into the 1570s). 'Morality' plays, single plays on Christian and Humanist virtues, were approved and performed in noblemen's and city halls; schools, universities and Inns of Court encouraged improving dramatic performances (e.g., the Senecan state tragedy *Gorboduc*, 1561). Plays also went on in animal-baiting arenas and inn-yards. Clearly, there was money to be made from playing if it could be organized properly (and despite Puritans' and employers' suspicions). The demands of the Court for entertainment were voracious, and noblemen vied to have 'their' companies perform at Court.

The first purpose-built London theatre, The Theatre, was built in Shoreditch in 1576 by James Burbage, and was later dismantled and used as the framework of the Globe (1599 – rebuilt in 1614 after a fire) in Bankside, south of the river, with the Rose (1587), Swan (1595) and Paris Gardens (the bull- and bear-baiting hall) as neighbours; generally the players needed to be beyond the reach of the City authorities. Other theatres in north London included the Fortune (1600) and the Red Bull (1604). The sheer number suggests the demand. Marlowe's *Tamburlaine* (c. 1587) and Kyd's

The Spanish Tragedy (*c*. 1589) were the smash hits of their time. Some playscripts were even printed.

All these theatres were large amphitheatres (taking up to 3,000 playgoers), round or polygonal, with covered thrust stages, open central courtyards for the 'understanders' (for a penny each – equivalent to the price of a good cinema seat today) and covered galleries on two or three levels, with seats, for twopence or threepence. Such theatres generally received a wide social range, from courtiers, lawyers and gentry to tradesmen, artificers, servants and apprentices (if they could get off work), as well as citizens' wives (protected by servants), and whores and cutpurses (both after the better-off). Much more expensive and therefore socially exclusive were the indoor, hall theatres, artificially lit, such as Paul's Boys, and the second Blackfriars (1596), within the City and also owned by Burbage: these seated some six hundred, at a minimum price of sixpence, with a stageside box costing much more; for extra payment, one could sit on the stage itself.

Different theatres tended to appeal to different playgoers and writers: while the Globe operated throughout the year (plague permitting), the Blackfriars closed from May to September while the Court was out of town and the courts not in session. The Red Bull and Fortune were rather down-market; Lyly, Marston and Jonson preferred the hall playhouses, while Shakespeare and Middleton could be seen at the Globe, which seems to have had the widest repertoire and social range, and became dominant. Eventually, there were only two companies; in 1604 King James made Shakespeare's company the King's Company – not that Elizabeth or James ever went to the theatre. The players performed at Court, particularly during Christmastide celebrations; but Court taste was less and less the popular taste. Drama was no longer a folk ritual, or religious or moral instruction, but, increasingly, entertainment, and business. 'For oh, for oh, the hobby-horse is forgot.' (*Hamlet*, 1600)

GOLDEN SYRUP

Only the poet . . . lifted up with the vigour of his own invention, doth grow in effect into another nature, in making things either better than Nature bringeth forth, or, quite anew, forms such as never were in Nature, as the heroes, demigods, cyclops, chimaeras, furies and such like; so as he goeth hand in hand with Nature, not enclosed within the narrow warrant of her gifts but freely ranging only within the zodiac of his own wit.

Nature never set forth the earth in so rich tapestry as divers poets have done, neither with pleasant rivers, fruitful trees, sweet-smelling flowers, nor whatsoever else may make the too much loved earth more lovely. Her world is brazen, the poets only deliver a golden. . . .

Of all the sciences . . . is our poet the monarch. For he doth not only show the way [to virtue] as will entice any man to enter into it. . . . He beginneth not with obscure definitions, which must blur the margins with interpretations, and load the memory with doubtfulness, but he cometh to you with words set in delightful proportion, either accompanied with, or prepared for, the well enchanting skill of music; and with a tale forsooth he cometh unto you, with a tale which holdeth children from play and old men from the chimney corner. And, pretending no more, doth intend the winning of the mind from wickedness to virtue; even as the child is often brought to take most wholesome things by hiding them in such other as have a pleasant taste.

Sir Philip Sidney, *An Apologie for Poetry* (1595)

A POT POET

Is the dregs of wit, yet mingled with good drink may have some relish. His inspirations are more real than others', for they do but feign a god, but he has his by him. His verse runs like the tap, and his invention, as the barrel, ebbs and flows at the mercy of the spigot. In thin drink he aspires not above a ballad, but a cup of sack inflames him, and sets his muse and nose afire together. The press is his mint, and stamps him now and then a sixpence or two in reward of the baser coin, his pamphlet. His works would scarce sell for three halfpence, though they are given oft for three shillings, but for the pretty title that allures the country gentleman; for which the printer maintains him in ale a fortnight. His verses are like his clothes, miserable centos [collocations, anthologies] and patches, yet their pace is not altogether so hobbling as an almanac's. The death of a great man or the burning of a house furnish him with an argument, and the nine muses are out straight in mourning gowns, and Melpomene [tragedy] cries, 'Fire, fire!'. He is a man now much employed in commendations of our navy, and a bitter inveigher against the Spaniard. His frequentest works go out in single sheets, and are chanted from market to market to a vile tune and a worse throat, whilst the poor country wench melts like her butter to hear them. And these are the stories of some men at Tyburn [execution place], or a strange monster out of Germany; or, sitting in a bawdy-house, he writes God's judgements. He drops away at last in some obscure painted cloth, to which himself made the verses, and his life, like a can too full, spills upon the bench. He leaves twenty shillings on the score, which my hostess loses.

John Earle, *Micro-cosmographie* (1628)

THE WRITER ROBERT GREENE (DIED PENNILESS, SEPTEMBER 1592)

(I)

I was altogether unacquainted with the man, and never once saluted him by name; but who in London hath not heard of his dissolute and licentious living; his fond [foolish] disguising of a Master of Art with ruffianly hair, unseemly apparel and more unseemly company; his vainglorious and thrasonical braving [boastful swaggering]; his piperly [like a street-piper] extemporising and Tarletonising [clowning, like Tarleton]; his apish counterfeiting of every ridiculous and absurd toy [fashion]; his fine cozening [cheating] of jugglers, and finer juggling with cozeners; his villainous cogging and foisting [cheating at cards and dice]; his monstrous swearing, and horrible forswearing; his impious profaning of sacred texts; his other scandalous and blasphemous raving; his riotous and outrageous surfeiting; his continual shifting of lodgings; his plausible mustering [insinuating], and banqueting of roisterly acquaintance at his first coming; his beggarly departing in every hostess's debt; his infamous resorting to the Bankside, Shoreditch, Southwark and other filthy haunts; his obscure lurking in basest corners; his pawning of his sword, cloak and what not, when money came short; his impudent pamphleting, fantastical interluding and desperate libelling when other cozening shifts failed; his employing of Ball (surnamed [nicknamed], Cutting Ball), till he was intercepted at Tyburn, to levy a crew of his trustier companions to guard him in danger of arrests; his keeping of the foresaid Ball's sister, a sorry ragged quean [whore], of whom he had his base [bastard] son, Infortunatus Greene; his forsaking of his own wife, too honest for such a husband; particulars are infinite; his contemning of superiors, deriding of others, and defying of all good order?

Gabriel Harvey, Four Letters (1592)

(II)

In short terms thus I demur upon thy long Kentish-tailed [there was a legend that Kentishmen had tails] declaration against Greene.

He inherited more virtues than vices; a jolly long red peak, like the spire of a steeple, he cherished continually without cutting, whereat a man might hang a jewel, it was so sharp and pendant.

Why should art answer for the infirmities of manners? He had his faults, and thou thy follies.

Debt and deadly sin, who is not subject to? With any notorious crime I never knew him tainted [attainted, charged] (and yet tainting [treating with ointment] is no infamous surgery for him that hath been in so many hot skirmishes [fights or sexual encounters]).

A good fellow he was, and would have drunk with thee for more angels [coins] than the Lord thou libelledst on gave thee in Christ's College [Cambridge]; and in one year he pissed as much against the walls as thou and thy two brothers spent in three.

In a night and a day would he have yarked up a pamphlet as well as in seven year, and glad was that printer that might be so blest to pay him dear for the very dregs of his wit.

He made no account of winning credit by his works, as thou dost; thou dost no good works, but think'st to be famoused by a strong faith of thy own worthiness. His only care was to have a spell in his purse to conjure up a good cup of wine with at all times.

For the lousy circumstance of his poverty before his death, and sending that miserable writ to his wife, it cannot be but thou liest, learned Gabriel.

I and one of my fellows, William Monox (hast thou never heard of him and his great dagger?), were in company with him a month before he died, at that fatal banquet of Rhenish wine and pickled herring (if thou wilt needs have it so), and then the inventory of his apparel came to more than three shillings (though thou sayest the contrary).

Thomas Nashe, *Strange News or The Four Letters Confuted* (1592)

FISHY TALES AND RED HERRINGS: FINDING FOOD FOR THE PRESSES

Homer, of rats and frogs hath heroicked it [*The Battle of the Frogs and Mice*]. Other oaten pipers after him, in praise of the gnat [*Culex*, attributed to Virgil], the flea [Ovid], the hazel-nut, the grasshopper [Aesop], the butterfly [Spenser, *Muiopotmos*], the parrot, the popinjay [Skelton, *Speke Parrot*], Philip-sparrow [Skelton], and the cuckoo; the wantoner sort of them sing descant on their mistress's glove, her ring, her fan, her looking-glass, her pantofle [slipper], and on the same jury I might empanel Johannes Secundus with his book of the two hundred kinds of kisses. Philosophers come sneaking in with their paradoxes of poverty, imprisonment, death, sickness, banishment and baldness, and as busy as they are about the bee, the stork, the constant turtle, the horse, the dog, the ape, the ass, the fox and the ferret. Physicians deafen our ears with the *Honorificabilitudinitatibus* [in Dante] of their heavenly panacea, their sovereign guaiacum [medicinal bark], their glisters [enemas], their treacles [medicinal compounds], their mithridates [homeopathic medicine] of forty several poisons compacted, their bitter rhubarb and torturing stibium [antimony].

The posterior [later, bottom] Italian and German cornugraphers [writers on cuckoldry] stick not to applaud and canonise unnatural sodomitry, the strumpet errant, the gout, the ague, the dropsy, the sciatica, folly, drunkenness and slovenry. The Galli Gallinacei, or cocking French, swarm every pissing while in their primer editions, *Imprimeda iour duy* [*Imprimé aujourd'hui*], of the unspeakable healthful conducibleness of the Gomorrian great *Poca, a poco* [little by little process of gonorrhoea], their true countryman every inch of him, the prescript laws of tennis or balloon (which is most of their gentlemen's chief livelihoods), the commodity of hoarseness, blear eyes, scabbed hams, threadbare cloaks, poached eggs and panados [spiced boiled bread]. Amongst our English harmonious calinos [popular singers] one is up with the excellence of the brown bill [halberd] and the long bow [Ascham, *Toxophilus*]; another plays his prizes in print, in driving it home with all weapons in right of the noble science of defence; a third writes passing inamorately of the nature of white-meats [cheese and dairy produce], and justifies it under his hand, to be bought and sold everywhere, that they exceed nectar and ambrosia; a fourth comes forth with something in praise of nothing [Passerat, *Nihil*, Shakespeare, *Much Ado About Nothing*?]; a fifth, of an inflamed zeal to Coppersmiths' Hall, all-to-berhymes it of the diversity of red noses, and the hierarchy of the rose magnificat. A sixth sweeps behind the door all earthly felicities and makes baker's malkins [oven-mops] of them, if they stand in competency of a strong dozen of points; marry, they must be points of the matter, you must consider, whereof the foremost codpiece point [tie] is the crane's proverb in printed cloths, 'Fear God and obey the King'; and the rest, some have tags [additions, codpiece ties] and some have none. A seventh sets a tobacco pipe instead of a trumpet to his mouth, and of that divine drug proclaimeth miracles. An eighth capers it up to the spheres in commendation of dancing [Sir John Davies, *Orchestra*]. A ninth offers sacrifice to the goddess Cloaca, and disports himself very scholarly and wittily about the reformation of close-stools [Sir John Harington, *The Metamorphosis of Ajax*]. A tenth sets forth remedies of toasted turfs against famine. . . .

The application of this whole catalogue of waste authors is no more but this: *Quot capita tot sententiae* ('so many heads, so many whirligigs' [spinning toys]). And if all these have terlery-ginked it so frivolously of they recked not what, I may *cum gratia et privilegio* [with grace and favour, like a Papal pronouncement] pronounce it, that a red herring is wholesome in a frosty morning, and rake up some few scattered syllables together in the exornation [embellishing] and polishing of it.

Thomas Nashe, *Nashe's Lenten Stuffe, In Praise of the Red Herring*
(1599)

A MORAL INTERLUDE

In the city of Gloucester, the manner is (as I think it is in other like corporations) that when players of interludes come to town, they first attend the mayor, to inform him what noblemen's servants they are, and so to get licence for their public playing; and if the mayor like the actors, or would show respect to their Lord and master, he appoints them to play their first play before himself and the aldermen and common council of the city; and that is called the mayor's play, where everyone that will, comes in without money, the mayor giving the players a reward as he thinks fit to show respect unto them.

At such a play, my father took me with him, and made me stand between his legs as he sat upon one of the benches, where we saw and heard very well. The play was called *The Cradle of Security*, wherein was personated a king or some great prince, with his courtiers of several kinds, amongst which three ladies were in special grace with him; and they, keeping him in delights and pleasures, drew him from his graver counsellors, hearing of sermons, and listening to good counsel and admonitions, that in the end they got him to lie down in a cradle upon the stage, where these three ladies joining in a sweet song rocked him asleep, that he snored again, and in the meantime closely conveyed under the cloths wherewithal he was covered, a vizard like a swine's snout upon his face, with three wire chains fastened thereunto, the other end whereof being holden severally by those three ladies, who fell to singing again, and then discovered his face, that the spectators might see how they had transformed him, going on with their singing. Whilst all this was acting, there came forth of another door at the farthest end of the stage, two old men, the one in blue, a sergeant at arms, with his mace on his shoulder, the other in red, with a drawn sword in his hand, and leaning with the other hand upon the other's shoulder; and so they two went along in a soft pace round about by the skirt of the stage, till at last they came to the cradle, when all the Court was in the greatest jollity; and then the foremost old man with his mace struck a fearful blow upon the cradle; whereat all the courtiers, with the three ladies and the vizard, all vanished; and the desolate prince starting up bare-faced, and finding himself thus sent for to judgement, made a lamentable complaint of his miserable case, and so was carried away by wicked spirits. This prince did personate in the moral, the wicked of the world; the three ladies, Pride, Covetousness and Luxury [lechery]; the two old men, the end of the world, and the Last Judgement.

This sight took such impression in me, that when I came towards man's estate it was as fresh in my memory as if I had seen it newly acted. From whence I observe out of mine own experience, what great care should be had in the education of children, to keep them from seeing spectacles of ill examples . . . And withal we may observe, how far unlike the plays and harmless morals of former times are to those which have succeeded; many of which (by report of others) may be termed schoolmaster of vice, and provocations to corruptions.

R. Willis, *Mount Tabor* (1639)

MOCK MAYGAMES

[SATIRISTS AGAINST BISHOPS – 'MARTIN MARPRELATES' –
COMPARED TO AN OLD ROBIN HOOD PLAY]

How whorishly Scriptures are alleged by them, I will discover (by God's help) in another new work which I have in hand, and entitled it, *The May-game of Martinism*, very deftly set out with pomps, pageants, motions, masques, scutcheons [decorated shields], emblems, impreses [allegorical pictures], strange tricks and devices, between the ape and the owl, the like was never yet seen in Paris Garden [where plays were sometimes performed]. Penry the Welshman is the foregallant [leader] of the morris, with the treble bells, shot through the wit with a woodcock's [gamebird's, simpleton's] bill. I would not, for the fairest horn-beast [goat, cuckold] in all his country that the Church of England were a cup of metheglin [Welsh mead] and came in his way when he is overheated; every bishopric would prove but a draught, when the mazer [bowl] is at his nose. Martin himself is the Maid Marian, trimly dressed up in a cast gown and a kerchief of Dame Lawson's, his face handsomely muffled up with a diaper napkin to cover his beard, and a great nosegay in his hand, of the principalest flowers I could gather out of all his works. Wiggenton dances round about him in a cotton coat, to court him with a leather pudding and a wooden ladle. Paget marshalleth the way with a couple of great clubs, one in his foot, another in his head, and he cries to the people with a loud voice, 'Beware of the man whom God hath marked!'. I cannot yet find any so fit to come lagging behind, with a budget [bag] on his neck, to gather the devotion of the lookers-on, as the stock-keeper of the Bridewell-house [house of correction] of Canterbury; he must carry the purse, to defray their charges, and then he may be sure to serve himself.

[It was probably performed at The Theatre in May, 1589]

Anon., *The Returne of the renowned Cavaliero Pasquill of England* (1589)

ARTS AND PLEASURES

PLEASURES

Without the city are some theatres, where English actors represent almost every day comedies and tragedies to very numerous audiences; these are concluded with variety of dances, accompanied by excellent music and the excessive applause of those that are present. . . .

There is still another place, built in the form of a theatre, which serves for the baiting of bears and bulls. They are fastened behind, and then worried by those great English dogs and mastiffs, but not without great risk to the dogs from the teeth of the one and the horns of the other; and it sometimes happens they are killed upon the spot. Fresh ones are immediately supplied in the places of those that are wounded or tired. To this entertainment there often follows that of whipping a blinded bear, which is performed by five or six men, standing in a circle with whips, which they exercise upon him without any mercy. Although he cannot escape from them because of his chain, he nevertheless defends himself, vigorously throwing down all who come within his reach and are not active enough to get out of it, and tearing the whips out of their hands and breaking them. At these spectacles and everywhere else, the English are constantly smoking the nicotian weed which in America is called Tobacco (others call it Paetum) and generally in this manner: they have pipes of purpose made of clay, into the farther end of which they put the herb, so dry that it may be rubbed into powder, and, lighting it, they draw the smoke into their mouths, which they puff out again through their nostrils, like funnels, along with it plenty of phlegm and defluxion from the head. In these theatres, fruits, such as apples, pears and nuts, according to the season, are carried about to be sold, as well as wine and ale.

Paul Hentzner, *Travels in England* (1598; pub. 1757)

IN PUBLIUM

Publius, student at the common law,
Oft leaves his books, and for his recreation,
To Paris Garden doth himself withdraw;
Where he is ravished with such delectation,
As down among the dogs and bears he goes,

Where whilst he skipping cries, 'To head, to head,'
His satin doublet and his velvet hose
Are all with spittle from above bespread.
Then is he like his father's country hall,
Stinking with dogs, and muted all with hawks.   [dunged]
Which for such filthy sports his books forsakes,
And rightly too on him this filth doth fall,
Leaving old Plowden, Dyer and Brooke alone,   [law books]
To see old Harry Hunks and Sackerson.   [a famous
bear, and dog]

Sir John Davies, *Epigrams and Elegies* (1590)

A PURITAN VIEW OF THE THEATRE

In our assemblies at plays in London, you shall see such heaving and
shoving, such itching and shouldering, to sit by women; such care for
their garments that they be not trod on; such eyes to their laps, that
no chips light in them; such pillows to their backs, that they take no
hurt; such masking in their ears, I know not what; such playing at
foot saunt [cent-foot, a card game] without cards; such tick[l]ing, such
toying, such smiling, such winking and such manning them home
when the sports are ended, that it is a right comedy to mark their
behaviour, to watch their conceits, as the cat for the mouse, and as
good as a course at the game itself, to dog them a little, or follow
aloof by the print of their feet, and so discover by slot [track] where
the deer taketh soil [refuge]. If this were as well noted as ill seen, or
openly punished as secretly practised, I have no doubt but the cause
would be feared to dry up the effect, and these pretty rabbits very
cunningly ferreted from their burrows. For they that lack customers
all the week, either because their haunt is unknown, or the constables
and officers of their parish watch them so narrowly that they dare not
queatch [move], to celebrate the Sabbath, flock to theatres, and there
keep a general market of bawdry. Not that any filthiness indeed is
committed within the compass of that ground, as was done in Rome,
but that every wanton and his paramour, every man and his mistress,

every John and his Joan, every knave and his quean, are there first acquainted, and cheapen the merchandise [bargain] in that place, which they pay for elsewhere as they can agree.

Stephen Gosson, The Schoole of Abuse (1579)

REVEL

'Speak, gentlemen, what shall we do today?
Drink some brave health upon the Dutch carouse?
Or shall we go to the Globe and see a play?
Or visit Shoreditch, for a bawdy house?
Let's call for cards or dice, and have a game,
To sit thus idle is both sin and shame.'

This speaks Sir Revel, furnished out with fashion,
From dish-crowned hat unto th'shoes' square toe,
That haunts a whorehouse but for recreation,
Plays but at dice to coney-catch, or so;   [to trick the gullible]
Drinks drunk in kindness, for good fellowship,
Or to the play goes but some purse to nip.

Samuel Rowlands, *The Letting of Humours Blood in the Head-Vaine* (1600)

AT HAND, QUOTH PICK-PURSE

A tradesman's wife of the Exchange, one day when her husband was following some business in the City, desired him he would give her leave to go see a play, which she had not done in seven years. He bade her take his apprentice along with her, and go; but especially to have a care of her purse; which she warranted him she would. Sitting in a box amongst some gallants and gallant wenches, and returning when the play was done, returned to her husband and told him she had lost her purse.

'Wife,' quoth he, 'did I not give you warning of it? How much money was there in it?'

Quoth she, 'Truly, four [gold] pieces, six shillings and a silver tooth-picker.'

'Quoth her husband, 'Where did you put it?'

'Under my petticoat, between that and my smock.'

'What,' quoth he, 'did you feel nobody's hand there?'

'Yes,' quoth she, 'I felt one's hand there, but I did not think he had come for that.'

Henry Peacham, *The Compleat Gentleman* (1634)

ADVICE FOR THE FASHIONABLE THEATREGOER

Present not yourself on the stage, especially at a new play, until the quaking prologue hath, by rubbing, got colour in his cheeks, and is ready to give the trumpets their cue that he's upon point to enter: for then is the time, as though you were one of the properties, or that you dropped out of the hangings, to creep from behind the arras [back-cloth curtain], with your tripos or three-footed stool in one hand, and a teston [sixpence] mounted between a forefinger and a thumb in the other. For if you should bestow your person upon the vulgar when the belly of the house is but half full, your apparel is quite eaten up, the fashion lost, and the proportion of your body in more danger to be devoured than if it were served up in the counter amongst the poultry; avoid that as you would the baston [cudgel].

It shall crown you with rich commendation to laugh aloud in the midst of the most serious and saddest scene of the terriblest tragedy, and to let that clapper, your tongue, be tossed so high that all the house may ring of it. Your lords use it; your knights are apes to the lords, and do so too; your Inns of Court man is zany [mimic or servant] to the knights, and (marry, very scurvy) comes likewise limping after it: be thou a beagle to them all, and never lin [stop] snuffing till you have scented them. For, by talking and laughing (like a ploughman in a morris) you heap Pelion upon Ossa, glory upon glory. As first, all the eyes in the galleries will leave walking after the players, and only follow you; the simplest dolt in the house snatches up your name, and when he meets you in the streets, or that you fall into his hands in the middle of a watch, his word shall be taken for you, he'll cry, 'He's such a gallant!', and you pass. Secondly, you publish your temperance to the world, in that you seem not to resort thither to taste vain pleasures with a hungry appetite, but only as a gentleman, to spend a foolish hour or two, because you can do nothing else. Thirdly, you mightily disrelish the audience and disgrace the author: marry, you take up (though it be at the worst hand) a strong opinion of your own judgement, and enforce the poet to take pity of your weakness, and, by some dedicated sonnet, to bring you into a better paradise, only to stop your mouth.

Now sir, if the writer be a fellow that hath either epigrammed you, or hath had a flirt at your mistress, or hath brought either your feather or your red beard, or your little legs, etc. on the stage, you shall disgrace him worse than by tossing him in a blanket, or giving him the bastinado [cudgelling] in a tavern, if in the middle of his play, be it pastoral or comedy, moral or tragedy, you rise with a screwed and discontented face from your stool to be gone. No matter whether the scenes be good or no, the better they are the worse do you distaste them; and, being on your feet, sneak not away like a coward, but salute all your gentle acquaintance, that are spread either on the rushes or on stools about you, and draw what troop you can from the stage after you. The mimics are beholden to you, for allowing them elbow room, their poet cries, perhaps, 'A pox go with you!', but care not for that, there's no music without frets.

Marry, if either the company, or indisposition of the weather, bind you to sit it out, my counsel is then that you turn plain ape, take up a rush, and tickle the earnest ears of your fellow gallants, to make other fools fall a-laughing; mew at passionate speeches, blare at merry, find fault with the music, whew at the children's action, whistle at the songs; and, above all, curse the sharers, that whereas the same day you had bestowed forty shillings on an embroidered felt and feather (Scotch fashion) for your mistress in the Court, or your punk [whore] in the City, within two hours after, you encounter with the very same block [mould of hat] on the stage, when the haberdasher swore to you the impression was extant but that morning.

Thomas Dekker, *The Gulls Horn-Booke* (1609)

ABSURDITY AND DELIGHT

Our tragedies and comedies (not without cause cried out against), observing rules neither of honest civility nor of skilful poetry, excepting *Gorboduc* [Norton and Sackville, 1561] (again, I say, of those that I have seen), which, notwithstanding as it is full of stately speeches and well-sounding phrases, climbing to the height of Seneca his style, and as full of notable morality, which it doth most delightfully teach, and so obtain the very end of poesy, yet in troth it is very defectious in the circumstances; which grieveth me, because it might not remain as an exact model of all tragedies. For it is faulty both in place and time, the two necessary companions of all corporeal actions. For where the stage should always represent but one place, and the uttermost time presupposed in it should be, both by Aristotle's precept and common reason, but one day, there is both many days and many places inartificially [unskilfully] imagined. But if it be so in *Gorboduc*, how much more in all the rest? Where you shall have Asia of the one side and Afric of the other, and so many other under-kingdoms, that the player, when he cometh in, must ever begin with telling where he is, or else the tale will not be conceived. Now ye shall have three ladies walk to gather flowers, and then we must believe the stage to be a garden; by and by, we hear news of shipwreck in the same place, and then we are to blame if we accept it not for a rock.

Upon the back of that, comes out a hideous monster with fire and smoke, and then the miserable beholders are bound to take it for a cave; while in the meantime two armies fly in, represented with four swords and bucklers, and then what hard heart will not receive it for a pitched field? Now of time they are much more liberal, for ordinary it is that two young princes fall in love. After many traverses, she is got with child, delivered of a fair boy, he is lost, groweth a man, falls in love, and is ready to get another child, and all this in two hours' space; which how absurd it is in sense, even sense may imagine, and art hath taught, and all ancient examples justified, and at this day the ordinary players in Italy will not err in. . . .

But besides these gross absurdities, how all their plays be neither right tragedies nor right comedies, mingling kings and clowns, not because the matter so carrieth it, but thrust in clowns by head and shoulders, to play a part in majestical matters, with neither decency nor discretion, so as neither the admiration nor commiseration nor the right sportfulness is by their mongrel tragi-comedy obtained. . . . [W]here the whole tract of a comedy should be full of delight, as the tragedy should be still maintained in a well-raised admiration. But our comedians think there is no delight without laughter, which is very wrong, for though laughter may come with delight, yet cometh it not of delight, as though delight should be the cause of laughter; but well may one thing breed both together, nay rather in themselves they have as it were a kind of contrariety. For delight we scarcely do but in things that have a conveniency to ourselves or to the general nature. Laughter almost ever cometh of things most disproportioned to ourselves and nature. Delight hath a joy in it, either permanent or present. Laughter hath only a scornful tickling.

Sir Philip Sidney, An Apologie for Poetry (1595)

Dancing As Concord

It is diligently to be noted that the associating of man and woman in dancing, they both observing one number and time in their movings, was not begun without a special consideration, as well for the necessary conjunction of those two persons as for the intimation of sundry virtues which be by them represented. And forasmuch as by the association of a man and woman in dancing may be signified matrimony, I could in declaring the dignity and commodity of that sacrament make entire volumes, if it were not so commonly known to all men, that every friar limitour [licensed to beg] carrieth it written in his bosom. . . .

But now to my purpose. In every dance, of a most ancient custom, there danceth together a man and a woman, holding each other by the hand or the arm, which betokeneth concord. Now it behoveth the dancers and also the beholders of them to know all qualities incident to a man, and also all qualities to a woman likewise appertaining.

A man in his natural perfection is fierce, hardy, strong in opinion, covetous of glory, desirous of knowledge, appetiting by generation to bring forth his semblable [reproduce himself]. The good nature of a woman is to be mild, timorous, tractable, benign, of sure remembrance, and shamefast. Divers other qualities of each of them might be found out, but these be most apparent, and for this time sufficient.

Wherefore, when we behold a man and woman dancing together, let us suppose there to be a concord of all the said qualities, being joined together as I have set them in order. And the moving of the man would be more vehement, of the woman more delicate and with less advancing of the body, signifying the courage and strength that ought to be in a man and the pleasant soberness that should be in a woman. And in this wise [manner], fierceness joined with mildness maketh severity; audacity with timorosity maketh magnanimity; wilful opinion and tractability (which is to be shortly persuaded and moved) maketh constancy a virtue; covetousness of glory adorned with benignity causeth honour; desire of knowledge with sure remembrance procureth sapience; shamefastness joined to appetite of generation maketh continence, which is a mean between chastity and inordinate lust. These qualities in this wise being knit together, and signified in the personages of man and woman dancing, to express or set out the figure of very [true] nobility; which in the higher state it is contained, the more excellent is the virtue in estimation.

Sir Thomas Elyot, *The Boke named the Gouernour* (1531)

A NEW DANCE, AND THE OLD

Duchess Aurelia.	We will dance. Music! We will dance.
Courtier Guernino.	*Les Guerino*, Lady, *Pensez bien, Passa regis*, or Beancha's brawl? [Names of dances]
Aurelia.	We have forgot the brawl.
Courtier Ferrardo.	So soon? 'Tis wonder.
Guernino.	Why, 'tis but two singles on the left, two on the right, three doubles forward, a traverse of six round; do this twice, three singles side, galliard trick of twenty, coranto pace; a figure of eight, three singles broken down, come up, meet two doubles, fall back, and then honour [bow or curtsy].
Aurelia.	O Daedalus, thy maze, I have quite forgot it!
Maquerelle [Court bawd].	Trust me, so have I, saving the falling back, and then honour [on her].

John Marston, *The Malcontent* (1604)

YOUR MERRY HEART GOES ALL THE WAY

[The comedian Will Kemp morris-danced from London to Norwich in nine (non-consecutive) days, in 1599]

In this town of Sudbury, there came a tall lusty fellow, a butcher by his profession, that would in a morris keep me company to Bury. I, being glad of his friendly offer, gave him thanks, and forward we did set; but ere ever we had measured half a mile of our way, he gave me over in the plain field, protesting that if he might get hundred pound he would not hold out with me; for indeed my pace of dancing is not ordinary.

As he and I were parting, a lusty country lass being among the people called him faint-hearted lout, saying,

'If I had begun to dance, I would have held out one mile though it had cost my life.'

At which words many laughed.

'Nay,' saith she, 'if the dancer will lend me a leash of his bells, I'll venture to tread one mile with him myself.'

I looked upon her, saw mirth in her eyes, heard boldness in her words, and beheld her ready to truss up her russet petticoat. I fitted her with bells, which she, merrily taking, garnished her thick short legs, and with a smooth brow bade the taborer begin. The drum struck, forward marched I with my merry Maid Marian, who shook her fat sides and footed it merrily to Melford, being a long mile. There parting with her, I gave her (besides her skinful of drink) an English crown to buy more drink, for, good wench, she was in a piteous heat. My kindness she requited with dropping some dozen of short curtseys, and, bidding God bless the dancer, I bade her adieu; and to give her her due, she had a good ear, danced truly, and we parted friendly.

Will Kemp, *Nine Days Wonder* (1600)

GAMES AND SPORTS

Man, I dare challenge thee to throw the sledge,   [hammer]
To jump or leap over a ditch or hedge,
To wrestle, play at stoolball, or to run,   [like rounders or baseball]
To pitch the bar, or to shoot off a gun,
To play at loggets [throwing sticks at a staff], nineholes or tenpins,
At ticktack [like backgammon], Irish, noddy, maw and ruff,   [card
At hotcockles [blindfold guessing], leapfrog, or blindman-buff; games]
To play at base [prisoner's base], or pen-and-inkhorn Sir John,
To dance the morris, play at barley-break;   [where couples play catch]
At all exploits a man can think or speak:
At shove-groat, venter point or cross and pile,   [tossing coins]

At 'Beshrew him that's last at yonder stile',
At leaping o'er a Midsummer bonfire,
Or at the drawing Dunne [a log] out of the mire;
At any of these, or all these presently,
Wag but your finger, I am for you, I . . .

Samuel Rowlands, *The Letting of Humours Blood in the Head-Vaine* (1600)

SELLING BALLADS AT A COUNTRY FAIR

Clown [yokel]. What hast here? Ballads?

Mopsa [country girl]. Pray now, buy some. I love a ballad in print a-life, for then we are sure they are true.

Autolycus [pedlar]. Here's one to a very doleful tune: how a usurer's wife was brought to bed of twenty money-bags at a burden, and how she longed to eat adders' heads and toads carbonadoed.

Mopsa. Is it true, think you?

Autolycus. Very true, and but a month old.

Dorcas [country girl]. Bless me from marrying a usurer!

Autolycus. Here's the midwife's tale to't, one Mistress Taleporter, and five or six honest wives that were present. Why should I carry lies abroad?

Mopsa. Pray you now, buy it.

Clown. Come on, lay it by; and let's first see mo[r]e ballads; we'll buy the other things anon.

Autolycus. Here's another ballad, of a fish that appeared upon the coast on Wednesday the fourscore of April, forty thousand fathom above water, and sung this ballad against the hard hearts of maids. It was thought she was a woman, and was turned into a cold fish for she would not exchange flesh with one that loved her. The ballad is pitiful, and as true.

Dorcas. Is it true too, think you?

Autolycus. Five justices' hands at it; and witnesses more than my pack will hold.

Clown. Lay it by too. Another.

Autolycus.	This is a merry ballad, but a very pretty one.
Mopsa.	Let's have some merry ones.
Autolycus.	Why, this is a passing merry one, and goes to the tune of 'Two maids wooing a man'. There's scarce a maid westward but she sings it; 'tis in request, I can tell you.
Mopsa.	We can both sing it. If thou'lt bear a part, thou shalt hear; 'tis in three parts.
Autolycus.	I can bare my part; you know 'tis my occupation. Have at it with you.

Shakespeare, *The Winter's Tale* (1611)

POPULAR MUSICS

Those small and popular musics sung by *Cantabanqui* [ballad-singers] upon benches and barrels' heads, where they have none other audience than boys or country fellows that pass them by in the street, or else by blind harpers or suchlike tavern minstrels that give a fit of mirth for a groat, and their matters being for the most part stores of old time, as the *Tale of Sir Topas*, the reports of *Bevis of Southampton, Guy of Warwick*, and *Clymme of the Clough* and such other old romances or historical rhymes, made purposely for recreation of the common people at Christmas dinners and bride-ales, and in taverns and alehouses and such other places of base resort, also . . . be used in carols and rounds and such light or lascivious poems, which are more commodiously uttered by these buffoons or vices in plays than by any other person.

George Puttenham, *The Arte of English Poesie* (1589)

BOWLING

A bowl-alley is the place where there are three things thrown away besides bowls, to wit, time, money and curses, and the last, ten for one. The best sport in it is the gambler's, and he enjoys it that looks on and bets not. It is the school of wrangling, and worse than the schools, for men will cavil here for an hair's breadth, and make a stir where a straw would end the controversy. No antic [clown] screws men's bodies into such strange flexures, and you think them here senseless to speak sense to their bowl, and put their trust in entreaties for a good cast. The betters are the factious noise in the alley, or the gamesters' beadsmen that pray for them. They are somewhat like those that are cheated by great men, for they lose their money and must say nothing. It is the best discovery of humours, especially in the losers, where you have fine variety of impatience, whilst some fret, some rail, some swear and others more ridiculously comfort themselves with philosophy. To give you the moral of it: it is the emblem of the world, or the world's ambition, where most are short, or over, or wide, or wrong-biased, and some few jostle in to the Mistress Fortune. And it is here as in the Court, where the nearest are most spited, and all blows aimed at the 'toucher'.

John Earle, *Micro-cosmographie* (1628)

THE BEAUTIFUL GAME

Oswald.   I'll not be strucken, my lord.
Kent.   Nor tripped neither, you base football player.

Shakespeare, *King Lear* (1606)

As concerning football playing, I protest unto you, it may rather be called a friendly kind of fight than a play or recreation, a bloody and murdering practice than a fellowly sport or pastime.

For doth not everyone lie in wait for his adversary, seeking to overthrow him and to pick [pitch] him on his nose, though it be upon hard stones, in ditch or dale, in valley or hill or what place soever it be, he careth not so he have him down. And he that can serve the most of this fashion, he is counted the only fellow, and who but he? So that by this means, sometimes their necks are broken, sometimes their backs, sometimes their legs, sometimes their arms, sometimes one part thrust out of joint, sometimes another, sometimes the noses gush out with blood, sometimes their eyes start out; and sometimes hurt in one place sometimes in another. But whatsoever 'scapeth away, the best goeth not scot free, but is either sore wounded, crazed and bruised, so as he dieth of it, or else 'scapeth very hardly; and no marvel, for they have the sleights to meet one betwixt two, to dash him against the heart with their elbows, to hit him under the short ribs with their griped [clenched] fists, and with their knees to catch him upon the hip and to pick him on his neck, with a hundred such murdering devices. And hereof groweth envy, malice, rancour, choler, hatred, displeasure, enmity and what not else; and sometimes fighting, brawling, contention, quarrel picking, murder, homicide and great effusion of blood, as experience daily teacheth.

Philip Stubbes, *The Anatomy of Abuses* (1583)

CARNIVAL

But now stand off, my friends, give room I say, for here must enter that waddling, straddling, bursten-gutted carnifex [butcher] of all Christendom, vulgarly entitled Shrove-Tuesday, but more pertinently, sole Monarch of the Mouth, High Steward to the Stomach, chief Ganymede to the Guts, prime Peer of the Pullets, first Favourite of the Frying-pans, greatest Bashaw to the Batter-bowls, Protector of the Pancakes, first Founder of the Fritters, Baron of Bacon Flitch, Earl of Egg-baskets, and, in the least and last place, Lower Warden of the Stink Ports.

Anon., *Vox Graculi, or Jack Dawes Prognostication* (1622)

THE VIRTUES OF SHERRY SACK

Falstaff. There's never none of these demure boys come to any proof; for thin drink doth so over-cool their blood, and making many fish-meals, that they fall into a kind of male green-sickness; and then, when they marry, they get wenches. They are generally fools and cowards, which some of us should be, too, but for inflammation. A good sherris-sack hath a twofold operation in it. It ascends me into the brain; dries me there all the foolish and dull and cruddy [curdled] vapours which environ it; makes it apprehensive, forgetive [creative], full of nimble, fiery and delectable shapes; which, delivered o'er to the voice, the tongue, which is the birth, becomes excellent wit. The second property of your excellent sherris is the warming of the blood; which before, cold and settled, left the liver white and pale, which is the badge of pusillanimity and cowardice; but the sherris warms it, and makes it course from the inwards to the parts' extremes. It illumineth the face, which, as a beacon, gives warning to all the rest of this little kingdom, man, to arm; and then the vital commoners and inland petty spirits muster me all to their captain, the heart, who, great and puffed up with this retinue, doth any deed of courage: and this valour comes of sherris. So that skill in the weapon is nothing without sack, for that sets it a-work; and learning, a mere hoard of gold kept by a devil till sack commences it and sets it in act and use. Hereof comes it that Prince Harry is valiant: for the cold blood he did naturally inherit of his father, he hath, like lean, sterile and bare land, manured, husbanded and tilled, with excellent endeavour of drinking good and good store of fertile sherris, that he is become very hot and valiant. If I had a thousand sons, the first humane principle I would teach them should be to forswear thin potations, and to addict themselves to sack.

Shakespeare, *Henry IV, Part II* (1598)

DRUNKARDS

Nor have we one or two kind of drunkards only, but eight kinds. The first is ape drunk, and he leaps and hollers and danceth for the heavens. The second is lion drunk, and he flings the pots about the house, calls his hostess whore, breaks the glass windows with his dagger, and is apt to quarrel with any man that speaks to him. The third is swine drunk, heavy, lumpish and sleepy, and cries for a little more drink and a few more clothes. The fourth is sheep drunk, wise in his own conceit when he cannot bring forth a right word. The fifth is maudlin drunk, when a fellow will weep for kindness in the midst of his ale, and kiss you, saying, 'By God, Captain, I love thee; go thy ways, thou dost not think so often of me as I do of thee. I would, if it pleased God, I could not love thee so well as I do,' and then he puts his finger in his eye and cries. The sixth is martin drunk, when a man is drunk and drinks himself sober ere he stir. The seventh is goat drunk, when in his drunkenness he hath no mind but on lechery. The eighth is fox drunk, when he is crafty drunk, as many of the Dutchmen be, that will never bargain but when they be drunk. All these species and more I have seen practiced in one company at one sitting, when I have been permitted to remain sober amongst them, only to note their several humours. He that plies any one of them hard, it will make him to write admirable verses and to have a deep-casting mind, though he were never so very a dunce before.

Gentlemen, all you that will not have your brains twice sodden, your flesh rotten with the dropsy, that love not to go in greasy doublets, stockings out at the heels, and wear alehouse daggers at your backs, forswear this slavering bravery that will make you have stinking breaths and your bodies smell like brewers' aprons. Rather keep a snuff [small drop] in the bottom of the glass to light you to bed withal than leave never an eye in your head to lead you over the threshold. It will bring you in your old age to be companions with none but porters and carmen, to talk out of a cage, railing as drunken men are wont, a hundred boys wondering about them; and to die suddenly, as Fol Long the fencer did, drinking aqua vitae.

Thomas Nashe, *Pierce Penniless his Supplication to the Devil* (1592)

TOBACCO

And for the vanities committed in this filthy custom, is it not both great vanity and uncleanness, that at the table, a place of respect, of cleanliness, of modesty, men should not be ashamed to sit tossing of tobacco pipes, and puffing of the smoke of tobacco one to another, making the filthy smoke and stink thereof to exhale athwart the dishes, and infect the air, when very often men that abhor it are at their repast? Surely smoke becomes a kitchen far better than a dining chamber, and yet it makes a kitchen also oftentimes in the inward parts of men, soiling and infecting them, with an unctuous and oily kind of soot, as hath been found in some great tobacco takers, that after their death were opened. And not only meat time, but no other time or action is exempted from the public use of this uncivil trick: so as if the wives of Dieppe were to list contest with this nation for good manners, their worst manners would in all reason be found at least not so dishonest as ours are in this point. The public use whereof, at all times and in all places, hath now so far prevailed, as divers men very sound both in judgement and complexion [temperament] have been at last forced to take it also, without desire, partly because they were ashamed to seem singular. . . . And is it not a great vanity, that a man cannot heartily welcome his friend now, but straight they must be in hand with tobacco? No, it is become in place of a cure, a point of good fellowship, and he that will refuse to take a pipe of tobacco among his fellows (though by his own election he would rather feel the savour of a sink [sewer]) is accounted peevish and no good company, even as they do with tippling in the cold eastern countries. Yea, the mistress cannnot in a more mannerly kind entertain her servant than by giving him out of her fair hand a pipe of tobacco. But herein is not only a great vanity, but a great contempt of God's good gifts, that the sweetness of man's breath, being a good gift of God, should be wilfully corrupted by this stinking smoke, wherein I must confess it hath too strong a virtue, and so that which is an ornament of nature, and can neither by an artifice be at the first acquired, nor, once lost, be recovered again, shall be filthily corrupted with an incurable stink, which vile quality is as directly contrary to that wrong opinion which is holden of the wholesomeness thereof, as the venom of putrefaction is contrary to the virtue preservative.

Moreover, which is a great iniquity, and against all humanity, the husband shall not be ashamed to reduce thereby his delicate, wholesome and clean complexioned wife to that extremity, that either she must also corrupt her sweet breath therewith, or else resolute to live in a perpetual stinking torment.

Have you not reason then to be ashamed, and to forbear this filthy novelty, so basely grounded, so foolishly received and so grossly mistaken in the right use thereof? In your abuse thereof sinning against God, harming yourselves both in persons and goods, and taking also thereby the marks and notes of vanity upon you; by the custom thereof making yourselves to be wondered at by all foreign civil nations, and by all strangers that come amongst you, to be scorned and contemned [despised]. A custom loathsome to the eye, hateful to the nose, harmful to the brain, dangerous to the lungs, and in the black stinking fume thereof nearest resembling the horrible stygian smoke of the pit that is bottomless.

King James VI and I, *A Counterblaste to Tobacco* (1604)

10

POVERTY, CRIME AND PUNISHMENT

Perhaps 2 per cent of the population controlled most of the nation's land and wealth, some with incomes ranging up to over £50,000 a year; yeomen had incomes of £100 to £50 a year; a schoolmaster might get £16 a year, a labourer a shilling (£¹/₂₀th) a day; there were plenty who received less than that. Poverty was increasingly widespread: in the country, small husbandmen and farmworkers were broken by enclosures, higher rents and the decline in real wages; in the town, industrial changes, export problems, immigrant workers and disease increased the difficulties. Bad harvests produced malnutrition; there were riots (demonstrations) against deprivation of commonland rights, or lack of affordable food (as in *Coriolanus*); the poor suffered disproportionately from rickets, scurvy, influenza, tuberculosis, typhus and smallpox. Generally, 4 to 5 per cent of the population obtained poor relief, but in crisis times this proportion could reach 20 per cent locally.

Three groups of poor were generally recognized. The 'impotent' (widows, orphans, the sick) were traditional recipients of charity. The labouring, able-bodied poor, in worryingly increasing numbers, were those willing but unable to support themselves: the lowest wages might not sustain an average family, so women worked (in the cloth business, or in domestic or farm labouring), as did children from the age of seven; they might be put to work in houses of correction, or given a dole, or moved on. Then there were 'the idle', 'rogues and vagabonds', dramatized and feared as carriers of disease and threats to good order, to be flogged and driven off. Most wanderers were actually seeking work, whether seasonal or permanent; some were runaway apprentices or soldiers returning from impressment in Ireland or the Netherlands, or pedlars or beggars (as in *King Lear*).

215

Partly in the interests of social stability and political security, the state increasingly recognized responsibility for the nation's poor (the Poor Law was passed in 1601), arranging for grain supplies in times of dearth, establishing poor rates on a parochial basis, the compulsory apprenticeship of poor children, and houses of correction, with attempts to find work for the deserving poor. Riots and vagrancy were severely punished.

There was much — largely unfounded — fear of crime and disorder, as increasing economic strains, deprivation and the breakdown in traditional 'good-neighbourliness' and custom produced greater social stress, with petty crime, intolerance and violence. The turn of the century marked a peak in bastardy and infanticide, as poverty and worklessness prevented many poor people's intended marriages. The most frequent offences included poaching, housebreaking, horse-thieving, petty theft, highway robbery; women were charged with petty theft, scolding, witchcraft and prostitution. Despite enjoyably shocking stories of beggar gangs, cutpurses and prostitutes, there was little evidence of organized crime outside London.

Nationally, most legal administration was conducted at the county Quarter Sessions and Assizes, while Church courts dealt with religious matters, sexual irregularity, drunkenness and misconduct. Punishment for offences under the degree of felony included flogging, fining and stocking, while felony led to death, and forfeiture of property (which could be retained for one's family by refusing to plead and being crushed to death — 'peine forte et dure'). There were over 1,000 hangings in England and Wales annually. Those who could read the 'neck verse' (Psalm 50, v. 1) could plead 'benefit of clergy' and, like Ben Jonson (charged with manslaughter), be branded rather than hanged.

> In London and within a mile, I ween,
> There are of jails and prisons full eighteen,
> And sixty whipping-posts, and stocks and cages,
> Where sin with shame and sorrow hath due wages,

wrote John Taylor (*The Praise and Vertue of a Jayle and Jaylers*, 1623). Prison generally was considered no great disgrace; the population varied widely – political prisoners in the Tower, debtors in Ludgate or the Counters, religious and maritime offenders in the Marshalsea, petty local peacebreakers in the Clink, whores and vagabonds in Bridewell. The prisons were run for the gaolers' profit; well-off prisoners could have private rooms, meals sent up, wives (and others) to visit, and even have leave; others shared beds and messrooms; the impoverished slept promiscuously on the floor and fed on scraps from the alms basket, gathered at the gates of the charitable rich.

THE POOR

There is no commonwealth at this day in Europe wherein there is not great store of poor people, and those necessarily to be relieved by the wealthier sort, which otherwise would starve and come to utter confusion. With us, the poor is commonly divided into three sorts, so that some are poor by impotency, as the fatherless child, the aged, blind and lame, and the diseased person that is judged incurable; the second are poor by casualty, as the wounded soldier, the decayed householder and the sick person visited with grievous and painful diseases; the third consisteth of thriftless poor, as the rioter that hath consumed all, the vagabond that will abide nowhere but runneth up and down the place (as it were seeking work and finding none), and finally the rogue and strumpet, which are not possible to be divided in sunder, but run to and fro over all the realm, chiefly keeping the champion soils in summer, to avoid the scorching heat, and the woodland grounds in winter, to eschew the blustering winds.

For the first two sorts, that is to say, the poor by impotency and the poor by casualty, which are the true poor indeed, and for whom the Word doth bind us to make some daily provision, there is order taken throughout every parish in the realm that weekly collection shall be made for their help and sustentation, to the end they should not scatter abroad and by begging here and there annoy both town and country. . . . But if they refuse to be supported by this benefit of the law and will rather endeavour, by going to and fro, to maintain their idle trades, then are they adjudged to be parcel of the third sort, and so, instead of courteous refreshing at home, are often corrected with sharp execution and whip of justice abroad. . . .

Idle beggars are such, either through other men's occasion, or through their own default. By other men's occasion (as one way, for example), when some covetous man espying a further commodity [opportunity] in their commons, holds and tenures, doth find such means as thereby to wipe many out of their occupyings and turn the same unto his private gains. Hereupon it followeth, that although the wise and better minded do either forsake the realm for altogether, and seek to live in other countries, as France, Germany, Barbary [North Africa], India, Moscovia [Russia] and very Calicut [southern India], complaining of no room to be left for them at home, [or] do so behave themselves that they are worthily to be accounted among the second sort; yet the greater part, commonly having nothing to stay upon, are wilful, and thereupon do either prove idle beggars or else continue stark thieves till the gallows do eat them up. . . .

Such as are idle beggars through their own default are of two sorts, and continue their estates either by casual or more voluntary means; those that are such by casual means are in the beginning justly to be referred either to the first or second sort of poor aforementioned. . . . The voluntary means proceed from outward causes, as by making of corrosives and applying the same to the more fleshy parts of their bodies; and also laying of ratsbane, spearwort, crowfoot and suchlike unto their whole members, thereby to raise pitiful and odious sores, and move the hearts of goers-by such places where they lie, to yearn [lament] at their misery, and thereupon bestow large alms upon them. How artificially they beg, what forcible speech, and how they select and choose out words of vehemency, whereby they do in manner conjure or adjure the goer-by to pity their cases, I pass over to remember . . .

Unto this nest is another sort to be referred, more sturdy than the rest, which, having sound and perfect limbs, do yet notwithstanding sometimes counterfeit the possession of all sorts of diseases. Divers times in their apparel also they will be like serving-men or labourers; oftentimes they can play the mariners, and seek for ships which they never lost. But in fine, they are all thieves and caterpillars in the commonwealth, and by the Word of God not permitted to eat, sith they do but lick the sweat from the true labourers' brows, and bereave the godly poor of that which is due unto them, to maintain their excess, consuming the charity of well-disposed people bestowed upon them after a most wicked and detestable manner.

William Harrison, *Description of England* (1587)

ROGUES AND VAGABONDS: A GUIDE

AN ABRAHAM MAN

An abraham man is he that walketh bare-armed and bare-legged, and feigneth himself mad, and carrieth a pack of wool, or a stick with bacon on it, or suchlike toy, and nameth himself Poor Tom [as in *King Lear*].

A RUFFLER

A ruffler goeth with a weapon to seek service, saying he hath been a servitor in the wars, and beggeth for his relief. But his chiefest trade is to rob poor wayfaring men and market-women.

A PRIGMAN

A prigman goeth with a stick in his hand like an idle person. His property is to steal clothes off the hedge [laundry airing], which they call storing of the rogueman [see Autolycus in *The Winter's Tale*]; or else filch poultry, carrying them to the alehouse, which they call the boozing inn, and there sit playing at cards and dice, till that is spent which they have so filched.

AN UPRIGHT MAN

An upright man is one that goeth with the truncheon of a staff, which staff they call a filchman. This man is of so much authority that, meeting with any of his profession, he may call them to account and command a share or snap unto himself of all that they have gained by their trade in one month. And if he do them wrong, they have no remedy against him, no, though he beat them, as he useth commonly to do. He may also command any of their women, which they call doxies, to serve his turn. He hath the chief place at any market walk and other assemblies, and is not of any to be controlled.

A CURTAL

A curtal is much like to the upright man, but his authority is not fully so great. He useth commonly to go with a short cloak, like to grey friars, and his women with him in like livery, which he calleth his altham, if she be his wife, and if she be his harlot, she is called his doxy.

A JACKMAN

A jackman is he that can write and read, and sometime speak Latin. He useth to make counterfeit licences which they call gybes, and sets to seals, in their language called jarks.

A KITCHIN MORTS

A kitchin morts is a girl; she is brought at her full age to the upright man to be broken, and so she is called a doxy, until she comes to the honour of an altham.

A PATRIARCH CO

A patriarch co doth make marriages, and that is until death depart the married folk, which is after this sort: when they come to a dead horse or any dead cattle, then they shake hands and so depart, every one of them a several way.

John Awdely, *The Fraternitie of Vagabondes* (1575)

TEACH YOURSELF ROGUES' CANT

Upright man.   *Bene lightmans to thy quarrons. In what libken hast thou libbed in this darkmans, whether in a libbege or in the strummel?*

Good morrow to thy body. In what house has thou lain in all night, whether in a bed or in the straw?

Rogue.   *I couched a hogshead in a skipper this darkmans.*

I laid me down to sleep in a barn this night.

Man.   *I tour the strummel trine upon thy nab-cheat and togman.*

I see the straw hang upon thy cap and coat.

Rouge.   *I say by the Solomon I will lage it off with a gage of bene booze. Then cut to my nose watch.*

I swear by the mass I will wash it off with a quart of good drink. Then say to me what thou wilt.

Man.	*Why, hast thou any lour in thy bung to booze?*
	Why, hast thou any money in thy purse to drink?
Rougue.	*But a flag, a win and a make.*
	But a groat, a penny and a halfpenny.
Man.	*Why, where is the ken that hath the bene booze?*
	Where is the house that hath the good drink?
Rogue.	*A bene-mot hereby at the sign of the prancer.*
	A goodwife hereby at the sign of the Horse.
Man.	*I cut it is queer booze. I boozed a flag the last darkmans.*
	I say it is small and naughty drink. I drank a groat there the last night.
Rogue.	*But booze there a bord, and thou shalt have beneship.*
	But drink there a shilling, and thou shalt have very good.
	Tour ye. Yonder is the ken. Dup the jigger and maund that is beneship.
	See you. Yonder is the house. Open the door and ask for the best.
Man.	*This booze is as beneship as Rome-booze.*
	This drink is as good as wine.
	Now I tour that bene booze makes nase nabs.
	Now I see that good drink makes a drunken head.
	Maund of this mort what bene peck is in her ken.
	Ask of this wife what good meat she hath in her house.
Rogue.	*She hath a cackling-cheat, a grunting-cheat, ruff-peck, cassan and poplar of yarrum.*
	She hath a hen, a pig, bacon, cheese and milk-porridge.
Man.	*That is beneship to our watch.*
	That is very good for us.
Rogue.	*Now we have well boozed, let us strike some cheat.*
	Now we have well drunk, let us steal something.
Man.	*Younder dwelleth a queer cuffin. It were beneship to mill him.*
	Yonder dwelleth a hoggish and churlish man. It were very well done to rob him.
Rogue.	*Now bing we a waste to the high-pad, the ruffmans is by.*
	Nay, let us go to the highway, the woods is at hand.
Man.	*So may we happen on the harmans, and cly the jerk, or to the queer-ken and scour queer cramp-rings, and so to trining on the chats.*

So we may chance to set in the stocks, either be whipped, either had to prison-house, and there be shackled with bolts and fetters, and then to hang on the gallows.

Rogue.   *Gerry gan! the ruffian cly thee!*

A turd in thy mouth! the devil take thee!

Man.   *What! stow your bene, cove, and cut benat whids! And bing we will to Rome-vill, to nip a bung. So shall we have lour for the boozing-ken. And when we bring back to the dews-a-vill, we will filch some duds off the ruffmans, or mill the ken for a lag of duds.*

What! Hold your peace, good fellow, and speak better words! And go we to London, to cut a purse. Then shall we have money for the alehouse. And when we come back again into the country, we will steal some linen clothes off some hedges, or rob some house for a buck [bundle] of clothes.

Thomas Harman, *A Caveat for Commen Cursetors* (1567)

A CANTING LOVE-SONG

1.	Doxy O! Thy glaziers shine	[eyes]
	As glimmer! By the Solomon,	[fire; Mass]
	No gentry mort hath prats like thine,	[lady; genitals]
	No dell e'er wapped with such a one.	[copulated]
2.	White thy fambles, red thy gan,	[hand; lip]
	And thy quaroms dainty is.	[body]
	Couch a hogshead with me, then,	[sleep]
	In the darkmans clip and kiss.	[night; embrace]
3.	What though I no caster wear	[cloak]
	Nor commission, no, nor slate?	[shirt; sheet]
	Store of strommel we'll have here	[straw]
	And i'th'skipper lib in state.	[barn; lie]
4.	Niggling thou, I know, dost love,	[sexual play]
	Else the Ruffian cly thee, mort.	[Devil; whip; woman]
	From thy stampers then remove	[shoes]
	Thy drawers and let's prig in sport.	[stockings; copulate]

5.   When the lightmans up does call   [dawn]
        Margery prater from the nest   [hen]
      And her cackling cheats withal,   [fellows]
        In a boozing ken we'll feast.   [alehouse]

6.   There if I lower want, I'll mill   [money; steal]
        A gage or nip for thee a bung.   [quart pot; steal a purse]
      Bene booze thou shalt booze thy fill,   [good ale; drink]
        And crash a grunting cheat that's young.   [kill a suckling
                                                        pig]

7.   Bing awast to Romeville, then,   [get you hence to London]
        O my doxy, O my dell.
      We'll heave a booth and dock again,   [rob; copulate]
        And trining 'scape, and all is well.   [hanging]

Thomas Dekker, *English Villainies Discovered by Lantern and Candlelight*
(1608–16)

SLEEP FOR VAGABONDS

Now I think it not unnecessary to make the reader understand how and in what manner they lodge a-nights in barns or bakehouses, and of their usage there, forasmuch as I have acquainted them with their order and practices a-daytimes. The arch and chief walkers, that hath walked a long time, whose experience is great because of their continuing practice, I mean all morts and doxies for their handsomeness and diligence for making of their couches. The men never trouble themselves with that thing, but takes the same to be the duty of the wife. And she shuffles up a quantity of straw or hay into some pretty corner of the barn where she may conveniently lie and well shaketh the same, making the head somewhat high, and drives the same upon the sides and feet like a bed; then she layeth her wallet, or some other little pack of rags or scrip under her head in the straw, to bear up the same, and layeth her petticoat or cloak upon and over the straw, so made like a bed, and that serveth for the blanket. Then she layeth her slate (which is her sheet) upon that. An she have no sheet, as few of them go without, then she spreadeth some

223

large clouts or rags over the same and maketh her ready, and layeth her drowsily down. Many will pluck off their smocks and lay the same upon them instead of their upper sheet, and all her other pelt and trash upon her also; and many lieth in their smocks. And if the rest of her clothes in cold weather be not sufficient to keep her warm, then she taketh straw or hay to perform the matter. The other sort, that have not slates, but tumble down and couch a hogshead in their clothes, these be still lousy, and shall never be without vermin, unless they put off their clothes and lie as is abovesaid. If the upright man come in where they lie, he hath his choice, and creepeth in close by his doxy. The rogue has his leavings if the morts or doxies lie or be lodged in some farmer's barn, and the door be either locked or made fast to them, then will not the upright man press to come in, unless it be in barns and out-houses standing alone, or some distance from houses which be commonly known to them . . .

Sometime shall come in some rogue, some picking knave, a nimble prig. He walketh in softly a-nights, when they be at their rest, and plucketh off as many garments as may be aught worth that he may come by, and worth money, and may easily carry the same, and runneth away with the same with great celerity, and maketh port-sale [auction] at some convenient place of theirs, that some be soon ready in the morning, for want of their casters and togmans [cloaks and coats]: where instead of blessing is cursing, in place of praying, pestilent prating with odious oaths and terrible threatenings. . . .

And in this barn do lie forty upright men with their doxies together at one time. And this must the poor farmer suffer, or else they threaten him to burn him and all he hath.

A DOXY

These doxies be broken and spoiled of their maidenhead by the upright men, and then have they their name of doxies and not afore. And afterward she is common and indifferent for any that will use her, as *homo* is a common name to all men. Such as be fair and somewhat handsome keep company with the walking morts [whores], and are ready always for the upright men, and are chiefly maintained by them for others shall be spoiled for their sakes. The other inferior sort will resort to noblemen's places, and gentlemen's houses, standing at the gate either lurking on the back-side about bakehouses, either in hedgerows, or some other thicket, expecting their prey which is for the uncomely company of some courteous guest, of whom they be refreshed with meat and some money, where exchange is made, ware for ware. This bread and meat they use to carry in their great hosen; so that these beastly bribering [thieving] breeches serve many times for bawdy purposes.

I chanced, not long sithence, familiarly to common with a doxy that came to my gate, and surely a pleasant harlot, and not so pleasant as witty, and not so witty as void of all grace and goodness. I found by her talk that she had passed her time lewdly eighteen years in walking about. I thought this a necessary instrument to attain some knowledge by. And before I would grope her mind, I made her both eat and drink well. That done, I made her faithful promise to give her some money if she would open and discover to me such questions as I would demand of her, and never bewray her neither to disclose her name.

'An you should,' saith she, 'I were undone.'

'Fear not that,' quoth I. 'But, I pray thee,' quoth I, 'say nothing but truth.'

'I will not,' saith she.

'Then first tell me,' quoth I, 'how many upright men and rogues dost thou know, or hast thou known and been conversant with, and what their names be?'

She paused awhile, and said, 'Why do you ask me, or wherefore?'

'For nothing else,' as I said, 'but that I would know them when they came to my gate.'

'Now by my troth,' quoth she, 'then are ye never the near, for all mine acquaintance for the most part are dead.'

'Dead,' quoth I, 'how died they? For want of cherishing, or of painful diseases?'

Then she sighed, and said they were hanged.

'What, all,' quoth I, 'and so many walk abroad, as I daily see?'

'By my troth,' quoth she, 'I know not past six or seven by their names,' and named the same to me.

'When were they hanged?' quoth I.

'Some seven years agone, some three years and some within this fortnight,' and declared the place where they were executed, which I knew well to be true by the report of others.

'Why,' quoth I, 'did not this sorrowful and fearful sight much grieve thee, and for thy time long and evil spent?'

'I was sorry,' quoth she, 'by the mass. For some of them were good loving men. For I lacked not when they had it, and they wanted not when I had it, and divers of them I never did forsake, until the gallows departed us.'

'O merciful God!' quoth I, and began to bless me.

'Why bless ye?' quoth she. 'Alas, good gentleman, every one must have a living.'

A KINCHIN MORT

A kinchin mort is a little girl. The morts their mothers carries them at their backs in their slates, which is their sheets, and brings them up savagely, till they grow to be ripe: and soon ripe, soon rotten.

Thomas Harman, *A Caveat for Commen Cursetors* (1576)

THE CUTPURSE'S BOAST

(I)

I pray you what finer quality, what art is more excellent, either to try the ripeness of the wit, or the agility of the hand, than that for him that will be master of his trade must pass the proudest juggler alive the points of legerdemain; he must have an eye to spy the bung, and then a heart to dare to attempt it – for this by the way, he that fears the gallows shall never be good thief while he lives. He must as a cat watch for a mouse, and walk Paul's, Westminster, the Exchange, and such common-haunted places, and there have a curious eye to the person, whether he be gentleman, citizen or farmer, and note, either where his bung lies, whether in his hose or pockets, and then dog the party into a press where his stall with heaving and shoving shall so molest him, that he shall not feel when we strip him of his bung, although it be never so fast or cunningly couched about him. What poor farmer almost can come to plead his case at the bar, to attend upon his lawyer's at the bench, but, look he never so narrowly to it, we have his purse, wherein sometime there is fat purchase, twenty or thirty pounds.

Robert Greene, *A Disputation, Between a Hee Conny-catcher, and a Shee Conny-catcher* (1592)

POVERTY, CRIME AND PUNISHMENT

(II)

HOW NED BROWNE KISSED A GENTLEWOMAN AND CUT HER PURSE

Thus, gentlemen, being in my dumps, I saw a brave [fine] country gentlewoman coming along from St Bartholomew's in a satin gown, and four men attending upon her. By her side she had hanging a marvellous rich purse embroidered, and not so fair without but it seemed to be as well lined within. At this my teeth watered, and, as the prey makes the thief, so necessity and the sight of such a fair purse began to muster a thousand inventions in my head how to come by it. To go by her and nip it I could not, because she had so many men attending on her; to watch her into a press, that was in vain, for, going towards St John's Street, I guessed her about to take horse to ride home, because all her men were booted. Thus perplexed for this purse, and yet not so much for the bung as the shells, I at last resolutely vowed in myself to have it, though I stretched a halter for it. And so, casting in my head how to bring my fine mistress to the blow, at last I performed it thus. She standing and talking awhile with a gentleman, I stepped before her and leaned at the bar till I saw her leave him, and then stalking towards her very stoutly as if I had been some young cavalier or captain, I met her, and courteously saluted her, and not only greeted her, but, as if I had been acquainted with her, I gave her a kiss, and so in taking acquaintance closing very familiarly to her I cut her purse. The gentlewoman seeing me so brave [smart] used me kindly, and blushing said, she knew me not.

'Are you not, mistress,' quoth I, 'such a gentlewoman, and such a man's wife?'

'No truly, sir,' quoth she, 'you mistake me.'

'Then I cry you mercy,' quoth I, 'and am sorry that I was so saucily bold.'

'There is no harm done, sir,' said she, 'because there is no offence taken.'

And so we parted, I with a good bung, and my gentlewoman with a kiss, which I dare safely swear, she bought as dear as ever she did a thing in her life; for what I found in the purse, that I keep to myself.

Robert Greene, *The Blacke Bookes Messenger* (1592)

IN PRISCUM

'Mongst the monopolists on London's Burse,
Priscus was ta'en for cutting of a purse,
And being reviled, made this bold question, 'Why
Are these monopolists excused, since I
Did cut but one man's purse, while they cut all?'
But thus we see, the weakest goes to th' wall.

Richard Niccols, *The Furies* (1614)

A Whore that Crossbit [Swindled] a Gentleman of the Inns of Court

A certain quean belonging to a close nunnery about Clerkenwell, lighting in the company of a young puny [novice] of the Inns of Court, trained him home with her to her hospital, . . . there covenanting for so much to give him his houseroom all night. To bed they went together like man and wife. At midnight a crew of her copesmates kept a knocking and bustling at the door. She, starting suddenly out of her sleep, arose and went to the window to look out; wherewith she, crying out to him, said that a Justice was at the door with a company of bills [halberdiers] and came to search for a [Catholic] seminary priest, and that there was no remedy but she must open unto them. Wherefore either he must rise and lock himself in a study that was hard by, or they should be both carried to Bridewell. The poor silly youth in a trance, as one new start out of sleep and that knew not where he was, suffered her to lead him whither she would, who hastily thrust him into the study, and there locked him, and went to let them in.

Then entered Sim Swashbuckler, Captain Gogswounds and Lawrence Longswordsman, with their appurtenances, [and] made enquiry, as if they had been officers indeed, for a young seminary priest that should be lodged there that night. She simpered it, and made curtsy, and spake reverently unto them, as if she had never seen them before and that they had been such as they seemed, and told them she knew of none such, and that none lay there but herself. With that, through signs that she made, they spied where his clothes were fallen down between the chest and the wall. Then they began to rail upon her, and call her a thousand whores, saying they would make her an example, aye, marry would they, and use her like an infidel for her lying, nor would they stand searching any longer, but she would be constrained to bring him forth; and that they might be sure he should not start, they would carry away his clothes with them. As for the closet, because it was a gentleman's out of town, they would not rashly break it open, but they would set watch and ward about the house till the morning, by which time they would resolve further what to do. So out of doors go they with his clothes, doublet, hose, hat, rapier, dagger, shoes, stockings and twenty marks that he had in his sleeve which he was to pay upon a bond the next day for his father, to a merchant in Canning Street, and left Nicholas Novice starving and quaking in that doghole.

The morning grew on, and yet the young ninnyhammer, though he was almost frozen to death, stood still and durst not stir, till at length the goodwife of the house came and let him out, and bade him shift for himself, for the house was so belayed [besieged] that it was not possible for him to escape, and that she was utterly undone through his coming thither. After many words it grew to this upshot, that he must give her a ring worth thirty shillings, which he then had on his finger, only to help him out at a back door, and in so doing she would lend him a blanket to cast about him. Which being performed, like an Irish beggar he departed on the backside of the fields to his chamber, vowing never to pay so dear for one night's lodging during his life.

Samuel Rowlands, *Greenes Ghost Haunting Conlecatchers* (1602)

MAN'S TRADE, WOMAN'S OCCUPATION

Freevill. Alas, good creatures, what would you have them do? Would you have them get their living by the curse of man, the sweat of their brows? So they do; every man must follow his trade, and every woman her occupation. A poor decayed mechanical man's [manual worker's] wife, her husband is laid up; may not she lawfully be laid down, when her husband's only rising is by his wife's falling? A captain's wife wants means [lacks money]; her commander lies in open field abroad; may not she lie in civil arms at home? A waiting gentlewoman that had wont to take say [fine cloth] to her lady, miscarries or so: the Court misfortune throws her down; may not the City courtesy take her up? Do you know no alderman would pity such a woman's case? Why is charity grown a sin?

Or relieving the poor and impotent an offence? You will say beasts take no money for their fleshly entertainment; true, because they are beasts, therefore beastly. Only men give to lose, because they are men, therefore manly; and indeed, wherein should they bestow their money better? In land, the title may be cracked; in houses, they may be burned; in apparel, 'twill wear; in wine, alas for pity, our throat is but short. But employ your money upon women, and a thousand to one some one of them will bestow that on you which shall stick by you as long as you live. They are no ungrateful persons; they will give quit for quo [tit for tat]; do ye protest, they'll swear; do you rise, they'll fall; do you fall, they'll rise, do you give them the French crown, they'll give you the French [French coin; bald patch caused by pox] — *O justus, justa, justum* [Latin: just]. They sell their bodies; do not better persons sell their souls? Nay, since all things have been sold, honour, justice, faith, nay, even God himself,

> Ay me, what base ignobleness is it
> To sell the pleasure of a wanton bed?

John Marston, *The Dutch Courtesan* (1605)

CRIME AND PUNISHMENT

In cases of felony, manslaughter, robbery, murder, rape, piracy and such capital crimes as are not reputed for treason or hurt of the estate, our sentence pronounced upon the offender is, to hang till he be dead. For of other punishments used in other countries we have no knowledge or use; and yet so few grievous crimes committed with us as elsewhere in the world. To use torment also, or question by pain and torture, in these common cases, with us is greatly abhorred . . .

The greatest and most grievous punishment used in England, for such as offend against the state, is drawing from the prison to the place of execution upon an hurdle or sled, where they are hanged till they be half dead, and then taken down and quartered; after that, their members and bowels are cut from their bodies, and thrown into a fire provided near hand and within their own sight, even for the same purpose. [Holinshed, *Chronicles*, 1586: On the one and twentieth day of January, two seminary priests (before arraigned and condemned) were drawn to Tyburn, and there hanged, bowelled and quartered.

Also on the same day a wench was burned in Smithfield, for poisoning her aunt and mistress . . .] Sometimes, if the trespass be not the more heinous, they are suffered to hang till they be quite dead. And whensoever any of the nobility are convicted of high treason, this manner of their death is converted into the loss of their heads only, notwithstanding that the sentence do run after the former order. In trial of cases concerning treason, felony or any other grievous crime, not confessed, the party accused doth yield, if he be a nobleman, to be tried by an inquest (as I have said) and his peers; if a gentleman, by gentlemen; and an inferior, by God and the country, and being condemned of felony, manslaughter, etc., he is eftsoons hanged by the neck till he be dead, and then cut down and buried. But if he be convicted of wilful murder, done either upon pretended malice, or in any notable robbery, he is either hanged alive in chains near the place where the fact was committed, or else first strangled with a rope, and so continueth till his bones consume to nothing. [Holinshed, 1578–9: The seventeenth of February, an Irishman, for murdering of a man in a garden of Stepney parish, was hanged in chains on the common called Mile End Green.]

Under the word felony are many grievous crimes contained, as: breach of prison, disfigurers of the prince's liege people; hunting by night with painted faces and visors; rape, or stealing of women and maidens; conspiracy against the person of the prince; embezzling of goods committed by the master to the servant, above the value of forty shillings; carrying of horses or mares into Scotland; sodomy and buggery; stealing of hawks' eggs; conjuring, sorcery, witchcraft and digging up of crosses; prophesying upon arms, cognisances, names and badges; casting of slanderous bills; wilful killing of a soldier from the field; departure of a soldier from the field; diminution of coin, all offences within case of *praemunire*, embezzling of records, goods taken from dead men by their servants, stealing of whatsoever cattle, robbing by the highway, upon the sea, or of dwelling houses, letting out of ponds, cutting of purses, stealing of deer by night, counterfeiters of coin [Holinshed, 1569–70: The seven and twentieth of January, Philip Mestrell, a Frenchman, and two Englishmen, were drawn from Newgate to Tyburn, and there hanged, the Frenchman quartered, who had coined gold counterfeit], evidences, charters and writings, and divers other, needless to be remembered. . . . Perjury is punished by the pillory, burning in the forehead with the letter P, and loss of all his moveables.

Many trespasses also are punished by the cutting of one or both ears from the head of the offender, as the utterance of seditious words against the magistrates, fray-makers, petty robbers, etc. Rogues are burned through the ears; carriers of sheep out of the land, by the loss of their hands; such as kill by poison are either scalded to death in lead or seething water. Heretics are burned quick [alive, not necessarily quickly; Holinshed, 1583: On the eighteenth day of September, John Lewes, who named himself Abdoit, an obstinate heretic, denying the godhead of Christ, and holding divers other detestable heresies . . . was burned at Norwich]; harlots and their mates, by carting, ducking and doing of open penance in sheets, in churches and market steads, are often put to rebuke. . . . The dragging of some of them over the Thames between Lambeth and Westminster at the tail of a boat, is a punishment that most terrifieth them which are condemned thereto . . .

Rogues and vagabonds are often stocked and whipped; scolds are ducked upon cucking-stools in the water. Such felons as stand mute, and speak not at their arraignment, are pressed to death by huge weights laid upon a board that lieth over their breast, and a sharp stone under their backs, and these commonly hold their peace thereby to save their goods unto their wives and children, which, if they were condemned, should be confiscated to the prince. Thieves that are saved by their books and clergy [prove themselves literate] are burned in the left hand, upon the brawn of the thumb, with an hot iron, so that if they be apprehended again that mark bewrayeth them to have been arraigned of felony before, whereby they are sure at that time to have no mercy. . . .

Pirates and robbers by sea are condemned in the Court of the Admiralty, and hanged on the shore at low water mark, where they are left till three tides have over-washed them [Holinshed, 1577–8: On the ninth of March, seven pirates were hanged at Wapping in the Ouse, beside London]. . . .

Certes there is no greater mischief done in England than by robberies, the first by young shifting gentlemen, which oftentimes do bear more port [live to a higher standard] than they are able to maintain [*Henry IV, Part I*?]. Secondly by serving-men, whose wages cannot suffice so much as to find them breeches, wherefore they are now and then constrained either to keep highways and break into the wealthy men's houses with the first sort, or else to walk up and down in gentlemen's and rich farmers' pastures, there to see and view which horses feed best, whereby they many times get something, although with hard adventure; it hath been known by their confession at the gallows, that some one such chapman hath had forty, fifty or sixty stolen horses at pasture here and there abroad in the country at a time, which they have sold at fairs and markets afar off . . .

Our third annoyers of the commonwealth are rogues, which do very great mischief in all places where they become. For whereas the rich only suffer injury by the first two, these spare neither rich nor poor; but whether it be great gain or small, all is fish that cometh to net with them; and yet I say, both they and the rest are trussed up apace. For there is not one year commonly, wherein three hundred or four hundred of them are not devoured and eaten up by the gallows in one place and another.

William Harrison, *Description of England* (1587)

A Constable

Is a viceroy in the street, and no man stands more upon't that he is the king's officer. His jurisdiction extends to the next stocks, where he has commission for the heels only, and sets the rest of the body at liberty. He is a scarecrow to that alehouse where he drinks not his morning draught, and apprehends a drunkard for not standing in the king's name. Beggars fear him more than the Justice, and as much as the whip-stock, whom he delivers over to his subordinate magistrates, the bridewell-man and the beadle. He is a great stickler in the tumults of double-jugs [arguments over drink], and ventures his head by his place, which is broke many times to keep the peace. He is never so much in his majesty as in his night-watch, where he sits in his chair of state, a shop-stall, and, environed with a guard of halberds, examines all passengers. He is a very careful man in his office, but if he stay up after midnight you shall take him napping.

John Earle, *Micro-cosmographie* (1628)

SHAKESPEARE'S ENGLAND

GUIDANCE FOR MAGISTRATES, ON RAPE

To ravish a woman where she doth neither consent before nor after is a felony [a capital offence]. But a woman that is ravished ought presently [promptly] to levy hue and cry, or to complain thereof presently to some credible persons. . . . If the woman at the time of the supposed rape do conceive with child by the ravisher, this is no rape, for a woman cannot conceive with child except she do consent. If a man ravish a woman who consenteth for fear of death or duress, yet this is a ravishment against her will, for that consent ought to be voluntary and free . . . it is a good plea, in an appeal of rape, to say that before the ravishment supposed, she was his concubine . . . and yet to ravish a harlot against her will is felony . . . The taking away of a maid under sixteen years of age without the consent of her parents . . . or deflowering her, is no felony, but yet shall be punished with long imprisonment without bail, or grievous fine. But unlawfully and carnally to know and abuse any woman child under the age of ten years is felony, although such child consents before.

M. Dalton, *The Countrey Justice* (1618)

A PRIEST ASTRAY

Now for the punishment of priests in my youth, one note and no more. John Atwood, draper, dwelling in the parish of St Michael upon Cornhill, directly against the church, having a proper woman to his wife, such a one as seemed the holiest among a thousand, had also a lusty chantry priest, of the said parish church, repairing to his house, with the which priest the said Atwood would sometimes after supper play a game at tables [backgammon] for a pint of ale. It chanced on a time, having haste of work and his game proving long, he left his wife to play it out, and went down to his shop; but, returning to fetch a pressing iron, he found such play to his misliking that he forced the priest to leap out at a window, over the penthouse [awning, outhouse], into the street, and so to run to his lodging in the churchyard. Atwood and his wife were soon reconciled, so that he would not suffer her to be called in question, but the priest being apprehended and committed, I saw his punishment to be thus. He was

234

on three market days conveyed through the high street and markets of the City with a paper on his head wherein was written his trespass. The first day he rode in a carry [small cart], the second, on a horse, his face to the horsetail, the third, led betwixt twain, and every day 'rung with basins' [loud 'rough music'] and proclamations made of his fact [deed] at every turning of the streets, and also before John Atwood's stall, and the church door of his service, where he lost his chantry of twenty nobles the year, and was banished the City for ever.

John Stow, *The Survay of London* (1598, 1603)

Dyer's Stain

[Justices' report of an examination to establish paternity of an
illegitimate child]

Agnes Bourman the harlot saith on the play day at Bradford John Dyer met her in the churchyard of West Buckland, and they went together into the church porch and there he had the use of her body, and at that time she delivered him VId [sixpence]. It is confessed that Dyer dwelleth near the same churchyard. She also saith that Dyer hath divers times met her in Burt's Close [enclosed pastureland] in the night. Agnes . . . saith that between Whitsuntide and Midsummer last, as they were going into the field, Dyer took her about the middle and carried her aside by the hedge and tumbled with her. It was about seven o'clock at night. Thomas Bartlett saith that on Sunday after Trinity Sunday, half an hour after candle-lighting, he saw Dyer and Agnes Bourman in Buckland churchyard together and he saw him kiss her.

The proofs at that time for Dyer [his defence]: Emlyn Way saith that she heard Dyer say, rather than he would father another man's child he would buy himself a suit of apparel and run away. Peter Chuff saith he saw Agnes Bourman in the dyke of Bye's Close and a man with her in a white cut doublet, and then affirmed upon his salvation, what the man was he knew not, nor would not nor could not for hundred pounds say that it was Robert Bye. . . . Abel Levering the minister . . . of Buckland saying Dyer prayed him that he would keep his counsel, which was that he heard Agnes Bourman was with child, and that she would charge him to be the father, and therefore he would be gone.

Alexander Burt saith Agnes Bourman did wish that the ground would open and that she might sink in, if ever she knew whether John Dyer were a man or woman.

Somerset Session Rolls, 1611
[By permission, Somerset Record Office]

[Quaife (see Further Reading) records that Dyer ran away, before being adjudged the father; Agnes Bourman's child became a charge on the parish, and she herself was sentenced to be 'openly whipped upon some festival day'.]

PRISON LIFE

I am with dim water-colours to line a chart and in it to lay down the bounds of those tempestuous seas in which ten thousand are every day tossed, if not overwhelmed. Some do but cross over the waters and are sea-sick but not heart-sick; such are happy. To others it is longer than an East Indian voyage and far more dangerous, for, in that, if of threescore men twenty come home it is well, but in this, if fourscore of a hundred be not cast overboard it is a wonder.

More now than a three years' voyage have I made to these Infortunate Islands [Dekker was committed to the King's Bench Prison, for debt, in 1612 and released in 1619]. A long lying have I had under hatches, during which time my compass never went true, no star of comfort have I sailed by, no anchor to cast out. Topsail, foresail, spritsail, mizzen, mainsheet, bowlines and drabblers [extra canvas attached to sails] are all torn by the winds, and the barque itself so weatherbeaten that I fear it shall never touch at the Capo Buona Speranza. What have I hereby gotten but a sad experience of my own and others' miseries? I can only say what I have seen and tell what others have felt. This man hath spread a full sail and by help of skilful pilots made a safe arrival. That man, having as fair a wind, hath been cast away in the same haven. A fly-boat [ship's boat] hath brooked that sea in which an argosy hath been drowned. For the greatest courages are here wrecked; the fairest revenues do here run aground; the noblest wits are here confounded.

So that I may call a prison an enchanted castle, by reason of the rare transformations therein wrought, for it makes a wise man lose his wits, a fool to know himself. It turns a rich man into a beggar, and leaves a poor man desperate. He whom neither snows nor alps can vanquish but hath a heart as constant as Hannibal's, him can the misery of a prison deject. And how brave an outside soever his mind carries, open his bosom and you shall see nothing but wounds. . . .

Art thou poor and in prison? Then art thou buried before thou are dead. Thou carriest thy winding-sheet on thy back up and down the house. Thou liest upon thy bier and treadest upon thy grave at every step. If there be any Hell on earth, here thou especially shalt be sure to find it. If there be degrees of torments in Hell, here shalt thou taste them. The body is annoyed with sickness, stench, hunger, cold, thirst, penury, thy mind with discontents, thy soul with inutterable sorrows; thine eye meets no object but of horror, wretchedness, beggary and tyranny. . . .

[A DEVIL'S VISIT TO PRISON]
Looking to hear there nothing but sighing, lamenting, praying and cryings-out of afflicted and forlorn creatures, there was no such matter, but only a clamorous noise of cursing creditors, drinking healths to their confusion, swaggering, roaring, striking, stabbing one another as if that all desperviews [the hopeless, destitute] of sixteen armies had been swearing together. Considering the desperate resolutions of some, he wished himself in his own territories, knowing more safety there than in the Hospital of Incurable Madmen, and could not till about dinner-time be persuaded but that the gaol was Hell, every room was so smoky with tobacco, and oaths flying faster about than tapsters could score up their frothy reckoning. But the time of munching being come, all the sport was to see how the prisoners, like sharking soldiers at the rifling of a town, ran up and down to arm themselves against that battle of hunger, some whetting knives that had meat, others scraping trenchers aloud that had no meat, some ambling downstairs for bread and beer meeting another coming upstairs carrying a platter more proudly aloft, full of powder beef and brewis [bread and gravy], than an Irishman does his enemy's head on the top of his sword, every chamber showing like a cook's shop where provant [provisions] was stirring, and those that had not provender in the manger nor hay in the rack walking up and down like starved jades new over-ridden in Smithfield. This set at maw [card-game; eating] being played out, all seemed quiet. The water under London Bridge at the turning was not more still.

But locking-up being come, that every cock must go to his roost, the music of that (in the judgement of the black spy) might well enough serve to rock Gran Beelzebub asleep. For nothing could be heard but keys jingling, doors rapping, bolts and locks barring in, gaolers hoarsely and harshly bawling for prisoners to their bed, and prisoners reviling and cursing gaolers for making such a hellish din. Then to hear some in their chambers singing and dancing, being half drunk, others breaking open doors to get more drink to be whole drunk, some roaring for tobacco, others raging and bidding Hell's plague on all tobacco because it hath so dried up their mouths, with as many other frantic passions as there be several men. . . .

[SHARING A BED]

Thy companion haply may not be thy bedfellow. Call therefore him not thy bedfellow who is familiar with thee in thy chamber and scorns to look upon thee in the parlour; part sheets with such a man; the earthy smell of such dead familiarity turns thy bed into a grave wherein thou art buried alive. . . .

[THE GAOLER]

He that sails to the Indies must look to be sunburnt, and he that lives amongst the Goths and Vandals will smell of their harsh conditions. An officer of this character hath not a bosom like a dove's, all downy, but rather the back of a porcupine, stuck full of quills ready to be shot every minute, because every minute he shall be made angry. . . . The favour of a prison-keeper is like smoke out of Coldharbour chimneys [poor tenements], scarcely seen once in a year. He is a bell in time of sickness that more often rings out for burials than divine service. If his eye chance to glance out pity, it is but a painted gallipot in an apothecary's shop containing that in it that is able to kill thee.

['POLITIC BANKRUPTS', LIVING WELL IN PRISON ON FRAUDULENTLY-OBTAINED MONEY]

How many of them . . . are earthed in the King's Bench, the Fleet, and that abused sanctuary of Ludgate. Here they play at bowls, lie in fair chambers within the Rule [outside housing, technically part of the prison], fare like Dives [rich man in Luke XVI], laugh at Lazarus [poor man], can walk up and down many times by *habeas corpus* and jeer their creditors. There they lie, barricadoed within King Lud's bulwark against gunshot; there they strut up and down the prison like magnificoes in Venice on the Rialto, brave in clothes, spruce in ruffs, with gold-wrought nightcaps on their heads. They feed deliciously, plenteously, voluptuously, have excellent wines to drink, handsome wives to lie with when they please, who come not like the wives of prisoners but of the best and wealthiest citizens. These men command the stone walls, not the walls them. They scorn the poor miserable wretches who beg at the grate [for food] and live upon the charity of the house. . . .

To conclude, such a bankrupt has the head of a lamb, the eyes of a dove, the tongue of a nightingale, the arms of a freebooter, the hands of a hangman, the teeth of a lion, and the belly of an elephant.

Thomas Dekker, *English Villainies Discovered by Lantern and Candlelight* (1608–16)

11

OVER SEAS

Sir Francis Drake is still the most famous of Elizabethan sailors (though once 'every schoolboy' knew also of Hawkins, Frobisher, Cavendish and Sir Richard Grenville), chiefly for spectacular achievements such as his highly profitable privateering raids on the Spanish between 1572 and 1573, his journey of 1577–80 around the world, and his success against the Spanish Armada (1588). Many other men from the island of England were involved in sea-going. There was the busy inshore traffic, such as that transporting coal from Newcastle to London; also important was the fishing trade (encouraged by government requirements for fish-eating on Fridays and holy days): cod and herring from the North Sea (competing with the Dutch), pilchards from the southwest, and the increasingly important cod-fishing off Newfoundland (reportedly, one lowered buckets and scooped them up). Privateering, whether in the northern seas or the Spanish Main (especially from 1585 to 1602) was immensely profitable for individuals and the national economy. Above all, trade overseas was of major importance.

Exports, as with many developing countries, were mainly of primary goods (wool, tin – for pewter – and some grain, with finished cloth steadily becoming more important), while the chief imports increasingly included luxury consumption goods, mostly for the affluent – wines, fancy textiles, dried fruits, spices, sugar, pepper: these mostly from or via southern Europe; from America, later, came tobacco; from northern Europe came more utilitarian goods – timber, flax, nitre for gunpowder, metal wares. Earlier, trade had been funnelled mostly, via London, through Antwerp, the great North European entrepôt, but as that declined (partly as a consequence of war), and with the expulsion in 1598 of the Hanseatic League merchants, English merchants increasingly took control of the nation's commerce.

The luxury goods trade and its huge profits drove the merchants' little ships and their long-suffering, scurvy-ridden crews ever farther and farther: the Baltic (the Muscovy Company was founded in 1553), the Mediterranean, despite the dreaded corsairs (the Levant Company, 1593), Morocco, West Africa, through the Indian Ocean (the East India Company, 1600) and across the Atlantic. Portugal's control of direct access to the Far East led to searches for North-Eastern and North-Western Passages. England was slow off the mark in exploiting the Americas (theoretically a Spanish domain): Hawkins tried to get in on the slave trade from West Africa to America, and after war broke out, privateering against Spain boomed, bringing in wine, sugar, hides, bullion (and, as in the capture of the *Madre de Dios*, jewels, spices, perfumes, silks, calico, Oriental goods and ivory). One consequence of all this was the establishment of secure bases, and the foundation of settlements and colonies in the Americas.

Many of these, such as that in Jamestown, Virginia (1607), were essentially economic ventures, founded by English entrepreneurs, run by wealthy agents and planters, worked by poor indentured labourers (and slaves). These settlements struggled financially until tobacco was discovered as a valuable crop: production increased rapidly, transforming living conditions there, and the market in Europe. Other, later settlers went seeking religious freedom and a new life in the New World; they had to manage without the tobacco trade, but eventually developed their own mixed economy. Early in the seventeenth century, ships exported thousands of poor people to the Americas, to replace those killed off by harsh living conditions, disease, poor diet and hostile natives; other ships brought in Africans, as slaves; those returning from the southern plantations brought back tobacco and sugar, while others brought salt Newfoundland cod to the Indies or to Spain, before returning with wine, hides or salt.

This book deals with 'Shakespeare's England'; the question of England's identity and how that related to Wales, Scotland and Ireland was a complex one (as Shakespeare's *Henry V* hinted). Ireland is touched on here, as being literally over seas, though Englishmen generally regarded it as not a colony like Virginia but as part of the kingdom, if with alien customs, backward, troublesome and needing to be brought into good, recognizable order. Various political, military and administrative schemes were tried: 'surrender and regrant' sought to transform Irish chieftains into English noblemen, lordships into shires; English settlers and administrators were introduced; by 1590 English rule had theoretically been extended from 'the Pale' around Dublin throughout all Ireland except Ulster (to which James was later to encourage Scots settlers). Nevertheless, indecisive policy, insensitivity and religious conflict provoked frequent uprisings (some with Spanish armed assistance); the Earl of Essex's failure to defeat Hugh O'Neill, Earl of Tyrone, led indirectly to his own fall, but Lord Mountjoy's vigorous campaign crushed the rebellion. Shortly after Elizabeth's death, Tyrone surrendered, and the political unification of 'The Britannic Isles' seemed established – for the time being; but a new England was over the seas and far away.

THE NAVY

The navy of England may be divided into three sorts, of which the one serveth for the wars, the other for burden, and the third for fishermen, which get their living by fishing on the sea. How many of the first order are maintained within the realm, it passeth my cunning to express; yet sith it may be parted into the navy royal and common fleet, I think good to speak of those that belong unto the prince, and so much the rather for that their number is certain and well known to very many. Certes there is no prince in Europe that hath a more beautiful or gallant sort of ships than the Queen's Majesty of England at this present, and those generally are of such exceeding force that two of them, being well appointed and furnished as they ought, will not let to encounter with three or four of those of other countries, and either bowge them [stave in their sides, sink them] or put them to flight, if they may not bring them home.

Neither are the moulds of any foreign barks so conveniently made, to brook so well one sea as another lying upon the shore in any part of the continent as those of England. And therefore the common report that strangers make of our ships amongst themselves is daily confirmed to be true, which is, that for strength, assurance, nimbleness and swiftness of sailing, there are no vessels in the world to be compared with ours. The Queen's Highness hath at this present already made and furnished to the number of four or five and twenty great ships, which lie for the most part in Gillingham road, beside three galleys . . .

The number of those that serve for burden with the other, whereof I have made mention already, and whose use is daily seen, as occasion serveth, in time of the wars, is to me utterly unknown. Yet if the report of one record be anything at all to be credited, there are 135 ships that exceed 500 tons; topmen [crew] under 100 and above forty, 656; hoys, 100; but of hulks, ketches, fisherboats and crayers [small traders], it lieth not in me to deliver the just account, sith they are hardly to come by. Of these also there are some of the Queen's Majesty's subjects that have two or three; some, four or six; and (as I heard of late) one man, whose name I suppress for modesty's sake, hath been known not long since to have had sixteen or seventeen, and employed them wholly to the wafting in and out of our merchants, whereby he hath reaped no small commodity and gain. . . . Only this will I add, to the end all men shall understand somewhat of the great masses of treasure daily employed upon our navy, how there are few of those ships of the first and second sort, that, being apparelled and made ready to sail, are not worth one thousand pounds, or three thousand ducats at the least, if they should presently be sold. . . .

For the journeys also of our ships, you shall understand that a well builded vessel will run or sail commonly three hundred leagues or nine hundred miles in a week, or peradventure some will go 2,200 leagues in six weeks and a half. And surely, if their lading be ready against they come thither, there be of them that will be here, at the West Indies, and home again in twelve or thirteen weeks from Colchester, although the said Indies be eight hundred leagues from the cape or point of Cornwall, as I have been informed. This also I understand by report of some travellers, that if any of our vessels happen to make a voyage to Hispaniola or New Spain (called in time past Quinquezia and Haiti, and lieth between the north tropic and the Equator), after they have once touched at the Canaries (which are eight days' sailing, or two hundred and fifty leagues from St Lucas de Barameda in Spain) they will be there in thirty or forty days, and home again in Cornwall in other eight weeks, which is a goodly matter, beside the safety and quietness in passage.

William Harrison, *Description of England* (1587)

THE SPANISH ARMADA

(I)

QUEEN ELIZABETH'S SPEECH AT TILBURY:

My Loving People,

We have been persuaded by some that are careful of our safety, to take heed how we commit ourselves to armed multitudes, for fear of treachery; but I assure you, I do not desire to live to distrust my faithful and loving people.

Let tyrants fear; I have always so behaved myself that, under God, I have placed my chiefest strength and safeguard in the loyal heart and good will of my subjects, and therefore I am come amongst you, as you see, at this time, not for my recreation and disport, but being resolved in the midst and heat of the battle, to live or die amongst you all, to lay down for my God, and for my kingdoms, and for my people, my honour and my blood, even in the dust.

I know I have the body but of a weak and feeble woman; but I have the heart and stomach of a king, and of a king of England too; and think foul scorn that Parma or Spain, or any prince of Europe should dare to invade the borders of my realm; to which, rather than any dishonour should grow by me, I myself will take up arms, I myself will be your general, judge and rewarder of every one of your virtues in the field.

I know already, for your forwardness you have deserved rewards and crowns; and we do assure you on the word of a prince, they shall be duly paid you. In the mean time my lieutenant-general shall be in my stead, than whom never prince commanded a more noble or worthy subject; not doubting but by your obedience to my general, by your concord in the camp, and your valour in the field, we shall shortly have a famous victory over those enemies of my God, of my kingdoms, and of my people.

First pub., Cabala, 1651.

(II)

1588. The Spanish navy so long looked for doth now at last show itself over against our coasts, upon our 20 of July, where it is foughten withal upon the morrow, only with 50 sail of our English ships under the conduct of the Lord Admiral and Sir Francis Drake; afterward by our whole navy of 150 sail, for the space of 2 days together; in th'end thereof they are put to flight before Calais, and driven to return home about by

Scotland, with great loss, so that, of 160 sail and more which came out of Spain, scarcely 40 returned again in safety unto that king, God himself so fighting for us that we lost not 80 men, neither was there so much as one vessel of ours sunk by the enemy or taken, in all these skirmishes. In their return also, and besides those 15 vessels which they lost in our seas, 17 other of them did either perish upon the coast of Ireland, or, coming thither for succour, were seized upon also to Her Majesty's use. The lieutenant of this great navy was the Duke Medina of Cydonia, and with him were 210 noblemen, among which, beside the King's bastard son, were 2 marquesses, one prince, one duke, 4 earls, and 3 lords, which came to seek adventures and win honour upon England, as they said; howbeit, as God would, they never touched the land, nor came near unto our shore by divers miles. The Duke of Parma should have assisted them at this present with 80 or 100 sail provided out of the Low Countries; but, being kept in by weather and a portion of our navy, and his mariners also forsaking him, he was enforced to stay and keep upon the land, where he abode in safety and out of the roaring gunshot. . . .

A general thanksgiving throughout England in every church, for the victory of the Almighty given by th'English over the Spanish navy; in which the Queen herself, and her nobility, came to St Paul's church in London, November the 19, where, after she had heard the divine service, and in her own person given solemn thanks to God, in the hearing of such as were present, she heard the sermon at the Cross [outside St Paul's] preached by the Bishop of Sarum [Winchester], and then dined with the Bishop of London in his palace thereunto annexed.

William Harrison, *Chronologie* for John Stow, *Annales* (1605)

HARD TO SWALLOW

Voyages of purchase or reprisals [trading], which are now grown a common traffic, swallow up and consume more sailors and mariners than they breed, and lightly not a slop of a rope-hauler they send forth to the Queen's ships but he is first broken to the sea in the herring-man's skiff or cockboat, where, having learned to brook all waters, and drink as he can out of a tarry can, and eat poor John [dried salt fish] out of sooty platters, when he may get it, without butter or mustard, there is no 'ho' with him [no stopping], but, once heartened thus, he will needs be a man of war, or a tobacco-taker, and wear a silver whistle. Some of these, for their haughty climbing, come home with wooden legs, and some with none, but leave body and all behind. Those that escape to bring news tell of nothing but eating tallow and young blackamoors, of five and five to a rat in every mess and the ship-boy to the tail, of stopping their noses when they drank stinking water that came out of the pump of the ship, and cutting a greasy buff jerkin in tripes and broiling it for their dinners. Divers Indian adventures have been seasoned with direr mishaps, not having for eight days' space the quantity of a candle's end among eight score to grease their lips with; and landing in the end to seek food, by the cannibal savages they have been circumvented and forced to yield their bodies to feed them.

Thomas Nashe, *Nashe's Lenten Stuffe* (1599)

A SAILOR'S YARN

Mendax [liar].   From thence we sailed to the great isle called Madagastat, in Scorea, where were kings, Mahometans by religion, black as devils. Some had no heads, but eyes in their breasts. Some, when it rained, covered all the body with one foot. That land did abound in elephants' teeth; the men did eat camels' and lions' flesh. Musk and civet in every place did abound, and the mother of pearl, whereof the people made their platters to put in their meat; they dwell among spice; the ground is moist with oil of precious trees. Plenty of wine out of grapes as big as this loaf; much pepper; they cannot tell what to do with sugar, but that their merchants of Malabar, twenty days' journey off, do come and take their goods frankly for nothing; but some of them do bring iron to make edge tools, for which they have for one pound, twenty pound of fine gold. Their pots, pans and all vessel are clean gold garnished with diamonds. I did see swine feed in them.

Civis [citizen].   Did you see no strange fowls there and fishes?

Mendax.   In the isle called Ruc, in the great Khan's land, I did see mermaids and satyrs, with other fishes, by night came four miles from the sea and climbed into trees, and did eat dates and nutmegs, with whom the apes and baboons had much fighting, yelling and crying. The people of that land do live by eating the flesh of women. . . . Also there are a people called Astomii, which live very long, and neither eat nor drink, but only live by air and the smell of fruits. In Selentide there are women, contrary to the nature of other women, do lay eggs and hatch them, from whom do children come fifty times greater than those which are born of women. There did I see Scipodes, having but one foot, which is so broad that they cover all their bodies for the rain and the sun.

Item, I did see men having feet like horse, called Hippopodes.

Item, I did see the satyrs, half men and half goats, playing upon cornets.

Item, I did see Apothami, half horse and half man.

Item, I played at tables with people called the Fanesii, whose ears were as long as cloaks, covering all their bodies; near them is the great city called O, four hundred miles within the wall; the wall was brass, two thousand gates, six hundred bridges as big as London Bridge; the city was paved with gold. Naked men dwell there with two heads and six hands every man. There did I see apes play at tennis.

Civis.   I pray you, is there any plenty of precious stones?

Mendax.   Very many, but hard to come by; but in the island Zanzibar is much plenty of ambergris, that they make clay for their houses withal; there, if we had holden together like friends, we might have gotten a world. When I do remember it, alas, alas, every man is but for himself. You may consider what division is. Emeralds, rubies, turquoises, diamonds and sapphires were sold when we came thither first for the weight of iron; a thousand rich turquoises were sold for three shillings four pence, to be short, one with another, after three shillings four pence a peck. Our men gathered up carbuncles and diamonds with rakes under the spice trees.

Civis.   How chance you brought none home into this realm?

Mendax.   Oh, sir, we filled two ships with fine gold, three ships with ambergris, musk and unicorns' horns, and two tall barks with precious stones, and sailed by the adamant stones, which will draw iron unto them, and so cast away the greatest riches in Heathenness or Christendom.

William Bullein, *A Dialogue against the Pestilence* (1573)

A MERCHANT

A worthy merchant is the heir of adventure, whose hopes hang much upon the wind. Upon a wooden horse he rides through the world, and in a merry gale he makes a path through the seas. He is a discoverer of countries and a finder out of commodities, resolute in his attempts and royal in his expenses. He is the life of traffic and the maintainer of trade, the sailor's master and the soldier's friend. He is the exercise of the exchange, the honour of credit, the observation of time and the understanding of thrift. His study is number, his care his accounts, his comfort his conscience, and his wealth his good name. He fears not Scylla and sails close by Charybdis, and having beaten out a storm, rides at rest in a harbour. By his sea gain he makes his land purchase, and by the knowledge of trade finds the key of treasure. Out of his travels he makes his discourses, and from his eye-observations brings the models of architecture. He plants the earth with foreign fruits, and knows at home what is good abroad. He is neat in apparel, modest in demeanour, dainty in diet and civil in his carriage. In sum, he is the pillar of a city, the enricher of a country, the furnisher of a court, and the worthy servant of a king.

Nicholas Breton, *The Good and the Badde* (1616)

VOYAGES OF TRADE AND EXPLORATION

(I)

Master John Hawkins with the *Jesus* of Lubeck, a ship of 700, and the *Salomon*, a ship of 140, the *Tiger* a bark of 50 and the *Swallow* of 30 tons, being all well furnished with men to the number of one hundred threescore and ten, as also with ordnance and victual requisite for such a voyage, departed out of Plymouth the 18 day of October, in the year of our Lord 1564, with a prosperous wind.

The fourth of November they had sight of the island of Madeira, and the sixth day of Tenerife, which they thought to have been the Canary. To speak somewhat of these islands: being called in old time *insulae fortunatae* [Fortunate Islands], by the means of the flourishing thereof, the fruitfulness of them doth surely exceed far all other: for they make wine better than any in Spain; for sugar, sweets, raisins of the sun, and many other fruits, abundance; for resin and raw silk, there is great store. They have many camels also, which, being young, are eaten of the people for victuals, and being old, they are used for carriage of necessaries; whose property is, as he is taught, to kneel at the taking of his load and unloading again. His nature is to engender backwards contrary to other beasts; of shape very deformed, with a little belly, long misshapen legs, and feet very broad. This beast liveth hardly, and is contented with straw and stubble, but of force strong, being well able to carry five hundredweight.

The 25th he came to Cabo Blanco, which is upon the coast of Africa, and a place where the Portuguese do ride, that fish there in the month of November especially, and is a very good place of fishing for mullet and dogfish. The people of that part of Africa are tawny, having long hair, without any apparel, saving before their privy members. Their weapons in wars are bows and arrows.

The 29th we came to Cape Verde. These people are all black, and are called negroes, without any apparel, saving before their privities; of stature goodly men.

The two and twentieth the captain went into the river called Callowsa, with the two barks, and the *John*'s pinnace, and the *Salomon*'s boat, leaving at anchor in the river's mouth the two ships, the river being twenty leagues in, where the Portuguese rode, and dispatched his business, and so returned with two caravels, laden with negroes [bought from a trader].

The captain was advertised by the Portuguese of a town of the negroes, where was not only great quantity of gold, but also that there were not above forty men, and an hundred women and children in the town, so that he might get an hundred slaves. He determined to stay before the town three or four hours, to see what he could do, and thereupon prepared his men in armour and weapon together, to the number of forty men well appointed, having to their guides certain Portuguese. We landing boat after boat, and divers of our men scattering themselves, contrary to the captain's will, by one or two in a company, for the hope that they had to find gold in their houses, ransacking the same, in the meantime the negroes came upon them, and hurt many, being thus scattered, whereas if five or six had been together, they had been able, as their companions did, to give the overthrow to forty of them. While this was doing, the captain, who with a dozen men went through the town, returned, finding 200 negroes at the water's side shooting at them in the boats, and cutting them in pieces which were drowned in the water. Thus we returned back somewhat discomforted, although the captain in a singular wise manner carried himself with countenance very cheerful outwardly, having gotten by our going ten negroes, and lost seven of our best men, and we had 27 of our men hurt.

We departed with all our ships from Sierra Leone towards the West Indies, and for the space of eighteen days we were becalmed, having now and then contrary winds, which happened to us very ill, being but reasonably watered for so great a company of negroes and ourselves, which pinched us all, and that which was worst, put us in such fear that many never thought to have reached to the Indies without great death of negroes and of themselves. But the Almighty God, who never suffereth his elect to perish, sent us, the sixteenth of February, the ordinary breeze, which is the northwest wind, which never left us till we came to an island of the cannibals called Dominica, where we arrived the ninth of March, upon a Saturday.

[The account further describes their travels through the Caribbean and to Florida, before their return in September 'with the loss of twenty persons in all the voyage, and with great profit to the venturers of the said voyage.']

(II)

On Whit Sunday, the six and twentieth of May 1577, Captain Frobisher departed from Blackwall, with one of the Queen's ships, called the *Aide*, of nine score tons, and two other little barks likewise, one called the *Gabriel* and the other the *Michael*, accompanied with seven score gentlemen, soldiers and sailors, well furnished with victuals, and other provisions necessary for one half year, on this his second voyage for the further discovering of the passage to Cathay, supposed to be on the north and northwest part of America; where through our merchants may have course and recourse with their merchandise, from these our northernmost parts of Europe to those Oriental coasts of Asia, in much shorter time and with greater benefit than any others, to their no little commodity and profit.

With a merry wind the 7th of June we arrived at the islands called Orcades, or vulgarly Orkney, where we made provision of fresh water . . . At our landing, the people fled from their poor cottages with shrieks and alarms . . . It seemeth they are often frighted with pirates. . . . We departed hence the 8th of June and followed our course until the 4th of July, all which time we had no night, but that easily and without any impediment we had, when we were so disposed, the fruition of our books, and other pleasures to pass away time. This benefit endureth in those parts not six weeks, while the sun is near the Tropic of Cancer.

We met great islands of ice, of half a mile, some more, some less in compass, showing above the sea 30 or 40 fathoms and, as we supposed, fast on the ground, where with our lead we could scarce sound the bottom for depth.

Here, in place of odoriferous and fragrant smells of sweet gums, and pleasant notes of musical birds, which other countries in more temperate zones do yield, we tasted the most boisterous Boreal [wintry] blasts mixed with snow and hail, in the months of June and July, nothing inferior to our untemperate winter: a sudden alteration.

All along this coast ice lieth as a continual bulwark, and so defendeth the country, that those that would land there incur great danger. Our general three days together attempted with the ship-boat to have gone on shore, which, for that without great danger he could not accomplish, he deferred it. All along the coast lie very high mountains covered with snow. Four days coasting along this land, we found no sign of habitation. Little birds came flying into our ships, which causeth us to suppose that the country is both more tolerable and also habitable within than the outward shore maketh show.

On July 16th we came with the making of land. Between two islands there is a large entrance or strait, called Frobisher's Strait, after the name of our general, the first finder thereof.

Whilst he was searching the country near the shore, some of the people of the country showed themselves, leaping and dancing, with strange shrieks and cries, which gave no little admiration to our men. Our general, desirous to allure them unto him by fair means, caused knives and other things to be proffered unto them, which they would not take at our hands, but being laid on the ground and the party going away, they came and took up, leaving some things of theirs to countervail the same. At length two of them, leaving their weapons, came down to our general and master, who did the like to them, commanding the company to stay, and went unto them; who after certain dumb signs and mute congratulations began to lay hands upon them, but they deliverly escaped and ran to their bows and arrows, and came fiercely upon them (not respecting the rest of our company which were ready for their defence), but with their arrows hurt divers of them: we took the one, and the other escaped.

The day following, being the 19th of July, our captain returned to the ship with report of supposed riches, which showed itself in the bowels of those barren mountains, wherewith we were all satisfied.

Within four days after we had been at the entrance of the straits, the northwest and west winds dispersed the ice into the sea, and made us a large entrance. We entered them, and our general and master with great diligence sought out and found out a fair harbour for the ship and barks to ride in, and brought the ship, barks and all their company to safe anchor, except one man, which died by God's visitation.

After the ship rode at anchor, our general, with such company as could well be spared from the ships, in marching order entered the land, having special care that we should all with one voice thank God for our safe arrival; secondly, beseech Him that it would please His divine majesty long to continue our Queen, for whom he and all the rest of our company in this order took possession of the contry; and thirdly, that by our Christian study and endeavour those barbarous people trained up in paganism and infidelity might be reduced to the knowledge of true religion and to the hope of salvation in Christ our Redeemer. . . .

The stones of this supposed continent with America be altogether sparkled, and glister in the sun like gold; so likewise doth the sand in the bright water, yet they verify the proverb: all is not gold that glistens.

[The account further relates their conflicts with the natives – apparently Inuits – and lack of success in the voyage.]

Richard Hakluyt, *The Principal Navigations . . . of the English Nation*
(1598–1600)

GOLDEN OPPORTUNITIES: GUIANA

The empire of Guiana is directly east from Peru towards the sea, and lieth under the equinoctial line, and it hath more abundance of gold than any part of Peru, and as many or more great cities than ever Peru had when it flourished most. . . . I have been assured by such of the Spaniards as have seen Manoa the imperial city of Guiana, which the

Spaniards call El Dorado, that for the greatness, for the riches, and for the excellent seat, it far exceedeth any of the world . . .

Undoubtedly those that trade Amazon return much gold . . . I had knowledge of all the rivers between Orinoco and Amazon, and was very desirous to understand the truth of those warlike women [Amazons], because of some it is believed, of others not. . . . They which are not far from Guiana do accompany with men but once in a year, and for the time of one month, which I gather by their relation to be in April. At that time all the kings of the borders assemble, and the queens of the Amazons, and after the queens have chosen, the rest cast lots for their valentines. This one month, they feast, dance, and drink of their wines in abundance, and the moon being done, they all depart to their own provinces. If they conceive and be delivered of a son, they return him to the father; if of a daughter, they nourish it, and retain it, and as many as have daughters send unto the begetters a present, all being desirous to increase their own sex and kind. But that they cut off the right dug of the breast I do not find to be true. It was further told me, that if in the wars they took any prisoners, that they used to accompany with those also at what time soever, but in the end for certain they put them to death . . . for they are said to be very cruel and bloodthirsty . . .

The Spanish, to the end that none of the people in the passage towards Guiana or in Guiana itself might come to speech with us, persuaded all the nations that we were cannibals, but when the poor men and women had seen us, and that we gave them meat, and to everyone something or other, which was rare and strange to them, they began to conceive the deceit and purpose of the Spaniards, who indeed (as they confessed) took from them both their wives and daughters daily, and used them for the satisfying of their own lusts. But I protest before the majesty of the living God, that I neither know nor believe that any of our company, by violence or otherwise, ever knew any of their women, and yet we saw many hundreds, and had many in our power, and of those very young and excellently favoured, which came among us without deceit, stark naked. . . .

I never saw a more beautiful country, nor more lively prospects, hills so raised here and there over the valleys, the river winding into divers branches, the plains adjoining without bush or stubble, all fair green grass, the ground of hard sand easy to march on either for horse or foot, the deer crossing in every path, the birds towards the evening singing on every tree with a thousand several tunes, cranes and herons of white, crimson and carnation perching in the river's side, the air fresh with a gentle easterly wind, and every stone that we stooped to take up promised either gold or silver by his complexion. . . .

Next unto Arui there are two rivers, Atoica and Caora, and on that branch which is called Caora are a nation of people whose heads appear not above their shoulders, which, though it may be thought a mere fable, yet for mine own part I am resolved it is true, because every child in the provinces of Arromaia and Camuri affirm the same. They are reported to have their eyes in their shoulders and their mouths in the middle of their breasts, and that a long train of hair groweth backward between their shoulders. . . . For mine own part I saw them not, but I am resolved that so many people did not all combine or forethink to make the report. . . . For the rest, which myself have seen, I will promise these things that follow and know to be true. Those that are desirous to discover and to see many nations may be satisfied within this river . . . above 200 miles east and west, and 800 miles north and south; and of these, the most either rich in gold or in other merchandises. The common soldier shall here fight for gold, and pay himself, instead of pence, with plates of half a foot broad, whereas he breaketh his bones in other wars for provant and penury. Those commanders and chieftains that shoot at honour and abundance, shall find there more rich and beautiful cities, more temples adorned with golden images, more sepulchres filled with treasure, than either Cortez found in Mexico or Pizarro in Peru, and the shining glory of this conquest will eclipse all those so far extended beams of the Spanish nation. . . .

Guiana is a country that hath yet her maidenhead, never sacked, turned, nor wrought, the face of the earth hath not been torn, nor the virtue and salt of the soil spent by manurance [cultivation], the graves have not been opened for gold, the mines not broken with sledges [hammers], nor their images pulled down out of their temples. It hath never been entered by any army of strength, and never conquered by any Christian prince. . . .

I hope, as we with these few hands have displanted the first [Spanish] garrison and driven them out of the said country, so Her Majesty will give order for the rest, and either defend it and hold it as tributary, or conquer and keep it as Empress of the same. . . . And where the south border of Guiana reacheth to the dominion and empire of the Amazons, those women shall hereby hear the name of a virgin which is not only able to defend her own territories and her neighbours, but also to invade and conquer so great empires and so far removed.

Sir Walter Raleigh, *The Discovery of Guiana* (1596)

TROUBLED VOICES: WHAT TO DO ABOUT IRELAND?

Eudoxus. But if that country of Ireland, whence you lately came, be so goodly and commodious a soil as you report, I wonder that no course is taken for the turning thereof to good uses, and reducing of that savage nation to better government and civility.

Irenaeus. Marry, so there have been divers good plots devised and wise counsels cast already about reformation of that realm; but they say it is the fatal destiny of that land that no purposes, whatsoever are meant for her good, will prosper or take good effect, which, whether it proceed from the very genius of the soil or influence of the stars, or that Almighty God hath not yet appointed the time of her reformation, or that he reserveth her in this unquiet state still for some secret scourge which shall by her come unto England, it is hard to be known but yet much to be feared. . . . I will then, according to your advisement, begin to declare the evils which seem to me most hurtful to the commonweal of that land, and first those which I said were most ancient and long-grown. And they also are of three kinds: the first in laws, the second in customs, and the third in religion . . . [He then provides a knowledgeable analysis of Irish law and custom, as not conducive to settled order and justice].

WHAT TO DO FIRST: NEITHER SWORDS NOR PLOUGHSHARES

Irenaeus. The first thing [to bring order] must be to send over into that realm such a strong power of men as that shall perforce bring in all that rebellious rout of loose people, which either do now stand out in open arms, or in wandering companies do keep the woods, spoiling the good subject.

Eudoxus. You speak now, Irenaeus, of an infinite charge to Her Majesty, to send over such an army as should tread down all that standeth before them on foot, and lay on the ground all the stiff-necked people of that land; for there is not but one outlaw of great reckoning, to wit the Earl of Tyrone, abroad in arms, against whom you see what great charges she hath been at, this last year, in sending of men, providing of victuals and making head against him; yet there is little or nothing at all done, but the Queen's treasure spent, her people wasted, the poor country troubled, and the enemy nevertheless brought unto no more subjection than he was, or not outwardly to show, which in effect is none, but rather a scorn of her power and an emboldening of a proud rebel, and an encouragement unto all like lewd-disposed traitors that shall dare to lift up their heels against their sovereign lady. Therefore it were hard counsel to draw such exceeding great charge upon her, whose event shall be so uncertain . . .

Irenaeus.   At the beginning of those wars, and when the garrisons are well planted and fortified, I would wish a proclamation were made generally and to come to their knowledge: that what persons soever would within twenty days absolutely submit themselves (excepting only the very principals and ring-leaders) should find grace . . . and that they then be not suffered to remain any longer in those parts; no, nor about the garrisons, but sent away into the inner parts of the realm, and dispersed in such sort as they shall not come together . . . afterwards I would have none received, but left to their fortune and miserable end. My reason is, for that those which will afterwards remain without, are stout and obstinate rebels, such as will never be made dutiful and obedient, nor brought to labour or civil conversation, having once tasted that licentious life, and, being acquainted with spoils and outrages will ever after be ready for the like occasions, so as there is no hope of amendment or recovery, and therefore needful to be cut off [from food supplies and other resources].

The end (I assure me) will be very short and much sooner than can be (in so great a trouble as it seemeth) hoped for, although there should be none of them fall by the sword nor be slain by the soldier, yet thus being kept from manurance and their cattle from running abroad, by this hard restraint they would quickly consume themselves and devour one another. The proof whereof I saw sufficiently ensampled in those late wars in Munster; for, notwithstanding that the same was a most rich and plentiful country, full of corn and cattle, that you would have thought they would have been able to stand long, yet ere one year and a half they were brought to such wretchedness as that any stony heart would have rued the same. Out of every corner of the woods and glens they came creeping forth upon their hands, for their legs could not bear them; they looked like anatomies of death, they spake like ghosts crying out of their graves; they did eat of the dead carrions, happy were they if they could find them; yea, and one another soon after, insomuch as the very carcasses they spared not to scrape out of their graves; and if they found a plot of water-cresses or shamrocks, there they flocked as to a feast for the time, yet not long able to continue therewithal; that in short space there were almost none left, and a most populous and plentiful country suddenly made void of man or beast; yet sure, in all that war there perished not many by the sword, but all by the extremity of famine which they themselves had wrought . . .

Eudoxus. I do now well understand you. But now when all things are brought to this pass and all filled with this rueful spectacle of so many wretched carcasses starving, goodly countries wasted, so huge a desolation and confusion, as even I that do but hear of it from you, and do picture it in my mind, do greatly pity and commiserate it, if it shall happen that the state of this misery and lamentable images of things shall be told and feelingly presented to her sacred Majesty, being by nature full of mercy and clemency, who is most inclinable to such pitiful complaints, and will not endure to hear such tragedies made of her people and poor subjects as some about her may insinuate; then she perhaps, for very compassion of such calamities, will not only stop the stream of such violence, and return to her wonted mildness, but also con them little thanks which have been the authors and counsellors of such bloody platforms.

In the Long Term

Irenaeus. Since Ireland is full of her own nation that may not be rooted out, and somewhat stored with English already, and more to be, I think it best by an union of manners and conformity of minds to bring them to be one people, and to put away the dislikeful conceit both of th'one and th'other, which will be by no means better than by their intermingling of them, that neither all the Irish may dwell together, nor all the English, but by translating of them and scattering them in small numbers among the English, not only to bring them by daily conversation unto better liking of each other but also to make both of them less able to hurt.

[Spenser was secretary to Lord Grey in Ireland in 1580, and lived there for sixteen years.]

Edmund Spenser, *A Vewe of the Present State of Ireland*
(registered 1598, published 1633)

FOUNDING VIRGINIA

Captain Bartholomew Gosnoll, one of the first movers of this plantation, having many years solicited many of his friends, but found small assistance, at last prevailed with some gentlemen, as Captain John Smith, Master Edward-Maria Wingfield, Master Robert Hunt and divers others, who depended a year upon his projects; but nothing could be effected till, by their great charge and industry, it came to be apprehended by certain of the nobility, gentry and merchants; so that His Majesty by his letters patent gave commission for establishing councils, to direct here, and to govern and execute there. To effect this was spent another year, and by that, three ships were provided, one of a hundred tons, another of forty, and a pinnace of twenty. The transportation of the company was committed to Captain Christopher Newport, a mariner well practised for the western parts of America. But their orders for government were put in a box, not to be opened nor the governors known until they arrived in Virginia.

On the nineteenth of December, 1606, we set sail from Blackwall, but by unprosperous winds were kept six weeks in the sight of England; all which time Master Hunt, our preacher, was so weak and sick that few expected his recovery. Yet although he were but twenty miles from his habitation (the time we were in the Downs), and notwithstanding the stormy weather, nor the scandalous imputations of some few (little better than atheists, of the greatest rank amongst us) suggested against him, all this could never force from him so much as a seeming desire to leave the business; but he preferred the service of God in so good a voyage before any affection to contest with his godless foes, whose disastrous designs (could they have prevailed) had even then overthrown the business, so many discontents did then arise, had he not with the water of patience and his godly exhortations (but chiefly by his true devoted examples) quenched those flames of envy and dissension.

We watered at the Canaries, we traded with the savages at Dominica, three weeks we spent in refreshing ourselves amongst the West India Isles; in Guadelupe we found a bath so hot, as in it we boiled pork as well as over the fire. And at a little isle called Monica we took from the bushes with our hands near two hogsheads-full of birds in three or four hours. In Nevis, Mona and the Virgin Isles we spent some time, where, with a loathsome beast like a crocodile called a gwayn [iguana], tortoises, pelicans, parrots and fishes, we daily feasted. . . .

The first land they made they called Cape Henry; where thirty of them, recreating themselves on shore, were assaulted by five savages, who hurt two of the English very dangerously.

That night was the box opened and the orders read . . . Until the thirteenth of May they sought a place to plant in; then the council was sworn, Master Wingfield was chosen president, and an oration made why Captain Smith was not admitted of the council as the rest.

Now falleth every man to work, the council to contrive the fort, the rest cut down trees to make place to pitch their tent; some provide clapboard to relade the ships, some make gardens, some nets, etc. The savages often visited us kindly. The president's overweening jealousy would admit no exercise at arms, or fortification but the boughs of trees cast together in the form of a half moon, by the extraordinary pains and diligence of Captain Kendall. . . . What toil we had with so small a power to guard our workmen a-days, watch all night, resist our enemies, and effect our business, to relade the ships, cut down trees, and prepare the ground to plant our corn, etc., I refer to the reader's consideration.

Six weeks being spent in this manner, Captain Newport (who was hired only for our transportation) was to return with the ships. Now Captain Smith all this time from their departure from the Canaries was restrained as a prisoner, upon the scandalous suggestions of some of the chief (envying his repute), who feigned he intended to usurp the government, murder the council and make himself king. . . . But . . . he wisely prevented their policies, though he could not suppress their envies; yet so well he demeaned himself in this business as all the company did see his innocency and his adversaries' malice, and those suborned to accuse him accused his accusers of subornation.

Many untruths were alleged against him, but, being so apparently disproved, begat a general hatred in the hearts of the company against such unjust commanders, that the president was adjudged to give him two hundred pounds (so that all he had was seized upon) in part of satisfaction, which Smith presently returned to the store for the general use of the colony. Many were the mischiefs that daily sprung from their ignorant yet ambitious spirits; but the good doctrine and exhortation of our preacher, Master Hunt, reconciled them, and caused Captain Smith to be admitted of the council.

The next day all received the communion, the day following the savages voluntarily desired peace, and Captain Newport returned for England with news, leaving in Virginia one hundred, the fifteenth of June 1607.

Captain John Smith, *The Generall Historie of Virginia* (1624)

TO THE VIRGINIAN VOYAGE

You brave heroic minds,
Worthy your country's name,
 That honour still pursue,
 Go, and subdue,
Whilst loitering hinds,
Lurk here at home, with shame.

Britons, you stay too long,
Quickly aboard bestow you,
 And with a merry gale
 Swell your stretchèd sail,
With vows as strong
As the winds that blow you.

Your course securely steer,
West and south forth keep,
 Rocks, lee shores, nor shoals,
 When Aeolus scowls,
You need not fear,
So absolute the deep.

OVER SEAS

And cheerfully at sea
Success you still entice
  To get the pearl and gold,
  And ours to hold,
VIRGINIA,
Earth's only paradise. . . .

Michael Drayton, *Odes*, (1619)

CODA

. . . These our actors,
As I foretold you, were all spirits, and
Are melted into air, into thin air;
And, like the baseless fabric of this vision,
The cloud-capped towers, the gorgeous palaces,
The solemn temples, the great globe itself,
Yea, all which it inherit, shall dissolve,
And, like this insubstantial pageant faded,
Leave not a rack behind. We are such stuff
As dreams are made on; and our little life
Is rounded with a sleep.

Shakespeare, *The Tempest* (1610)

FURTHER READING

Individual books, especially general studies, may be relevant to more than one section.

General Studies

Clay, C.G.A., *Economic Expansion and Social Change: England 1500–1700*. Vol. I: *People, Land and Towns*. Vol. II: *Industry, Trade and Government*, Cambridge University Press, 1984.

James, M., *Society, Politics and Culture. Studies in Early Modern England*, Cambridge University Press, 1986.

Morrill, J. (ed.), *The Oxford Illustrated History of Tudor and Stuart Britain*, Oxford University Press, 1996.

Nicoll, A. (ed.), *Shakespeare in his own Age*, Cambridge University Press, 1964.

Plowden, A., *Elizabethan England*, London, Reader's Digest, 1982.

Wrightson, K., *English Society, 1580–1680*, London, Hutchinson, 1982.

Women and Men

Cressy, D., *Birth, Marriage and Death. Ritual, Religion and the Life Cycle in Tudor and Stuart England*, Oxford University Press, 1997.

Ingram, M., *Church Courts, Sex and Marriage in England, 1570–1640*, Cambridge University Press, 1987.

McFarlane, A., *Marriage and Love in England, 1300–1840*, Oxford University Press, 1986.

Mendelson, S., and Crawford, P., *Women in Early Modern England*, Oxford, Clarendon Press, 1998.

Quaife, G.R., *Wanton Wenches and Wayward Wives. Peasants and Illicit Sex in Early Seventeenth-Century England*, London, Croom Helm, 1979.

House and Home

Girouard, M., *Robert Smythson and the Elizabethan Country House*, New Haven, Yale University Press, 1983.

Sim, A., *Food and Feast in Tudor England*, Stroud, Sutton Publishing, 1997.

———, *The Tudor Housewife*, Stroud, Sutton Publishing, 1998.

Summerson, J., *Architecture in Britain, 1530 to 1830*, rev. edn, Harmondsworth, Penguin, 1983.

Webster, C. (ed.), *Health, Medicine and Mortality in the Sixteenth Century*, Cambridge University Press, 1979.

Country Life

Laroque, F. (trans. J. Lloyd), *Shakespeare's Festive World*, Cambridge University Press, 1991.

Thirsk, J. (ed.), *The Agrarian History of England and Wales, Vol. IV, 1500–1640*, Cambridge University Press, 1967.

Underdown, D., *Revel, Riot and Rebellion*, Oxford University Press, 1985.

Education

Charlton, K., *Education in Renaissance England*, London, Routledge, 1965.

Curtiss, M.H., *Oxford and Cambridge in Transition, 1558–1642*, Oxford University Press, 1959.

Beliefs

Briggs, K.M., *Pale Hecate's Team*, London, Routledge, 1962.

Fletcher, A., and Roberts, P. (eds,), *Religion, Culture and Society in Early Modern Britain*, Cambridge University Press, 1994.

McFarlane, A., *Witchcraft in Tudor and Stuart England: A Regional and Comparative Study*, London, Routledge, 1970.

Thomas, K., *Religion and the Decline of Magic*, Harmondsworth, Penguin, 1971.

Tyacke, N. (ed), *England's Long Reformation*, London University Press, 1998.

The Court

Berry, P., *Of Chastity and Power*, London, Routledge, 1996.

Peck, L.L. (ed), *The Mental World of the Jacobean Court*, Cambridge University Press, 1991.

Further Reading

Thurley, S., *The Royal Palaces of Tudor England*, New Haven, Yale University Press, 1993.

London

Archer, I.W., *The Pursuit of Stability, Social Relations in Elizabethan London*, Cambridge University Press, 1991.

Beier, A.L., and Findlay, R. (eds), *London 1500–1700. The Making of the Metropolis*, London, Longman, 1986.

Holmes, M., *Elizabethan London*, London, Cassell, 1969.

Manley, L., *Literature and Culture in Early Modern London*, Cambridge University Press, 1995.

Arts and Pleasures

Barroll, J.L., and Leggatt, A., Hosley, R. and Kiernan, A. (eds), *The Revels History of Drama in English, Vol. III, 1576–1613*, London, Methuen, 1975.

Ford, B. (ed.), *A Guide to English Literature, Vol. II, The Age of Shakespeare* (rev. edn), Harmondsworth, Penguin, 1982.

Gurr, A., *Playgoing in Shakespeare's London*, Cambridge University Press, 1987.

Poverty, Crime and Punishment

Beier, A.L., *The Problem of the Poor in Tudor and Early Stuart England*, London, Methuen, 1983.

Sharpe, K.A., *Crime in Early Modern England, 1550–1750*, London, Longman, 1984.

Slack, P., *Poverty and Policy in Tudor and Stuart England*, London, Longman, 1988.

Over Seas

Foster, R.F. (ed), *The Oxford History of Ireland*, Oxford University Press, 1989.

Fuller, M., *Voyages in Print. English Travel to America, 1576–1624*, Cambridge University Press, 1995.

INDEX

INDEX